John Hawkesworth

John Hawkesworth, LL.D.

From an engraving by James Watson
after the painting by Sir Joshua Reynolds

John Hawkesworth)
Eighteenth-Century Man of Letters

John Lawrence Abbott

The University of Wisconsin Press

Published 1982

The University of Wisconsin Press
114 North Murray Street
Madison, Wisconsin 53715

The University of Wisconsin Press, Ltd.
1 Gower Street
London WC1E 6HA, England

First printing

Printed in the United States of America

For LC CIP information see the colophon

ISBN 0–299–08610–0

Publication of this book was made possible in part by grants from the
National Endowment for the Humanities, the University of Connecticut Research Foundation, and the Andrew W. Mellon foundation.

For Mary

Time, who is impatient to date my last paper, will shortly moulder the hand that is now writing it in the dust, and still the breast that now throbs at the reflection: but let not this be read as something that relates only to another; for a few years only can divide the eye that is now reading from the hand that has written. This awful truth, however obvious, and however reiterated, is yet frequently forgotten; for, surely, if we did not lose our remembrance, or at least our sensibility, that view would always predominate in our lives which alone can afford us comfort when we die.

—John Hawkesworth, *Adventurer* no. 140

It is much to be regretted that [Hawkesworth's] biography was not afterwards undertaken before all his friends passed away. Had his papers been preserved like those of Dr. Birch, they would have afforded the most valuable materials for the literary history of the last century.

—"Autobiography of Sylvanus Urban," *Gentleman's Magazine*, March 1857.

Johnson's feelings were more ordinary than fine, which indeed accounts for his popularity; more nervous than elevated; and I take Hawkesworth to have been at least his equal in sublimity, and that the author of the *Adventurer* deserves one history of his life.

—Robert Potter, *The Art of Criticism as Exemplified in Dr. Johnson's Lives of the Most Eminent English Poets* (1789)

Contents

Acknowledgments

I would like to thank Sir John FitzHerbert, Mrs. Donald F. Hyde, and Mr. Victor Montagu for permission to quote from materials in their possession. I am grateful to the following institutions for allowing me to quote from materials in their collections: the American Philosophical Society, the Bodleian Library, the British Library, the Bromley Central Library, the Folger Shakespeare Library, the Henry E. Huntington Library, the James Marshall and Marie-Louise Osborn Collection at Yale, the John Rylands University Library of Manchester, the Lambeth Palace Library, the National Library of Australia, and the Public Record Office, London.

Grants from the American Philosophical Society, the National Endowment for the Humanities, the Andrew W. Mellon Foundation, and the University of Connecticut Research Foundation made possible the research for and publication of this book. I would especially like to thank Dr. Hugh Clark for his support and the University of Connecticut for leaves of absence that enabled me to do research in England.

I could not have completed this volume without the help of a number of people. Professors Jeffrey Hart, James M. Kuist, and Richard B. Schwartz read this book in manuscript and offered many suggestions for revision, as did Ms. Carolyn Moser, who edited the manuscript for publication. The following scholars gave me valuable advice: Dr. D. G. C. Allan, Dr. J. D. Fleeman, Professors James Gray, Donald J. Greene, Philip Mahone Griffith, Duncan Isles, Paul J. Korshin, Michael Marcuse, and Dr. Helen Wallis. The late James L. Clifford assisted me in ways too numerous to mention here, and I will always be grateful for his many kindnesses. My greatest debt throughout this study is to Professor Arthur Sherbo. Without his example and encouragement this book would not have been written.

No one gave me more support in writing this study than my wife. It is with great pleasure that I dedicate it to her.

JLA

The University of Connecticut

Introduction

Poet, playwright, literary critic, essayist, editor and biographer of Swift, translator, writer of oriental and domestic tales, naval historian, and man-about-town in mid-eighteenth-century London, John Hawkesworth (1720–1773) has yet to find his biographer. No book, no article, has recorded fully his contribution to the Age of Johnson; no one has written the life of a man who was friend and associate of Samuel Johnson, David Garrick, Benjamin Franklin, Dr. Charles Burney, and Christopher Smart and the acquaintance of numerous celebrated figures of the time. Hawkesworth is best known to students of the period as a friend of Samuel Johnson, a member of Johnson's first club, the Ivy Lane, and the best imitator of the inimitable Johnsonian style. "Ingenious HAWKESWORTH to this school [Johnson's] we owe, / And scarce the pupil from the tutor know," John Courtenay wrote in his *Poetical Review of the Literary and Moral Character of Dr. Johnson* (1786). Johnson himself told Mrs. Piozzi that for knowledge of his early years biographers must look to "Jack" Hawkesworth. The extent of their friendship is reflected in the burial of Tetty Johnson in Hawkesworth's parish church at Bromley, Kent, in his handling of the funeral arrangements, and in his comforting of Johnson during a time of profound sorrow.

Hawkesworth participated vigorously in the literary, journalistic, and theatrical worlds of his day, and his writing is varied and extensive: it would be difficult to cite a literary genre or form that he did not attempt. His literary career began in 1741 with poetry contributions to the *Gentleman's Magazine*, and he continued to serve the publication in a variety of roles, emerging in the late 1740s as its literary and dramatic editor. The *Adventurer* (1754), co-authored with Johnson, was Hawkesworth's first literary success, bringing him recognition, financial reward, and identification not only as a moralist but as a fine stylist in the Johnson manner.

As Swift's editor and biographer at midcentury, Hawkesworth preserved and enhanced the reputation of one of the century's greatest writers: not only did his *Life of Swift* (1755) draw Johnson's highest praise, serving as a model for Johnson's commentary on the Dean in the *Lives of the English Poets*, but it was Hawkesworth who first published a major portion of the *Journal to Stella*. While Johnson helped Hawkesworth produce a fine sequel to the noble *Rambler*, David Garrick encouraged him to turn his talents to the theater. Hawkesworth was not only a friend, literary advisor, and defender of the great actor and theater manager, but revised for him Dryden's *Amphitryon* (1756) and Southerne's *Oroonoko* (1759), sparing theatergoers of the Age of Johnson the indelicacies of a grosser age no less than he appealed to their spirit of comedy in his original fairy tale, *Edgar and Emmeline.* In the latter entertainment disguise produces laughter at the same time it provides penetrating insights into the sexual stereotypes that bind men and women. It was not, however, as playwright that Hawkesworth made his greatest contribution to the theater of his day but rather as critic. For nearly three decades, as drama critic for the *Gentleman's Magazine*, he commented on the drama of his age and addressed a range of issues that pertained to it, from the nature of stagecraft to its moral mission.

Always with an eye on his mentor's success and conscious of the popularity of the genre itself, Hawkesworth published an oriental tale in 1761, *Almoran and Hamet.* It offers interesting parallels with *Rasselas* and was written with such finesse that Leigh Hunt ranked Hawkesworth with Addison and Johnson as one of the ablest practitioners of this form. If the young Johnson had found outlets for his great energies in translating from the French, an established Hawkesworth published in 1768 his *Telemachus*, translated from Fénelon's version. The subscribers' list reveals the global nature of culture at the time (copies were sent to Benjamin Franklin in Philadelphia and to others in Barbados), and Hawkesworth produced a work of such elegance that it remained the standard text for many years.

By the late 1760s Hawkesworth's literary career was at its peak, his success as a man of letters manifest. He had risen over several decades from the gloom of Grub Street to esteem and respect in the world of letters. His involvement in the literary life of his age was such that John Gough Nichols wrote in the "Autobiography of Sylvanus Urban" in the *Gentleman's Magazine*, "Had his papers been preserved like those of Dr. Birch, they would have afforded the most valuable materials for the literary history of the last century." Indeed, Hawkesworth's papers might have been preserved had not Mary Hawkesworth, for unexplained reasons, abandoned an edition of his collected works prepared by Johnson himself. Even this failure to publish his works might not have diminished Hawkesworth's place in literary history had he not become involved in a *cause célèbre* during the summer of 1773 which cost him his career, his reputation, and possibly his life.

In 1771 Lord Sandwich, the Admiralty's First Lord, commissioned Hawkesworth to prepare an account of the voyages to the South Seas undertaken by John Byron, Samuel Wallis, Philip Carteret, and James Cook, an assignment that he accepted with enthusiasm, since it promised enduring fame and certain financial reward. The public eagerly awaited publication of Hawkesworth's *Voyages* during the summer of 1773, but the completed text received widespread censure rather than the expected acclaim, and Hawkesworth was charged in private and public with blasphemy and immorality. He died in disgrace, his reputation as a writer and moralist in ruins.

Reassessment of Hawkesworth's contributions to the Age of Johnson has begun only in the twentieth century; studies already undertaken suggest that not only does a review of his life and work provide another angle of vision on a complex period of English literary and cultural history, but that Hawkesworth's role in this era is far greater than previously imagined. This is the first attempt to provide a definitive account of Hawkesworth's life and literary career. While he left no papers, as Nichols suggests—no diary, journal, or other material from which such a record could be constructed with ease—considerable evidence has survived, principally in Great Britain, though matter relating to Hawkesworth is scattered across the world, from New Haven to New Zealand. The first chapter details Hawkesworth's early years, apprenticeship, marriage, and removal to Bromley, Kent; subsequent chapters discuss important periods of his life and the literary works connected with them. Since his works are still inaccessible, I have tried to let Hawkesworth speak as much as possible for himself. His writing is still the best index to his worth.

Important Dates in Hawkesworth's Life

1720 Baptized in Old St. Pancras Church, son of John and Ann Hawkesworth (October 28)

1737 Apprenticed to John Harwood, attorney (March)

c. 1740 Meets Samuel Johnson

1741 First composition published, "The Fop, Cock and Diamond," in *Gentleman's Magazine* (June)

1744 Marries Mary Brown (May 12)

c. 1744 Hawkesworths occupy Thornhill Mansion in Bromley, Kent

1747 Joins Johnson in pictorial frontispiece to *Gentleman's Magazine*

1749 Joins Johnson's Ivy Lane Club (winter)

1752 Arranges for burial of Tetty Johnson at Bromley, Kent

First *Adventurer* paper appears (November)

1755 Publishes his life of Swift and edition of Swift's works (May)

1756 Alters Dryden's *Amphitryon* for Garrick (December)

Awarded a Lambeth doctor of laws by archbishop of Canterbury (December)

Accepts position of literary editor of *Gentleman's Magazine*

1759 Alters Southerne's *Oronooko* for Garrick (December)

1761 *Edgar and Emmeline* (January)

Almoran and Hamet, An Oriental Tale (June)

1766 Publishes Swift's correspondence (June)

1768 *Adventures of Telemachus* (May)

1771 Selected by Lord Sandwich to write Cook's *Voyages*

1773 Elected a director of East India Company (April)

Meets George III; publishes Cook's *Voyages* (June)

Dies (November 17)

John Hawkesworth

I EARLY YEARS AND REMOVAL TO BROMLEY, KENT, 1720–1744

He told my father that he had earned every thing he possessed by dint of labour and industry, except the last £6000—that he had had no education or advantage but what he had given himself.

Fanny Burney, *Early Diary*, 1773

During mid-October 1773 Dr. John Hawkesworth dined with Dr. Charles Burney, the famed musicologist, and his family in Queen Square. He was a frequent visitor at the Burney's, both at intimate family gatherings and as a guest at formal dinner parties that attracted people, like himself, of accomplishment and reputation. But this was no joyous evening for Hawkesworth and Burney. It is doubtful there was much discussion, as there often was, of the world of the arts in which both participated vigorously, enlightening not only the capital in which they worked, but the nation as a whole. Instead, there must have been gloomy reflection on the disaster that had befallen Hawkesworth during the preceding summer. The publication of his magnum opus, his account of Captain Cook's celebrated voyage to the South Seas, had brought, not public approbation, but extreme censure; the work that promised to be his career's capstone had produced instead heated condemnation and dark charges of obscenity and even heresy. Hawkesworth endured months of abuse, largely on his own as friends remained strangely silent in his time of stress. But Burney remained loyal, perhaps from a recognition that he had helped cause his friend's plight, but more likely from an essential decency of character. Certainly he saw at first hand the terrible toll the past months had taken on Hawkesworth, and Burney's daughter Fanny remarks of this period of the writer's life that she had never seen "a man more altered, thin, livid, harassed!"[1]

With Burney, at least, Hawkesworth could share thoughts that had remained almost exclusively his during the past summer, and with this friend there was probably genuine unburdening of profound grief. Hawkesworth spoke not as one simply weakened by a series of reverses, the cumulative effect of which bends, but does not break, the fabric of mind and body, but as one virtually destroyed by a single calamitous event that

3

made recovery almost impossible. He was unprepared for his special trial; nothing in his previous years remotely suggested that he would one day face it. It was a time, then, that inevitably called for reflection and even for final stocktaking. In a rare personal reference Hawkesworth told Burney "that he had earned every thing he possessed by dint of labour and industry, except the last £6000—that he had had no education or advantage but what he had given himself."[2] The tone here might seem one of self-justification, but it is better seen as the frame that contains the versatile career of an eighteenth-century man of letters. Fortunately, sufficient material remains to provide a fair reconstruction of the life and literary career of the man Samuel Johnson called friend, Sir Joshua Reynolds recorded in portrait, and an age looked to for general elevation of mind and spirit before his account of Cook's famous voyage unleashed vituperation that extinguished health and obliterated reputation.

Hawkesworth's early years are wrapped in obscurity. His previous biographers failed, in fact, to establish the year of his birth, and in the whole of his published work and correspondence there is scarcely a direct reference to his early life. Unlike some, Hawkesworth did not care to gild the success of later life with allusions to humble beginnings. Nevertheless, it is possible to provide a brief sketch of the time between his birth in 1720 and his removal as a young man to Bromley, Kent.[3]

Hawkesworth was baptized in Old St. Pancras Church by Edward De Chair on October 28, 1720, and one can assume he was born shortly before this date. His parents, John and Ann Hawkesworth (née Cornford) had been married by the same clergyman on July 22, 1716. Besides John they had a daughter, Honor, John's senior by about a year who was to marry John Ryland, a Johnson intimate, and another son, Thomas, baptized on September 28, 1722, who apparently did not survive long. A number of Hawkesworths, undoubtedly related to the writer's family, appear in the records of this parish, though precise connections cannot be established.[4]

Although the church of his baptism had not yet been swallowed up by the expanding metropolis, Hawkesworth probably spent his early years in or near the capital. His parents were, in fact, in residence at Tottenham Court at the time of his birth, and from then until his death he would be defined, like Johnson, by the kingdom's greatest city. It was in London that he would first encounter the world of letters and would meet Edward Cave of the *Gentleman's Magazine*, who drew aspiring writers like young Samuel Johnson to St. John's Gate; it was in London that Hawkesworth would attend meetings of Johnson's Ivy Lane Club; in London where his literary reputation would first be secured through his celebrated *Adventurer*; in London, finally, where the names of Cook and Hawkesworth would be joined in the latter's publication of an account of the captain's first Pacific voyage.

If Hawkesworth achieved prominence in the age that is marked by the name of its greatest writer and personality, he came of age in much the same world in which the young Johnson struggled to achieve fame. Shortly before Hawkesworth's birth George I had ascended the throne (1714), and the Old Pretender had unsuccessfully invaded Scotland (1715); shortly after his birth Walpole became prime minister (1721). George Frederick Handel first visited England in 1710, Defoe published *Robinson Crusoe* in 1719, and *Gulliver's Travels* appeared in 1726. Alexander Pope was the age's finest poet, and Hawkesworth's birth and early years are framed by Pope's various masterpieces—*The Rape of the Lock* was published in 1712, *An Essay on Man* in 1733, and *The Dunciad* in various versions from 1728 to 1743. The young Hawkesworth would, in fact, be as much influenced by Pope as the mature man was by Johnson.

Little is known about Hawkesworth's parents, though the Osborn sketch of his life at Yale suggests that his father was of Yorkshire descent. A piously educated man, he had a working knowledge of Latin and Greek and was "perfectly acquainted with French." By trade a watch-chaser and "so nice in his work, that he required more time than many others," his living was injured by the South Sea scheme of 1720. He contracted a debilitating disease "by too close application to his business, which gradually declining, he tried enamelling and other arts with still less success, and at length became [a] French usher in a small academy." Hawkesworth's father was, the sketch observes "always cheerful and agreeable." By education and conviction a Calvinistic Dissenter, he wrote one or two pamphlets "distinguished by deep thought and unaffected piety." Even less is known about Hawkesworth's mother, though the sketch provides the detail that she had "relations in affluence, but ruined by the consequences of the South Sea failure—highly exemplary in domestic virtues." Hawkesworth's origins, then, were humble, though there is no evidence that his early years were unhappy. Of his parents the sketch notes, "Dr. H. frequently said, that a faithful memorial of his father's and mother's lives might prove [of] higher importance than the history of his own."[5]

The Osborn Sketch also gives a brief insight into Hawkesworth's early education, commenting that he "learned only to write a fine hand, and the first rules of arithmetic, with a competent knowledge of his own language, chiefly from the Bible, from which text his parents diligently inculcated religious principles on his mind."[6] Yet for whatever advantages his parents could give him, even a father employed in a skilled trade with a knowledge of languages ancient and modern, Hawkesworth apparently felt to the end of his life the limitations of such a background.

To be mainly self-educated in the eighteenth century was no disgrace, though it was undoubtedly a handicap even in an age when few reached the university or were able to prepare for it. But far less than now was formal certification of educational attainment a necessity, and there were outlets for the talented, especially in London. No better example of a man who benefited from self-instruction exists than Johnson himself. In fact, in 1748 he wrote a fluent and graceful preface to Dodsley's *Preceptor*, a text designed not only for schools but for the enlightenment of those without access to regular instruction. Here, the title page suggests, the intellectually curious could encounter the diversity of human knowledge—reading, speaking, writing letters, geometry, astronomy, chronology, history, rhetoric, poetry, drawing, logic, natural history, ethics or morality, trade, commerce, laws and government, and human life and manners.

It was to such a text that Hawkesworth might have turned as a young man, though Sir John Hawkins in his *Life of Samuel Johnson, LL.D.*, provides a more extended, it somewhat negative, survey of his learning. While Hawkins concedes that Hawkesworth "had a good share of wit, and a vein of humour" and "more than a competent share of that intelligence which is necessary to qualify a man for conversation," he highlights the intellectual limitations of his fellow Ivy Lane Club member. "Hawkesworth was a man of fine parts," he suggests, "but no learning: his reading had been irregular and desultory" and "on no subject had he ever formed any system." Although Hawkins concludes that Hawkesworth's office of curator of the *Gentleman's Magazine* gave him "great opportunities of improvement, by an extensive correspondence with men of all professions," he sees a mind originally enriched by little more than the poems of Pope and the writings of modern French writers. "With the aid of Keill's Introduction, Chambers's Dictionary, and other such common books," Hawkins continues in his unflattering portrait, Hawkesworth "had attained such an insight into physics, as enabled him to talk on the subject." But he adds flatly: "In the more valuable branches of learning, he was deficient."[7]

While Hawkins's account can be trusted, it is marred by that special acidity that characterized the "unclubable knight" in assessments of his contemporaries. What he does reveal, though, is that Hawkesworth's intellectual interests, if somewhat haphazard, were wide and he possessed an inquisitive mind: one can hardly fault him for turning to such a work as John Keill's *Introduction to Natural Philosophy; or, Philosophical Lectures Read in the University of Oxford* . . . (1720), or Ephraim Chambers's *Cyclopaedia; or, An Universal Dictionary of Arts and Sciences* . . . *Compiled from the Best Authors* . . . (1728); and Pope provided an elegant summary of contemporary ethics. If by the "more valuable branches of learning" Hawkins means the classics, Hawkesworth was clearly deficient: his writing bore no stamp of Greece and Rome. Yet the English language received the full measure of his talents, and few writers of the time handled it with so much grace, force, and precision.

A more charitable summary of Hawkesworth's intellectual attainments appears in *Kentish Poets*, where R. Freeman writes in specific and even hostile response to Hawkins. "Hawkesworth had indeed no pretension to the character of a learned man, if by a learned man be meant one whose memory is loaded with all the literary lumber of schools," he asserts, "but that he derived from nature the finest capacity, that he had read much, and observed more, is amply proved by the number, variety, and the excellence of his productions."[8] Whether one accepts Hawkins's or Freeman's view of Hawkesworth's education, it is clear that his learning was more the result of his own efforts, of a quick and retentive mind, than of formal modes of instruction.

Although innate powers of composition manifested themselves early in his life, it was law rather than letters that engaged his energies for several years of young adulthood. Nearly all of Hawkesworth's biographers refer to his apprenticeship as a clerk to John Harwood, an attorney in Grocers' Alley in the Poultry, though none document his service. The articles of apprenticeship in the Public Record Office show that "John Son of John Hawkesworth" was apprenticed to John Harwood on Wednesday, the twenty-second of March, 1737, for five years nine months from the first of March. Five pounds were paid in consideration and a tax of two shillings sixpence.[9] At this time Hawkesworth was sixteen years old; his apprenticeship would have expired in November 1742. It does not appear to have been a happy or productive period in his life.

Freeman suggests that the character of Hawkesworth's handwriting reveals he worked as a mere transcriber in the attorney's office, and "it is certain," he comments, "that his occupation did not satisfy him, and that he took the earliest opportunity that offered to resign it, for the more congenial pursuits of literature." Whether he resigned or not, Hawkesworth met at this time with men of letters and wit, principally with John Ryland. Although confined in their work for long hours each day, they enjoyed each other's company on Sunday mornings or during the evening, sometimes at the home of Hawkesworth's father. "Otherwise," the Osborn Sketch comments, "they met only by stealth, and although living almost within sight of each other, . . . they chiefly conversed by the penny post under feigned signatures. In the office where H. wrote no fire was ever allowed, even during the severe winter of 1739." The last comment vividly highlights the difference between our age's attitude about life's basic amenities and that of Georgian England. An intense cold settled over England in January 1740, causing widespread suffering, especially in London. People froze in the streets—one, in fact, in Drury Lane—and the Thames itself solidified, depriving luckless watermen of their livelihood.[10]

The young attorney's clerk could not have chosen a friend more wisely; in Ryland he gained, eventually, not only a brother-in-law, but probably access to Cave and association with Johnson himself. Ryland was a lifelong Johnson intimate, a member of his first and last clubs, one who attended his final illness as well as his funeral. "Perhaps no man," John Nichols writes, "was more acquainted with Dr. Johnson's character, or better qualified to delineate it." Ryland was a good scholar, Nichols records, and "expressed himself, both in writing and speaking, in a peculiarly elegant and forcible manner. From long habits of intimacy he occasionally caught the expressions of his friends Johnson and Hawkesworth; but his mode of thinking was his own."[11] To have enjoyed the company of two such men must have partially compensated for Hawkesworth's lack of formal education, and there were benefits to be had at Ryland's and Johnson's table that even the best university could not provide.

While there are few references in Hawkesworth's writing or correspondence to his early years, *Adventurer* nos. 12, 13, and 14, the story of Opsinous, are probably based on his own experiences as a youth confronting the chaos, excitement, and dangers of the metropolis. Opsinous is the only son of a wealthy farmer zealous that his son learn Greek and Latin, but instead of sending him to boarding school (being unwilling to lose his son's company), he employs the local curate to be his tutor for ten pounds a year and board. From this good man Opsinous learns the classics and sciences and is taught "the theory of Christianity by his precepts, and the practice by his example."[12] Although the curate urges that Opsinous be sent to the university with a view to taking orders, a relation of his mother, an attorney of great practice in the Temple, declares: "If you have a mind your boy should make a figure in life, . . . put him clerk to me." (1:83). Opsinous leaves the purity of home for London's corruption and licentiousness, and his life begins to illustrate an "insensible deviation from felicity," which at last plunges him "in irremediable calamity." "I wish," he writes, "that others may escape perdition; and am, therefore, solicitous to warn them of the path, that leads to the precipice from which I have fallen" (1:79–80). Opsinous's London is the world of sealed, suffocating interiors that Richardson depicts so vividly in *Clarissa*, a world where the innocent are quickly initiated into new, diseased conditions of life. Opsinous's attorney relation keeps a mistress and challenges all ethical, moral, and religious assumptions. The young clerk is quickly caught up in the tainted atmosphere of the disputing clubs, frequented by apprentices, would-be wits, and men-about-town. There, he gains no ethical illumination but is gradually worn down and degraded by the atmosphere of blasphemy and moral relativism. "Instead of being confirmed in any principle," he comments, "I was diverted of all; the perplexity of my mind was increased, and I contracted such a habit of questioning whatever offered itself to my imagination, that I almost doubted of my own existence" (1:89). Opsinous's decline is rapid and absolute: he pursues sensuality and gratification of appetite; he seduces the attorney's lovely daughter, who dies from an abortion. Although acquitted of the crime, he becomes a prisoner of conscience, swallows poison, and composes his warning before expiring.

Opsinous's unhappy tale is obviously not Hawkesworth's, but there may be some parallels: Opsinous's early educational aspirations, his desire to attend the university and to take holy orders, may have been Hawkesworth's at the same age; Opsinous's tutor may be modeled on Edward De Chair, who married Hawkesworth's parents and baptized and married him. If not in specifics, surely in atmosphere and tone the story of Opsinous offers clues to Hawkesworth's early London years, and John Ryland himself asserted that Hawkesworth's vivid depiction of the disputing clubs was drawn from real life.[13] Perhaps, though, these *Adventurer* papers are as valuable in providing foreshadowing as background: some thirty years later Hawkesworth's career and reputation would be destroyed by his alleged heretical views on Providence expressed in his account of Cook's first Pacific voyage, and a number of critics would recall then the moral purity of the *Adventurer* while indulging themselves in extended commentary on the author's deviations from the true faith. Hawkesworth, it seems, had become an Opsinous. Perhaps the evenings spent in the disputing clubs left the man of letters more a participant than he realized.

Most of Hawkesworth's correspondence survives from the period when he became a public figure with a wide range of friends and associates, but two early letters exist, one written when he was around eighteen, the other when he was twenty-two. They provide an index, at least, to his mind and person and suggest that the character of the man was formed at a comparatively early age.

Sometime during 1738 Hawkesworth wrote to a "dear Friend" whose mother had recovered from a serious illness. He is profuse in his concern and reveals a sensibility often noted by commentators on his life. "After having drank of the poisonous draught contained in the first paragraph of your last letter," he comments, "I found myself in a very bad way, and in particular it so far affected my intellectuals and put my spirits into such disorder, that I could not understand and indeed I scarce gave myself leave to read the rest." Hawkesworth then refers to his own improved health—he was evidently of frail constitution throughout his life—and at length to his "Delia," possibly a reference to Mary Brown, whom he married several years later. The thought of her loss, he states, "awakens all the Springs of

Tenderness and concern, and renders the weakness of Reason, & the strength of passion too conspicuous." Her delicate state has moved him to compose a poem, a fervent expression of the necessity of enduring loss, a capacity his friend appears to have in greater measure than the poet:

> O! were my temper of a mould like thine
> How would my Soul adore the hand divine!
> Could I, like thee desolve in tears and flow
> Swift from beneath the pondrous weight of woe.
> As ebbing ruins, on the sandy shore,
> Elusive leave the weight their surface bore,
> Flow in glad Tides to friendly Ocean's breast,
> And find in realms, unknown, eternal Rest!
> But my rough Soul, half formed by hasty heav'n,
> Just rudely hewn, no after polish giv'n,
> Where fires unquenched, of burning anquish, live,
> Knows not the soft relief that Tears can give
> Mounts quick to wrath, and quickly bows to Love,
> As traytor passions still alternate move,
> And did a mortal hand oppress my fair,
> Grief would be rage, and vengeance my Despair
> But as 'tis power, which equal Goodness guides,
> My Soul submits to Heav'n, and Rage subsides,
> Yet wanting vent, within my tortur'd breast,
> Ten thousand warring passions Murder rest,
> And smother every infant dawn of peace.[14]

If not strong poetry, it is accomplished verse for one not yet twenty and reveals the literary potential soon to be realized in the poetry columns of the *Gentleman's Magazine*. Biographically it offers insight into Hawkesworth's character and suggests, as do many other sources, the emotional and religious sides to his nature. He was a man of feeling during an age when that word described the fabric of a man's character rather than a transitory emotional state. It is clear that the youth of eighteen reacted in much the same way to the prospect of "Delia's" death as the mature man did to the public outcry over his account of Cook's *Voyages*, when "Ten thousand warring passions" beset him and destroyed both peace of mind and health of body.

Several decades later in its "Sketch of the Character of the late Dr. Hawkesworth" the *Annual Register* assessed the writer in terms remarkably similar to those that he had used to describe himself in the poem above; there is little doubt in reading this eulogy that the young man and the seasoned man of letters were much the same. "Alive to every tender sentiment of friendship," the author of the sketch writes of Hawkesworth, "his heart dilated with joy whenever heaven put it in his power to be beneficial to those he loved." Unfortunately, "this feeling disposition was the means of leading him into such frequent though transient gusts of passion, as were too much for his delicate constitution to bear, without feeling the effects of them."[15]

If the 1738 letter provides insight into Hawkesworth's character, another, written in 1742, provides valuable supplementary evidence and specific details about his early life. It is in Hawkesworth's own hand, a clear one that changed little over the years; it is dated November 24, 1742, from No. 6 Plumtree Court, Holborn, possibly his residence at the time. It is addressed "To the Revd. Mr. Parry," who must have been a close friend. "My Father, Mother Sister M^r. Ryland & Miss Brown send each of them their compliment," Hawkesworth writes, and adds that "we frequently think of you talk of you & laugh at the Remembrance of the merry Evenings we spent with the Doctor." He continues: "Our Thursday Evening Society (of which your friend Mr Lewis is sometimes one) seldom fail of drinking your Health out of the very glass which was more than Once consecrated to Music & Wine in your presence at Islington & we flatter ourselves you sometimes remember us in the same benevolent way." The letter reveals the presence of his immediate family: his parents; his sister, Honor; and two who joined it, John Ryland and Mary Brown, who would become Mrs. Hawkesworth. Ryland had, in fact, already married Honor, as Hawkesworth notes, "I forgot to tell you that my friend Mr Ryland comenced my Brother last Whitsun Monday."[16] Besides references to his family, the letter also suggests Hawkesworth's strong social nature—there would be many Thursday evening societies during his life at which Hawkesworth joined not only family and close friends, but a number of the most notable figures of his time.

The 1742 letter also reflects Hawkesworth's literary interests, particularly in Pope; and it is not difficult to detect in the commentary of the young man in his early twenties the future literary critic of the *Gentleman's Magazine* who, for all his mildness of character and elegance of person, was an astringent arbiter of the literature of his period and of the authors who produced it. Even the greatest poet of the age is not immune from fairly severe criticism:

> As Mr Lewis (who is much better qualified) gives you from time to time an account of every Thing that deserves Notice in the Literary World I shou'd pass this intirely over if I cou'd help but saying that M^r. Pope with all his stock of Wit & knack at Versification is in my Eyes become almost contemptible for treating my Lord Shaftesbury (a Man every way his Superior) in the shameless manner he has done in his last Dunciad. It was a Crime I had forgiven him to steal from his Lordship's

writings without owning it which he had done almost throughout his
Ethic Epistles but to endeavour to lessen his Character after that is a
Villany of the same Nature as that of a felon's burning a House after he
has robb'd it to conceal the Theft & he seems to have acted from the
same Motive too for the less my Lord Shaftesbury is read the more M[r].
Popes works will be thought to be his own however the little gentleman
has been since sufficiently humbled on another Score as I doubt not but
you have heard.[17]

Hawkesworth's character, his religious and social nature, and his
interest in the world of letters are all revealed in these two letters, and one
suspects that however valuable other evidence might be in establishing a
full portrait of his early years, it would more likely complement than extend
or amend one's view of him. Of Hawkesworth one might say as Boswell
said of the young Johnson "that the boy is the man in miniature: and that the
distinguishing characteristicks of each individual are the same, through the
whole course of life."[18]

Some information has survived about Hawkesworth's life before he
became an established literary figure, especially about such important
events in his life as his marriage and his removal to and life in Bromley,
Kent. The Osborn sketch of his life comments that "his sister, whose heart
was congenial with his paid unremitting attention to his health, which
suffered from much close application, and hardships, and probably from
'stoln evenings spent with the choice spirits of the time.' " Hawkesworth,
the sketch continues, went to the country to repair his health and there met
his future wife, "to whose purse and unlimited affections, as well as to her
domestic economy and prudence he was indebted most materially for
comfort and support in the first unfavourable circumstances of his ensuing
life, and for whatever of ease and enjoyment attended it toward the close."[19]

Just when Hawkesworth first met Mary Brown is not clear, though it
was before November 1742, according to the letter quoted above. Their
first association may have been professional: Freeman notes that Mary
Brown and her mother kept a boarding school at Sydenham where
Hawkesworth officiated as a writing master. At the time of their marriage,
however, he gave his parish as Saint Andrew Holborn and she, Saint
Clement Danes, facts recorded in a license dated May 11, 1744. The
marriage took place the following day at the site of Hawkesworth's baptism,
the ceremony conducted by the incumbent, Edward De Chair. Mary,
Hawkesworth's wife, was the daughter of John Brown, a Bromley butcher.
She was from all evidence a woman of sensitivity and intelligence; their
marriage was by all accounts a genuinely happy union cemented by love,
affection, and deep religious conviction. Joseph Cradock, who knew them

well, spoke highly of Mary Hawkesworth. "His excellent and intelligent wife was always discreet," he writes, "and had the management of his great work, the 'Voyages,' been left *entirely* with her, nothing either immoral or offensive would ever have appeared before the public. I never knew, till lately, how much merit, in former publications, was due to her. She was an unassuming woman, of very superior talent."[20] She was also a woman of considerable energy and through her successful administration of a boarding school at Bromley apparently provided her husband with a secure enough financial base to build his literary career.

Sir John Hawkins, in fact, argues that Hawkesworth's first significant work, the *Adventurer*, was connected with this school, that it resulted from Hawkesworth's "desire of advantage in his then profession, which ostensibly was that of a governor of a school for the education of young females, by making himself known as a judge of life and manners, and capable of qualifying those of riper years for the important relations of domestic society." Philip Norman, author of undated manuscript notes preserved in the Bromley Central Library, gives specific information about the school's location: "Of girls' schools at Bromley the earliest, I believe about which we have any account is that kept by Mrs Hawkesworth in the famous old house a short distance north of the Bell." Freeman doubts there was any connection between this school and the publication of the *Adventurer* and also suggests that Mrs. Hawkesworth kept a second facility. "From private information of unquestioned authority," he writes, "we have since been assured that Mrs. Hawkesworth, after the death of her mother [around June 2, 1757] kept a boarding house for ladies, rather than a boarding school for children, to the latter of which, although of a superior order, the Doctor always expressed a great dislike, and never interfered in the management of it." Whatever special form they took, Mary Hawkesworth's enterprises must have spared her husband a first-hand confrontation with the awful Johnsonian truth that "slow rises worth, by poverty depress'd."[21]

The site of the school was also that of the Hawkesworths' home, "the famous old house" Norman refers to. Just when the Hawkesworths moved to this residence is not clear, but one suspects it was soon after their marriage in 1744. On June 20, 1773, Mary Hawkesworth wrote to Mrs. Garrick in an attempt to patch up the feud that had developed between their husbands over Hawkesworth's edition of Cook's *Voyages*. Here she mentions that "I am at length return'd to my peaceful Mansion at Bromley; Almost thirty years of enjoyment under this Roof has very much endear'd it to *me*."[22]

The Hawkesworths occupied, though Dr. Hawkesworth never owned, one of the most distinguished properties in Bromley, a home inhabited in the sixteenth century by the Knight family and in the seventeenth century by the Thornhills. It was known variously as the Thornhill Mansion or the Grete (Great) House. Late in the seventeenth century (1683) ownership passed to a Geoffrey Amhurst; for half of the eighteenth century it was held by the Blomer family, who sold it to William Scott in 1757. Assessment books reveal that he let it to the Hawkesworths for thirty-five pounds a year. Around 1776 Mary Hawkesworth acquired the property and at her death in 1796 owned the better portion of High Street East.[23] The sale of the property in 1757 caused Hawkesworth real consternation and a search for new accommodations. "The house in which I now live at this place, is lately sold with the estate to which it belongs," he writes to Joseph Highmore, the painter, "and I shall be obliged to quit it in about eight months." No move was necessary, however, and he was to pass the remainder of his life in one of Bromley's most handsome properties. It included several acres of land, a number of outbuildings, and the mansion itself, which stood on High Street just north of the Bell Hotel. Edward Walford in his *Greater London* writes that the house "stood in its own grounds inside heavy gates, the side posts of which were surmounted by globes of stone." Excavations in the spring of 1898 for electric-light works revealed the foundations of the old house and a massive garden wall with a succession of small arched recesses. Presumably the property included a stand of trees, for in a letter written on January 20 (no year indicated) Johnson commented that "you may by chance remember that I once mentioned in your grove the fitness of an epitome of Chambers Dictionary, which you said you would some time undertake."[24]

The reasons for the Hawkesworths' removal to Bromley are clear: for Mary Hawkesworth it was not only a source of livelihood from her boarding school, but native ground with family and friends nearby; for the aspiring man of letters it offered proximity to the full tide of human existence that could be found at Charing Cross as well as distance from the city's roar and turmoil. Stage connections were good, and if one chose, a return trip could be made in a day. Although Hawkesworth could not live without London, he did not appear to have a Johnsonian devotion to living in it. To his friend Joseph Highmore he wrote in 1760, for example, "I am almost overwhelmed with fatigue, and if I were to stay much longer in town, my life would not only be short but miserable." If Johnson could find refreshment merely by walking down Fleet Street to the Strand, Hawkesworth would have more eagerly boarded the stage to a town that Susanna Highmore, daughter of the famous artist, described in a letter of August 12, 1759, to Elizabeth Carter as possessing "every charm that a rural spot can boast, which is neither adorned by sea nor river."[25]

Hawkesworth's village would have been defined by the usual shops of the time to meet the domestic needs of the small resident population (his father-in-law was, in fact, a butcher) and was dominated by the parish church of St. Peter and St. Paul, the properties of the bishop of Rochester, the Bell Hotel, and the Hawkesworth mansion itself. All but the tower of the church was destroyed in an air raid in 1941, though the site is much as Hawkesworth viewed it, and it is not difficult to recreate in the mind's eye another chief landmark, the Bell. It occupied a central position on High Street, dominating the thoroughfare with its long frontage, identifying itself with its big black bell standing in its wrought-iron frame over its portico. It was the town's most important hostelry; when coaches still ran through Bromley they regularly stopped there, temporarily interrupting the quiet of High Street. Inside this ancient structure, whose pleasing, warm interiors generated good fellowship and good appetite, there were, an account records, "cosy bar parlors and a dining-room of ample dimensions, much requisitioned for big dinner and smokers. Much of the furniture was of the kind that excites the envy of the dealer in antiques, and in the quaint bedrooms upstairs were inlaid presses, toilet glasses &c., from the workshops of Sheraton and Chippendale." Johnson and his wife Tetty apparently were frequent visitors to Bromley and undoubtedly were entertained at the Hawkesworth home. But keeping in mind Johnson's assertion that "there is no private house . . . in which people can enjoy themselves so well, as at a capital tavern," one can imagine that Hawkesworth on occasion willingly succumbed to Johnson's urgings that the two of them walk the few steps to the Bell to enjoy such public felicity.[26]

If not its first citizen, Hawkesworth was surely among Bromley's most prominent citizens as the town's writer-in-residence in the eighteenth century (many years later it claimed the even more celebrated H. G. Wells). Hawkesworth's success as a writer and moralist excited great admiration. Susanna Highmore wrote to Elizabeth Carter on August 12, 1759, from Bromley, where she spent the summer months in the Hawkesworth household, that the doctor "associates very much with neighbors, who are all desirous of his company, and not a little proud of it." She had obtained, Freeman notes, "the intimate friendship of Young, Hawkesworth, and Richardson, a triumvirate rarely to be matched in any age or country." She undoubtedly joined those in Bromley who relished their association with the man of letters and valued the hours spent with such an estimable figure. "I am afraid when I return home," she continues, "I shall lament the not having sufficiently improved my time, where such opportunities are afforded for enriching the mind."[27]

However agreeable and gregarious a neighbor, Hawkesworth did not relish his more mundane involvement in parish affairs, and the vestry minutes in the parish church reveal something less than a public-spirited citizen eager to do service. In fact, he vigorously resisted service as a parish overseer, though vestry minutes show he ultimately capitulated. Hawkesworth apparently hoped to avoid such an assignment on the basis that he had been awarded a Lambeth doctorate, but according to the minutes for May 10, 1761, the vestry "resolved that it is the unanimous Opinion of this Vestry that notwithstanding the Reason alledged by the Dr he is not exempted by Law from serving parish Offices," and the best that Hawkesworth achieved was a delay until the spring of 1763. Vestry minutes and his own correspondence give some view of his work. To his friend Sir James Caldwell he wrote on July 2, 1763, "Today & to Morrow I shall be engaged in finishing a Contest by Arbitration that has been long in Litigation." In another letter written in the same month he reported, "I shall go thither from Bromley to Morrow in the afternoon, if I can credit the parish Accounts to Night which is what calls me away."[28]

What service Hawkesworth rendered was given rather grudgingly, and it is clear that London and the world of letters demanded the full measure of his intellectual and physical energies. Without excusing so manifest a lack of civic-mindedness, one can point out that the work of the vestry was necessarily pragmatic, concerned with the mundane concerns of parish life, particularly the administration of relief to the poor. And there were discussions, vestry minutes record, of very special problems—of wandering hogs and pollutions emanating from a butcher's work. These were hardly topics to sustain the interest of the author of elegant *Adventurer* papers, man-about-town in busy London, and member of Johnson's first club.

If vestry minutes provide a glimpse, at least, of Hawkesworth's life in Bromley, Mary's will presents another, perhaps broader picture. If not an art form of itself (though Richardson could make of Clarissa's will the matter of great art), the eighteenth-century will approaches a limited generic status and offers an ample index to a person's or a family's way of life. Mary Hawkesworth's is no exception, and in some eight densely written folio pages aspects of her life that she shared with her husband unfold. Among other details, the will shows that the Hawkesworths employed a number of servants and were themselves generously supplied with the material comforts of life and such luxuries as a harpsichord, rings, gold watches, and silver goblets. Mary leaves bequests not only of valuable rings, many of them diamond, as well as other personal possessions, but substantial gifts amounting to several thousand pounds—one bequest alone for two thousand pounds and several smaller ones for three hundred and five hundred pounds.[29]

By the late 1740s the chief outlines of Hawkesworth's life and character are clear: his childhood and youth were over, his apprenticeship was served, and a literary career was already in progress. A portrait by Sir

Joshua Reynolds provides evidence about his person. Although he sat for the painter late in life, the portrait is romanticized and suggests a younger man. Hawkesworth sits at a table with pen in his right hand, the left placed just within his fur-lined coat. The pose suggests the days of Grub Street penury were long over, and one views a man at ease in a context of culture and affluence. Behind Hawkesworth are stately volumes, perhaps his *Adventurer*, *Telemachus*, and other products of his pen. Reynolds records a man more than moderately handsome, clear featured, the nose straight and prominent, the chin somewhat small and receding, the hair well back from a sloping forehead. The picture might confirm Dr. Burney's reference to Hawkesworth's small stature when he wrote of the abbé DeLille that "his person is not very unlike little Hawkesworth's, but *più brutto*." And in Reynolds's portrayal of a man whose person conveys a certain delicacy of form one understands as well Goldsmith's comment that "Johnson would have made a *decent monk*, and Hawkesworth *a good dancing master*."[30]

Compared to generals and statesmen, makers of decisions affecting thousands, Hawkesworth might appear to have led a static life; yet pen and sword are more evenly matched than some might imagine. Many admire the later eighteenth century as much for its dedication to language and mind as for the vitality of its politics, commerce, battles, and explorations. While the contributions to this world of Johnson and his circle are well documented, Hawkesworth's have yet to be defined. To trace his activities is to see in action another shaper of British culture. By the late 1740s his circle of friends and associates had begun to grow; it included, or soon would include, such figures as Elizabeth Carter, the classicist so much admired by Johnson; the Reverend Francis Fawkes, the noted translator; and the Reverend John Duncombe, prolific author and graduate of Benet College, Cambridge. There was Joseph Highmore, the painter of Hogarth's school; John Stanley, the remarkable organist and composer who enjoyed Handel's esteem and friendship; and Fulke Greville, the aristocrat and man of fashion in whose employ Hawkesworth may have met another lifelong intimate, Charles Burney. This was the beginning of associations that would take Hawkesworth into the heart of the culture of his time: ahead lay friendship with David Garrick, Benjamin Franklin, Sir James Caldwell, Lord Shelburne, Lord Sandwich, and Christopher Smart.

To find such a life eventless, then, is to address surfaces rather than substance, to ignore the action of a man who as a youth charted the range and depths of the young Johnson and as a mature writer recorded Captain Cook's first Pacific voyage, in the latter giving vivid and dramatic embodiment to the heroic British colonial spirit in action at the earth's far corners. And beyond these links with two of the most celebrated men of his age there is John Hawkesworth, literary editor of the *Gentleman's Magazine*, who influenced a generation of readers of this popular publication. Of these experiences, none was so formative as his early association with Johnson, a friendship that culminated in their joint authorship of the *Adventurer*, at mid-century a worthy successor to the *Tatler*, the *Spectator*, and the *Rambler*. This work delivered Hawkesworth from Grub Street's obscurity into the happier station of one of London's most promising young writers.

II SAMUEL JOHNSON, THE *ADVENTURER*, AND DR. HAWKESWORTH

After my coming to London to drive the world about a
little, you must all go to Jack Hawkesworth for anecdotes.

Johnson to Mrs. Piozzi

Hawkesworth's literary career is framed by two of the greatest figures
of his age—Samuel Johnson and Captain Cook. He concluded his career
charting Cook's first voyage to the South Seas; he began it in the company of
Johnson. Hawkesworth knew Johnson years before Boswell appeared on
the scene. The precise date of their meeting is probably forever obscured,
and if Hawkesworth ever recorded his first impressions of the man destined
to dominate a world, that record has long since perished. Some evidence
that has survived describing their early relationship tends more to confuse
than to clarify. William Shaw states in his account of Johnson's life, for
example, that Hawkesworth, along with Garrick and others, was Johnson's
pupil at Lichfield and that Johnson had "mentioned with pleasure, that the
place of his education [Lichfield] had produced a Wollaston, a Newton, a
Willis, a Garrick, and a Hawkesworth," the last two of whom were his
schoolfellows.[1] While the difference in their ages might allow for the
tutor-pupil relationship Shaw suggests, it almost surely precludes the
other. Since Hawkesworth had no apparent contact with Johnson outside
of London, Shaw's assertion remains intriguing but unsubstantiated.

In her *Anecdotes* Mrs. Piozzi provides an even better-known reference
to Johnson and Hawkesworth's friendship when she and Johnson discussed
his possible biographers. "After my coming to London to drive the world
about a little," he told her, "you must all go to Jack Hawkesworth for
anecdotes: I lived in great familiarity with him (though I think there was not
much affection) from the year 1753 till the time Mr. Thrale and you took me
up."[2] There is again obvious confusion here—the period of intimacy must
have taken place primarily *before* 1753—and other evidence suggests that it
was marked by more "affection" than Johnson admits to here.

The *Universal Magazine* memoir of Hawkesworth's life and the Osborn
Sketch help establish, however, the probable place and approximate year of
their meeting. "In his connexion with Mr. Cave, he was introduced to the
acquaintance of Dr. Samuel Johnson," the anonymous but apparently

authoritative author of the memoir writes; and the Osborn Sketch notes that Hawkesworth's "frequent visits to M^r C about the year 1740 gave him the inestimable advantage of shining in conjunction with that star of the first magnitude during the Hanoverian Era, which is now setting at last."[3] There seems little doubt, then, that Hawkesworth and Johnson were equally attracted by the magnet of the *Gentleman's Magazine* and that it was at St. John's Gate their paths first crossed. Although it is possible that their meeting occurred before Johnson's country interlude in Leicestershire during 1739–40, it is more likely it took place after Johnson's return to London in what proved to be his permanent commitment to the metropolis.

Hawkesworth met a very different Johnson from the literary lion Boswell encountered in the back parlor of Tom Davies' bookshop—not one who flowed with honor through the nation's assemblies so much as the struggler rolling, it must have seemed to Johnson, "darkling down the torrent of his fate." For all his prodigious powers of mind Johnson had, in fact, failed at much he had hoped to accomplish: the months spent at Oxford had faded into memory, leaving the painful realization that he had failed to take a degree; a career in law or in holy orders seemed equally closed to him; and the most likely calling for one of his intellectual prowess—teaching—had resulted in the failure of his school at Edial and continued frustration as he failed to gain appointment after appointment. While marriage to Elizabeth Porter in July 1735 brought some change in Johnson's fortune, Tetty's modest resources were far from adequate, and only a retreat to London itself seemed to offer any prospect of success. And in London the brightest hope for one who would live by his pen lay at St. John's Gate, Clerkenwell, the home of the *Gentleman's Magazine*. For a number of years thereafter Johnson not only contributed a variety of writings to this publication that heralded greater productions to come, but served as Cave's principal editorial assistant. When he left for fuller devotion to the composition of the *Dictionary* and other literary pursuits, his friend Hawkesworth succeeded him and made of the *Gentleman's Magazine* one of the most important literary reviews of the age.[4]

A number of ties may have bound Hawkesworth and Johnson together during this period. Besides their mutual interest in Cave's periodical, Hawkesworth must have seen much in Johnson's life and aspirations to interest him: his friend had attended a great university, a fascinating world far removed from that of the son of a watch-chaser; he had already undertaken the composition of his tragedy *Irene* and undoubtedly discussed with his young friend the problems of stagecraft and the theatrical world in general, lessons that the future playwright and critic of drama must have attended carefully; and Johnson certainly would have shared with Hawkesworth anecdotes about some of his colorful friends—the notorious

Richard Savage, for example, the "artificial" bastard who claimed to be the illegitimate son of Earl Rivers and the countess of Macclesfield.

While it is not difficult to determine reasons for Hawkesworth's attraction to Johnson at this time, one might question more closely Johnson's interest in Hawkesworth. Although it is not possible to define those general affinities of spirit and personality that must have produced their friendship, it is likely that in Hawkesworth Johnson came to admire not only a singular devotion to the profession of letters but his special power to give shape to ideas through his extraordinary command of the English tongue. Indeed, Johnson might have agreed that the *Annual Register's* characterization of the mature writer applied equally to his youthful friend at St. John's Gate, that Hawkesworth's "fertile mind teemed with ideas, which he delivered in so clear, and yet concise a manner, that no one could be at a loss perfectly to comprehend his meaning, or ever tired by hearing him speak."[5]

There were practical reasons as well for a friendship that may have been primarily formed by a mutual reverence and capacity for language, not the least of which is that by the mid-1740s Hawkesworth made it possible for the Johnsons to escape the noise and pressures of the city for the peace of rural Bromley, Kent, some ten miles from London Bridge. It might be argued, in fact, that the Hawkesworths' Thornhill mansion served Johnson in somewhat the same manner in the 1740s as the Thrales' Streatham did from the 1760s. While Johnson claimed that "the happiness of London is not to be conceived but by those who have been in it," he and Tetty undoubtedly welcomed occasional surcease from the confusing admixture of overpowering contrasts of the city. For all the glories London presented to the eye fixed on general perspectives, there were assaults on even the toughest sensibilities. At mid-century London could be likened to an "enormous ant palace," and while it contained the kingdom's greatest treasures, it also harbored stews and stink and those Hogarthian scenes that would depress even the most devoted cosmopolite.[6]

Sarah Perrin (1745–95), one of five children of William Perrin and Frances Rooker, who lived near Bromley, documents Johnson's visits to the Hawkesworths at Bromley in the late 1740s and early 1750s. She writes, for instance: "My Sister Mary, the only Daughter living besides Myself, was sent to Mrs Hawkesworths at Bromley about a Mile from Beckenham, from her situation there[.] My Mother became slightly acquainted with Dr Johnson who at that time spent much of his time with Dr Hawkesworth." She continues: "My Brother when at home for the Hollidays had the Misfortune to cut his Leg with a Wood bill, which being across a Muscle occasioned so great a Wound, that My Mother sent him before the Coachman to Mr Blacking the Surgeon at Bromley where the D^r [Johnson] hapened to be when My Brother was taken in, and sat by during the Time the wound was sewed up." Sarah Perrin's "anecdotes and occurrences" not only place Johnson in Bromley, but suggest that he knew Hawkesworth's friends and acquaintances as well.[7] It is probable, for example, that at Bromley Johnson became well acquainted with Hawkesworth's curate, the Reverend Thomas Bagshaw, and Zachary Pearce (who became bishop of Rochester in 1756), both of whom contributed etymologies to the *Dictionary*.

If Johnson enjoyed the society of such figures at Bromley, he and Hawkesworth encountered a wider circle of friends in London, especially those connected with the literary world of St. John's Gate. Johnson's friends and acquaintances during this time are, in fact, a fairly accurate index to Hawkesworth's. "They were a strange group, those cronies of Johnson's in the early 1740's," James L. Clifford writes, "Bohemian poets, impractical idealists, reformed imposters, eager inventors, drunken rakes, and serious clergymen, many of them with only one tie in common, a compulsion to write."[8] Two particularly colorful members of this group were Samuel Boyse, a perennial ne'er-do-well who squandered money given him by sympathetic friends on gluttony; and George Psalmanazar, who perpetrated one of the celebrated hoaxes of the time by pretending to be a native of Formosa, inventing a complex alphabet and grammar of the language, teaching that "language" at Christ Church, Oxford, and publishing a history and geography of the island.[9]

While it is likely that Hawkesworth enjoyed the company of such figures as Boyse and Psalmanazar, it is certain that he met more frequently with those connected with the *Gentleman's Magazine*: the poet Moses Browne, now obscure but a person Cave felt warranted introduction to Johnson; "brisk" Tom Birch, one of Cave's chief advisors, who knew literary London as few other men (his unpublished correspondence in the British Library sheds light on this new age of authorship); a Scot, William Guthrie, who was involved with Johnson in the administration and editing of the periodical; and David Henry, Cave's brother-in-law and coadjutor, who assumed control of the magazine along with Richard Cave at Cave's death in 1754. Also attracted to the Gate, though not part of the magazine's staff, were Mark Akenside, the poet and physician; Richard Savage; and certainly Elizabeth Carter, the future bluestocking and contributor to Hawkesworth's first formal literary undertaking, the *Adventurer*. During the early 1740s Hawkesworth also met (perhaps through Johnson) a man destined to become one of the celebrated actors of the age—David Garrick. Hawkesworth might have met Garrick at his impromptu performance of the title role in Fielding's *Mock Doctor*, which was held during the summer of 1740 in the great room over the arch of St. John's Gate, though it is more likely that he knew him by the time Garrick gave his brilliant rendition of Richard III in Goodman's Fields on October 19, 1741. Whatever the date of the first meeting, their friendship developed quickly. While Johnson and Garrick gradually moved apart to different interests, Hawkesworth and Garrick forged a professional relationship and friendship of depth and duration, one that paired the drama's best performer with one of its most important critics.[10]

Of Hawkesworth's friendships during this period, however, none was of greater importance than Johnson's. Some measure of the latter's esteem for the young writer is seen during the winter of 1749 when he invited Hawkesworth to join the first of his clubs, the Ivy Lane, which met on Tuesdays at the King's Head, a famous beefsteak house in Ivy Lane between Paternoster Row and Newgate Street in the shadow of St. Paul's Cathedral. Other members included Dr. Samuel Salter, father of the late master of Charterhouse; John Ryland, Hawkesworth's brother-in-law, who would remain a Johnson intimate to his death; John Payne, a bookseller and later chief accountant of the bank; Samuel Dyer, a learned young man preparing for the dissenting ministry; three physicians, Dr. William M'Ghie, Dr. Edmund Barker, and Dr. Richard Bathurst; and of chief importance, John Hawkins, the celebrated magistrate and chairman of the Middlesex Quarter Sessions, who achieved literary fame through an edition of Walton's *Compleat Angler*, a pioneering *History of Music*, and, most notably, a biography of Johnson that provides a powerful complement to Boswell's masterpiece. Although the Ivy Lane Club was by no means as distinguished as the later Literary Club, though its membership included no Boswell, no Goldsmith, no Burke, no Reynolds, the group that met regularly at the King's Head included men wise to the ways of the world who spared Johnson evenings of restless dissipation at the same time that they provided young Hawkesworth instruction and stimulating conversation.

In the company of Samuel Dyer, for example, one could scarcely resist illumination of mind. "To speak of his attainments in knowledge," Hawkins, the club's best historian, writes, "he was an excellent classical scholar, a great mathematician and natural philosopher, well versed in the Hebrew, and master of the Latin, French and Italian languages." Admission to this, as to all of Johnson's clubs, was made not exclusively on the basis of qualities of mind but also on more general ones of person—conviviality, clubability, were essential to those who were to sit in his presence. Few, apparently, could grace a circle more than Richard Bathurst, a man greatly admired for both his character and manner. M'Ghie, a Scotsman in Johnson's life some years before Boswell, served on the side of the government in the rebellion of 1745 and had tales to tell about a skirmish that he had engaged in at Falkirk. He was, Hawkins records, "a learned, ingenious, and modest man; and of those few of his country whom Johnson could endure. To say the truth, he treated him with great civility, and may almost be said to have loved him."[11]

Johnson was actively composing the great *Dictionary* at this time, and Boswell observes, in explaining his attendance at the club, that his "enlarged and lively mind could not be satisfied without more diversity of employment, and the pleasure of animated relaxation." But in any company Johnson graced, conviviality would not produce weakness of wit or debilitating luxuriance of mind, and perhaps it was Hawkesworth himself who provided Johnson with the pleasant mental stimulation Boswell so aptly characterizes as "animated relaxation." Johnson, it is said, "delighted to make him sometimes an antagonist in that swordplay of wit and logic, which was his favourite amusement, sometimes the disciple of that wisdom, which in his triumphs of controversy he was accustomed to pour forth."[12] While no specific site is suggested for such an exchange between the two men, the Ivy Lane Club is a logical one, and it is certain that serious discussions did take place at the Tuesday meetings at the King's Head.

No subject interested club members more than the world of letters, and on one occasion several of its members—Johnson, Hawkesworth, and Payne—along with the *Gentleman's Magazine* became intimately involved in one of the famous literary scandals of the time perpetrated by a Scot named William Lauder. His life was marked by constant misfortune: at a young age he lost a leg to a wild shot while watching a golf match on Bruntsfield Links near Edinburgh—amputation followed the freak injury—and he spent his last days in obscurity and poverty in Barbados, where he died in 1771. For a few years, though, he stirred up the nation with his attacks upon the originality of Milton's *Paradise Lost* and in the process brought chagrin not only to the Ivy Lane Club's major, but to at least two of its less famous members. Lauder's commentaries on Milton appeared in the January, February, April, June, and August issues of the *Gentleman's Magazine* for 1747; rejoinders from Milton's irate supporters appeared through 1749. In this year Lauder's attack culminated in *An Essay on Milton's Use and Imitation of the Moderns in His "Paradise Lost,"* in which the great poet was charged with being an "unlicensed" plagiarist who failed to acknowledge his sources, known, of course, to one William Lauder himself. Johnson and Hawkesworth undoubtedly encouraged and kept the debate alive in the magazine during this period—Lauder's claims seemed to have merit, and controversy of this kind could only enhance circulation—and they must have informed fellow club members of latest developments. Not only were Johnson and Hawkesworth immediately involved, but John Payne himself as publisher of Lauder's *Essay*. It is possible that Payne brought proofs of the piece to the club meeting held on Tuesday, December 5, 1749, where members discussed and even endorsed Lauder's controversial assertions. If so, their faulty judgment was revealed the following year as John Douglas unmasked Lauder in *Milton Vindicated from the Charge of Plagiarism Brought Against Him by Mr. Lauder and Lauder Himself Convicted of Several Forgeries and Gross Impositions on the Public*, published on November 26, 1750. Johnson moved strenuously to dissociate himself from the fraud and in the end dictated Lauder's letter of confession and contrition to Douglas.[13]

Hawkesworth's role in this strange affair is less clear, though it could have been significant. He might have played a greater part in keeping the controversy boiling in the *Gentleman's Magazine* than Johnson and is a likely author of the somewhat strained explanation of the periodical's involvement in the matter in the December 1750 issue. This included an apology to Richard Richardson, whose warnings about Lauder, as well as other matter hostile to the fake, had been ignored or, worse, even temporarily suppressed by the editors. If Hawkesworth had occasion for some self-recrimination about his role in the Lauder forgeries, he must have taken some comfort from the fact his mentor had been equally duped; and he probably would have agreed with Johnson, who in 1780 wrote in the margin of a book attacking him for his aid to this rare Scot: "In the business of Lauder I was deceived, partly by thinking the man too frantic to be fraudulent."[14]

More often than not, though, the members of the Ivy Lane Club engaged in agreeable activities, none so enjoyable, perhaps, as a celebration, possibly during the summer of 1750, of the impending publication of Charlotte Lennox's novel *The Life of Harriot Stuart*. Johnson proposed a full night's festivities, and Hawkins, though a somewhat unwilling participant (he had never sat up a night in his life), left a vivid record of the occasion, which took place about eight in the evening with Mrs. Lennox, her husband, and friends assembled at the Devil Tavern. "Our supper was elegant," Hawkins states, "and Johnson had directed that a magnificent hot apple-pye should make a part of it, and this he would have stuck with bay-leaves, because, forsooth, Mrs. Lenox was an authoress, and had written verses; and further, he had prepared for her a crown of laurel, with which, but not till he had invoked the muses by some ceremonies of his own invention, he encircled her brows." The revels continued throughout the night and by morning "Johnson's face shone with meridian splendour, though his drink had been only lemonade," Hawkins continues. "It was not till near eight that the creaking of the street-door gave the signal for our departure." Although Hawkins later likened this evening to a "debauch," an unkind term generated, perhaps, by one of Puritan proclivities recollecting a night spent in profitless dissipation, it is likely that John Hawkesworth, a probable participant, remembered the celebration with real pleasure.[15]

It was not simply innocent amusement that Hawkesworth gained from membership in the Ivy Lane Club; it can be argued that this happy assembly did much to complete his education. Certainly it provided worthy examples for him in the solid learning of Dyer, in the worldly wisdom of Ryland and Payne, in the maturity and good sense of old Salter, and in the restless energy and discipline of Hawkins, who would have been a fine model for any who cared to get on in the age. Most centrally, there was Johnson himself, about whom the Osborn Sketch notes in reference to this period, "If any man departed without being wiser or better it certainly must have been his own fault."[16]

One suspects that Johnson's and Hawkesworth's friendship was most profoundly cemented, though, not so much through the conviviality of the club, or even through extraordinary affinities of mind, as through an event that always remained central to Johnson's life—the death of his wife, Tetty, which occurred on March 17, 1752 (O. S.). "The dreadful shock of separation took place in the night," Boswell records, "and he immediately dispatched a letter to his friend, the Reverend Dr. Taylor." Taylor rushed to Johnson and prayed with him, "and thus, by means of that piety which was ever his primary object, his troubled mind was, in some degree, soothed and composed." While the Reverend Dr. Taylor provided Johnson essential support in those awful first hours of bereavement, Hawkesworth offered valuable assistance thereafter. Tyers writes in his *Biographical Sketch of Dr. Samuel Johnson* that "Hawkesworth, one of the Johnsonian school, upon being asked, whether Johnson was a happy man, by a gentleman who had been just introduced to him, and wanted to know every thing about him, confessed, that he looked upon him as a most miserable being." The moment of inquiry, Tyers notes, was probably about the time that Tetty died, and he states that Johnson "sent for Hawkesworth, in the most earnest manner, to come and give him consolation and his company."[17]

Hawkesworth not only gave Johnson consolation and company, but also attended to the details of Tetty's burial itself, a fact both Hawkins and Boswell record, though neither elaborates on this important event in Johnson's life, and it is clear Boswell knew little about it. Writing long after the fact, Boswell merely suggests that Johnson "deposited the remains of Mrs. Johnson in the church of Bromley in Kent, to which he was probably led by the residence of his friend Hawkesworth at that place." Hawkins is more specific, stating that Johnson "intended also to have deposited her remains in the chapel in Tothill fields, Westminster, but, altering his mind, he committed the disposal of them to his friend, Hawkesworth, who buried her in his own parish church of Bromley in Kent, under a black marble stone."[18]

Johnson's decision to bury his wife at Bromley has elicited little interest from those who have otherwise found details of his marriage fascinating. Although Boswell includes unflattering references to Tetty in the *Life*, especially Garrick's description of her "as very fat, with a bosom of more than ordinary protuberance, with swelled cheeks, of a florid red, produced by thick painting, and increased by the liberal use of cordials," he pointedly tasks his rival for questioning Johnson's devotion to her. "Why Sir John Hawkins should unwarrantably take upon him even to *suppose* that Johnson's fondness for her was *dissembled* (meaning simulated or assumed,) and to assert, that if it was not the case, 'it was a lesson he had learned by rote,' I cannot conceive," Boswell writes, "unless it proceeded from a want of similar feelings in his own breast." It is no longer possible, though, to believe completely in Boswell's somewhat idealized portrait of the Johnson marriage; certainly, he and Tetty were often separated.[19] Dr. L. F. Powell once suggested to me that Johnson and Hawkesworth shared lodgings during their early London days, an indication, perhaps, that Johnson's devotion to his wife was less than absolute.

Tetty's burial at Bromley, then, might have raised questions Boswell preferred to ignore. Why, indeed, was she buried there? Can Johnson's friendship with Hawkesworth explain burial some distance from the home parish? Would it have been unusual at the time to transport a body some distance for burial? More ominously, perhaps, did Tetty actually die at Bromley (while visiting the Hawkesworths, presumably) during a separation from Johnson, and did this intensify his grief on this sad occasion? In the end, answers to these questions result in modest clarification rather than dramatic revelation. A recently discovered letter Johnson wrote to Charlotte Lennox on March 12, 1752, a few days before Tetty's death, suggests beyond doubt that she died at 17 Gough Square. In it Johnson writes, "Poor Tetty Johnson's Ilness will not suffer me to think of going any whither, out of her call. She is very ill, and I am very much dejected." Removal of remains for burial outside a home parish was not unusual at the time and contravened no civil or church law.[20] Although Johnson's choice of Bromley was undoubtedly determined by his friendship with Hawkesworth, as both Boswell and Hawkins record, neither was aware that a recent event in Hawkesworth's life made him uniquely suited to help his friend at this time.

Tetty was buried at Bromley on March 26, 1752, according to the Bromley burial register and one kept by John Dunn, the local undertaker. Both sources also record that on February 24, 1752, about a month before Tetty's funeral, a John Hawkesworth was buried there, probably Hawkesworth's father. Johnson surely knew about this death, and he must have recalled it when his wife died. An intimate friend who had recently arranged a funeral would be a logical person to turn to, and Hawkesworth apparently saw to the details of Tetty's as he had his father's a few weeks earlier. At no time was Johnson in greater need of assistance, suffering, it seems, not only from emotional shock but from a high fever that prevented him from attending his wife's services. At least he had the comfort of knowing that Tetty had been delivered to friends for final committal and to a site of rural tranquility that she undoubtedly loved. In Johnson's eyes it must have been an ideal haven and a reminder, perhaps, of the more stable times in his married life. And beyond the Hawkesworths, Bromley offered other friends with whom Johnson must have spent many pleasant hours—the Reverend Thomas Bagshaw, for example, who conducted Tetty's funeral service. A sensitive, learned man, Bagshaw appears as late as the last year of Johnson's life when, on July 12, 1784, Johnson wrote to him, requesting permission to place a stone over Tetty's remains. It was placed on the floor inside the church, "close by y[e] Charyty Childrens Pue," the Dunn register records.[21] Although the church was largely destroyed during World War II, the stone survived and stands today on the wall of the amulatory, left-hand side, a monument to Mrs. Johnson's memory and Johnson's deep affection for her at the same time that it remains a symbol of his friendship for Hawkesworth. In a time of great crisis he answered Johnson's call of distress and assisted him in those pragmatic details that a grieving man could not handle.

The meetings of the Ivy Lane Club must have provided Johnson some surcease from painful reflection on Tetty's death, and its members undoubtedly directed his thoughts to the world of letters that still gave life purpose. His literary accomplishments by this time—*London, Irene,* and *The Vanity of Human Wishes;* the *Rambler;* ongoing work on the *Dictionary*—testify that participants in the club benefited from his genius scarcely less than later members of the more famous Literary Club. The *Rambler,* published from March 20, 1750, to March 14, 1752, was of special interest to club members and a source of regular discussion. If they encouraged Johnson in this literary undertaking, though he composed the paper virtually unaided, they gave even more direct support to its successor, the *Adventurer,* a periodical that brought Hawkesworth's considerable literary abilities to the English reading public.

Two sources provide a clear idea of this paper's genesis in the context of the Ivy Lane Club. The Osborn Sketch records that Hawkesworth engaged in the *Adventurer* at the urging of John Payne, the *Rambler's* publisher. The *Universal Magazine* memoir of Hawkesworth is more explicit:

> In the summer, after the conclusion of the Rambler, and when the collection of that work into volumes had probably begun to remove all uncertainty of its ultimate success, the counsels of the club in Ivy-Lane encouraged Hawkesworth to propose the plan of the Adventurer. Mr.

J. Payne agreed to become the publisher, at the price of two guineas a number, copy-money. Hawkesworth was to be the editor and principal author of the work.

Whoever initiated the work, it was clearly a product of the club, and a number of its members were involved in its production: from beginning to end Hawkesworth was its editor and principal author; Johnson later became extensively involved; Hawkins claims that Dr. Bathurst contributed papers, though Bonnell Thornton now seems a more likely author; M'Ghie, the Scotsman, made some effort to assist. John Payne, of course, was central. He was not only a patron of literature, but a businessman aware of what the reading public would buy; he undoubtedly felt that a sequel to the *Rambler*, especially one that benefited from some of the apparent mistakes of the great prototype, would succeed handsomely.[22]

There was much to recommend Hawkesworth to Payne as Johnson's successor: Payne had seen Hawkesworth frequently at close quarters in club meetings, undoubtedly noting how he held his own with its intelligent membership, including Johnson himself. Hawkesworth, moreover, had already established himself in the literary marketplace of the day, having completed a number of years of service for Edward Cave's *Gentleman's Magazine*; and Payne must have known from Hawkesworth's reviews for this publication, as well as from other writings, that in clarity and force his prose style bore remarkable similarities to Johnson's. In short, Payne could find few better qualified to undertake such a project, and he probably felt certain that if trouble prevailed, Johnson would not abandon two close friends. In this assumption Payne's faith was amply sustained.

Among the literary forms the eighteenth century perfected, the periodical essay ranks high. In format and content it appealed to sophisticated readers as well as to those whose literacy was of no long duration, giving to all almost equal measure of instruction and pleasure. At mid-century Johnson's *Rambler* harkened back to the papers of Addison and Steele, though his was no mere imitation: readers used to the light, satirical tone of the *Tatler* and *Spectator* contended in his paper with complicated sentences often flavored with "hard" words. But generations of readers, if not Johnson's contemporaries generally, have seen in the *Rambler* the fullest illustration of his thought and stylistic powers and have agreed with Boswell "that in no writings whatever can be found *more bark and steel for the mind.*"[23]

Although Hawkesworth hoped to emulate the *Rambler*, especially its moral mission, he tried to improve upon it, implying in his concluding paper, no. 140, that Johnson's periodical resounded too much with a single voice, Johnson's magisterial voice, perhaps too unwilling to conform to public taste. If subsequent readers applaud him for resisting pressures to animadvert upon sprightlier, more entertaining issues, Hawkesworth realized the short-term worth, at least, of variety in voice and composition. "I did not, however, undertake to execute this scheme alone," he explains, "not only because I wanted sufficient leisure but because some degree of sameness is produced by the peculiarities of every writer." Hawkesworth hoped that enlisting others in composition "whose pieces should have a general coincidence with mine, would produce a variety, and by increasing entertainment facilitate instruction." In this essay he not only details a strategy of composition but announces that from the outset the *Adventurer* aimed for the permanence only a book format could give. "When this work was first planned, it was determined," Hawkesworth writes, "that whatever might be its success, it should not be continued as a paper, till it became unwieldy as a book." There was agreement, he adds, "that four volumes, when they should be printed in a pocket size, would circulate better than more, and that scarce any of the purposes of publication could be effected by less: the work, therefore, was limited to four volumes, and four volumes are now completed."[24]

Although he served throughout as the *Adventurer*'s editor and composed some half of its contents, Hawkesworth received assistance from a number of writers, principally Johnson, Joseph Warton, and the author of eight papers signed "A." While much light has been shed on authorship in the *Adventurer*, problems remain. Thomas Warton and his sister Jane are now known to have been involved in papers once confidently assigned to Joseph Warton. The author of the "A" papers has resisted positive identification to this day. The first to assist Hawkesworth (he apparently contracted with him to contribute regularly to the publication), A was identified by Hawkins as Richard Bathurst, a member of the Ivy Lane Club. Alexander Chalmers, who included the *Adventurer* in his *British Essayists* (1802), accepted this designation, then switched to Bonnell Thornton in his preface to the latter's paper, the *Connoisseur*, published in the same series, also in 1802. Subsequent debate over the authorship of the "A" papers has focused exclusively on these two figures. Recent evidence points strongly to Thornton.[25]

In spite of Hawkins' membership in the circle that helped produce the paper, his citation of Bathurst has been challenged, especially by the discovery of a letter Joseph Warton wrote on November 17, 1752, to his brother Thomas, just three days after the publication of *Adventurer* no. 3, the first of the papers signed "A." "Thornton called & seemed piqued I should say to Johnson that He wrote the *Adventurer*," Warton notes. "I told him I heard it at a Coffee house openly from 20 people which is true." David Fairer, a perceptive student of Hawkesworth's paper, argues that "Thornton's reaction will reasonably bear only one interpretation. He 'seemed piqued' because the secret had escaped so early." Some years later, on March 30, 1790, Warton suggested in a letter to Boswell that "it was *Thornton*, not *Colman*, who wrote several papers. And it was always imagined, tho I have not positive proof, that Thornton wrote all the papers marked A." If this evidence is not conclusive, at least it is convincing; and when it is shown that parallels exist between the "A" *Adventurer* papers and Thornton's own periodical, the *Connoisseur*, Bathurst's case is further weakened, since no sample of his writing survives for such comparisons.[26]

Hawkesworth carried the burden of the authorship of the first volume virtually alone. Undoubtedly he had prepared some papers ahead of time, but when A's contributions became sporadic and eventually failed, Hawkesworth needed help. Neither the spirit of the paper, which precluded a single author, nor Hawkesworth's own energies, since the *Gentleman's Magazine* demanded much time from him, would permit such a pattern to continue. He might have felt keenly the truth of Johnson's words in his final *Rambler*—that the burden of regular composition can cause a writer to "bring to his task an attention dissipated, a memory embarassed, an imagination overwhelmed, a mind distracted with anxieties, a body languishing with disease." Although Hawkesworth suffered less alarming symptoms, apparently nothing worse than a pain in his face, he required assistance and turned to his friend Samuel Johnson. Johnson contributed his first paper on March 3, 1753, *Adventurer* no. 34, signed "T," the first of twenty-nine submissions that greatly supported Hawkesworth's paper no less than they enriched the Johnson canon. Through Johnson, Hawkesworth also secured the services of a distinguished scholar and critic, Joseph Warton. In a letter written on March 8, 1753, rich in details about the *Adventurer*'s composition, Johnson told Warton: "I hope this proposal will not be rejected, and that the next post will bring us your Compliance."[27]

Warton answered Johnson's appeal and embellished the *Adventurer* with some twenty-four papers that included distinguished criticism of ancient and modern literature, especially his essays on Shakespeare's *King Lear* and the *Tempest*. Joining the principal contributors were several other writers: Hester Mulso, George Colman, Catherine Talbot, and Elizabeth Carter. Hamilton Boyle has been suggested as another possible contributor, and even Sarah and Henry Fielding have been linked, undoubtedly erroneously, with the publication. Samuel Richardson himself was approached to contribute, but though his circle was well represented in the figures of Hester Mulso, Catherine Talbot, and Elizabeth Carter, he disclaimed any role in a letter to Lady Bradshaigh on October 9, 1754. "Had I wrote *Adventurers*," he comments, "I should have acquainted your Ladiship. . . . I was applied to on that Head: but never found Leisure to oblige the Appliers."[28] Thus, if the *Adventurer* was guided and written principally by Hawkesworth, it was sustained by a larger community that invested it with a variety of voices and a vitality of spirit, ensuring its appeal to a large and appreciative audience. While Johnson's and Warton's contributions have received deserved attention over the years, the papers of Hawkesworth, who more than any other writer gave the *Adventurer* its tone and ensured its popular success, deserve a brief review.

Only eight months after Johnson completed his last *Rambler* essay, the first *Adventurer* paper appeared, on Tuesday, November 7, 1752, printed on a folio sheet and a half, single column, for J. Payne, at Pope's Head, in Paternoster Row, where letters to the *Adventurer* were received. It entertained a nation thereafter every Tuesday and Saturday until March 9, 1754, and in bound volumes throughout the century; to the present day it can be read, at least in part, in a variety of formats. Readers found both entertainment and enlightenment: in literary criticism, potential elevation of taste and judgment; in fiction of many forms—dream visions, satirical adventure stories, fables and fairy tales, oriental and domestic apologues—escape and delight; in philosophical and religious material, elevation of mind and soul; in critiques of the current scene, of the "Town," reminiscent of the genial satire of Addison and Steele, incentives to "correct" behavior. Hawkesworth excelled in all of these forms, and he contributed a range of essays to the *Adventurer* that was matched by no other author.[29]

In his essays on literary criticism, especially *Adventurers* nos. 4 and 16, Hawkesworth delineates a view of art that marks all of his writing, not only in the periodical itself, but in the review canon in the *Gentleman's Magazine*, and ultimately in his rendition of Cook's *Voyages*. While Hawkesworth notes in his fourth *Adventurer* that writers of history, voyages, and biography are confined to facts that require primarily faithful transcription, he observes in his sixteenth paper that the writer of fiction "has unbounded liberty to select, to vary and to complicate" in such a way that he engages not simply the mind but the passions. Given this power, then, he argues that the writer of fiction should "principally consider the moral tendency of his work, and that when he relates events he should teach virtue" (*Adventurer*, 1:108). Man's moral nature is so weak, Hawkesworth believes, that fiction should stress that "virtue alone is sufficient to confer honour upon the lowest character, and that without it nothing can preserve the highest from contempt" (1:111). To support this view Hawkesworth presents a fictional portrait of two youths, Florio and Benevolus.

Florio is a splendid young man: learned in Latin and Greek, he studied at Westminster, attended the university, made the Grand Tour, and obtained a place at court. Graceful of person and polite of manner, he made many conquests among the ladies and "killed in a duel an officer, who upbraided him with a breach of promise of marriage, confirmed by an oath, to a young beauty whom he kept in great splendour as a mistress" (*Adven-*

turer, 1:112). Benevolus, on the other hand, is dull, something of a clod; he lacks polish in both dress and manner. Although he is remarkable for the most uniform virtue and unaffected piety, he "is the jest of an assembly, and the aversion of ladies" (1:112). Florio, then, emerges as a dashing, witty figure; Benevolus, for all his qualities, is something of a prig and undoubtedly a bore. "Which of these two characters wouldst thou choose for thy own?" Hawkesworth asks; "whom dost thou most honour, and to whom hast thou paid tribute of involuntary praise? Thy heart has already answered with spontaneous fidelity in favour of Florio" (1:113). He is, of course, correct, and we recognize that the creative artist can make us look favorably at "a scoundrel, who by perjury and murder has deserved the pillory and the gibbett" (1:113) and with scorn at a pious and decent man whose chief fault is dullness. Hawkesworth, then, has demonstrated not only a moral theme—that mankind too often prefers a want of virtue to a want of parts—but the more important idea that art and morality are inextricably joined. Caught in his clever fictional trap, then, we are forced to see that it was not through intrinsic worth that we admired Florio but mere artistic manipulation, and, at least for a time, we are on guard against the next writer who would lure us from moral values that we know to be just.

Hawkesworth's stand in *Adventurer* no. 16 is no isolated one but part of a larger effort of a number of writers who attempted to construct a moral code suitable for the age, especially for the rising middle class, who rejected the older aristocratic values no less than they were horrified by the anarchy of the mob and the urban under-classes generally. Florio and Benevolus populate the worlds of the *Tatler* and the *Spectator* (Benevolus approximates Steele's Christian gentleman); they emerge with attenuated clarity in Richardson's *Clarissa* in the sober Hickman, who assures a sensible Anna Howe domestic regularity, while the fascinating Lovelace violates Richardson's heroine and damns himself; and they are virtually two halves of one of the century's most singular personalities, seen most honestly in the *London Journal 1762–1763*. Young James Boswell dashes about London, pulled alternately between the poles of a Florio and a Benevolus, eager to press himself upon the gay world while a voice within calls for sobriety, regularity—for him to be more *retenu* and less of a rattler.

Without mentioning specific authors or works, Johnson writes in his fourth *Rambler* paper in opposition to Fielding's comical and ironic assessment of the human condition and in support of Richardson's undiluted testaments of the heart, noting that:

> in narratives, where historical veracity has no place, I cannot discover why there should not be exhibited the most perfect idea of virtue; of virtue not angelical, nor above probability, for what we cannot credit

we shall never imitate, but the highest and purest that humanity can reach, which, exercised in such trials as the various revolutions of things shall bring upon it, may, by conquering some calamities, and enduring others, teach us what we may hope, and what we can perform.[30]

In his sixteenth *Adventurer* Hawkesworth not only announced the moral basis of his writing for the rest of his life but declared himself with equal vigor a member of Johnson's "school." The compliment paid the fourth *Rambler* by the sixteenth *Adventurer*, only by slight indirection that of the pupil to the tutor, could hardly have gone unnoticed.

If in *Adventurer* no. 16 Hawkesworth solidly aligns himself with Johnson and Richardson in his advocacy of the moral function of fiction, in his fourth paper he deliberates upon the effectiveness of various kinds of writing, noting the limitations of history, voyages and travels, biography, and the epic poem in gratifying curiosity and engaging the emotions. Even the novel, he suggests, has its limitations, "for it is confined within the narrower bounds of probability, the number of incidents is necessarily diminished, and if it deceives us more, it surprises us less" (*Adventurer*, 1: 21). In championing shorter fiction—the fable, or tale, especially of an oriental nature—Hawkesworth argues that it engages the passions and insists that a reader can admit the curious and fantastic provided that after the fact "the action of the story proceeds with regularity, the persons act upon rational principles, and such events take place as may naturally be expected from the interposition of superior intelligence and power: so that though there is not a natural, there is at least a kind of moral probability preserved, and our first concession is abundantly rewarded by new scenes to which we are admitted, and the unbounded prospect is thrown open before us" (1: 22). Writing in the very midlands of neo-classicism, Hawkesworth enunciates a principle that became the cornerstone of a revolution of mind and literature; his words here, in fact, may be the immediate source for one of the greatest critical statements in the language—Coleridge's "willing suspension of disbelief for the moment which constitutes poetic faith."[31]

Although even the most devoted modern connoisseur of arcane literary forms might find it hard to cultivate a taste for oriental fiction, its impact upon the English imagination was great. With the publication in English of Galland's *Arabian Nights* between 1704 and 1712, the *Turkish Tales* of 1708, and Pilpay's *Fables* in 1711, readers who viewed nothing more alarming from their windows than a restrained English countryside suddenly entered worlds populated by genies, flying carpets, blackstones, characters named Sinbad and Ali Baba, magical lamps, and commands of "Open Sesame." Throughout the century stories set somewhere between the

Islamic states on the eastern Mediterranean and the Far East enjoyed wide popularity and introduced the exotic and supernatural to an age officially wedded to restraint and reason. Addison helped popularize the form, and Johnson, hardly a man to be found east of Suez, turned to it in his "History of Seged" in the *Rambler* (nos. 204–5) and cast his greatest fiction, *Rasselas*, in an oriental frame in 1759.[32]

Hawkesworth was one of the age's ablest practitioners of this form, and his "Amurath: An Eastern Story," told in *Adventurer* nos. 20, 21, and 22, saw six reprintings. The story contains the inflated language demanded by the genre as well as obligatory references to a sultan, his harem, a moonlit desert landscape, and a hermit, though these are mere trappings to engage the passions of those needing moral amendment. In writing of Amurath, the "Sultan of the East, the judge of nations, the disciple of adversity," Hawkesworth addresses not simply the life of the potentate, but its larger significance for all mankind: "Let those who presumptuously question the ways of Providence," he writes in prologue to Amurath's trials, "blush in silence and be wise; let the proud be humble, and obtain honour; and let the sensual reform and be happy" (*Adventurer*, 1:135).

Upon his father's death, Amurath succeeds to the throne and is guided by Syndarac, a kind genius, who gives him a ruby ring that pricks his finger and grows pale when he commits evil acts. Amurath quickly descends from a high moral plane and indulges in a variety of villanies, attempting to seduce his betrothed, the princess Selima. Thereafter, he is transformed into a half-wolf, half-goat howling in the desert. As a man he had behaved like a beast, and now as a beast he understands what it means to be a man. As his soul is purged of vice and meanness, and moral sensitivity awakens within him, Amurath is gradually transformed back into his human form and is restored to Selima and his throne. His lesson must, obviously, be our own: "Of this is not thy heart a witness," Hawkesworth asks, "thou, whose eyes drink instruction from my pen? Hast thou not a monitor who reproaches thee in secret, when thy foot deviates from the paths of virtue?" He charges his audience not to neglect "the first whispers of this friend to thy soul; it is the voice of a greater than Syndarac, to resist whose influence is to invite destruction" (1:157–58).

The themes found in Amurath's tale are repeated throughout Hawkesworth's oriental fiction, whose titles reflect their principal concerns: in *Adventurer* no. 32, the story of Hassan suggests that "Religion [is] the only foundation of content"; in no. 38, Mirza, the servant of the mighty sovereign Abbas Carascan, learns that "No life [is] pleasing to God, that is not useful to man"; in nos. 72 and 73, the story of Nouraddin and Amana shows "The folly of human wishes and schemes to correct the moral government of the world"; and nos. 103 and 104, concerning Almerine and

Shelimah, reveal that "Natural and adventitious excellence, [is] less desirable than virtue." Such tales were enormously popular, and Hawkesworth undoubtedly boosted *Adventurer* sales with fiction that even in the nineteenth century Nathan Drake commended in noting that his "imagination was uncommonly fertile and glowing, his language clear and brilliant, yet neither gaudy nor over-charged, and he has always taken care to render the moral prominent and impressive."[33]

For a modern reader Hawkesworth's domestic tales are more entertaining, or at least they entertain to the degree that they offer abbreviated facsimiles of the worlds Pamela and Clarissa inhabited. Such fiction provides an interesting complement to the longer works of the great novelist, and it is clear they shared common concerns: like Richardson, Hawkesworth writes of people who are, or aspire to be, members of a moneyed middle class, and the values of this class are constantly extolled. In Hawkesworth's worlds one gains earthly happiness (and prospect of eternal bliss) through money, good marriage, piety, and caution in conduct, especially that involving the sexes; conversely, such an earthly paradise can be lost, and with it bliss in the hereafter, through imprudence, recklessness, high living, and defiance of revealed religion. (Ironically, at the end of his life Hawkesworth was charged with the last four and perhaps sent to an early death, the victim of an ethical system that he championed so vigorously in his *Adventurer* papers.)

Adventurer no. 7, entitled "Distress encouraged to hope; the history of Melissa," might just as well have been entitled "Melissa; or, Virtue Rewarded," for Melissa is clearly one of Pamela's many daughters. In Melissa's "eventful history," as Hawkesworth terms it, he presents events "from which the wretched may derive comfort, and the most forlorn may be encouraged to hope; as misery is alleviated by the contemplation of yet deeper distress, and the mind fortified against despair by instances of unexpected relief" (*Adventurer*, 1:40). Melissa's father, the younger son of a country gentleman, foolishly spurned the stable rewards of an apprenticeship and joined the army, hoping to realize dreams of adventure and glory. He compounded his folly by eloping with a young girl, who was then disinherited by her father. The issue of this romance is Melissa. She is variously cared for by a kind widow, a sympathetic English officer, an aunt and uncle, and a kind squire. Although by the age of thirteen she has felt every vicissitude of fortune, Melissa is the personification of probity, virtue, and courage: her life exemplifies the truth of the motto of the second installment—"Endure and conquer, live for better fate." The very "idea of virtue," as Johnson would say, Melissa resists the advances of the squire's son at the same time that she refuses even lawful offers of marriage because of her low station in life. After much trial, though, virtue is rewarded, and

Melissa comes into a large inheritance, making possible reconciliation with the squire (who had driven her from his home) and marriage to his son.

This story is characteristic of Hawkesworth's domestic fiction: he employs a straightforward narrative of the history of his protagonist, whose trials serve not simply to entertain but to instruct. His tales have little technical sophistication: there are no interpolated histories, no shifts between scenes and characters. Like Defoe's, Hawkesworth's suffering heroes and heroines as well as his villains move from youth to old age to chronology's strict cadences. In so writing, however, he avoided the faults of the novel, noted in *Adventurer* no. 4, in which "lovers compliment each other in tedious letters and set speeches; trivial circumstances are enumerated with minute exactness, and the reader is wearied with languid descriptions and impertinent declamations" (*Adventurer*, 1:21).

While Hawkesworth sketches Melissa's troubled life with some clarity, if not novelistic completeness, he constructs in *Adventurer* no. 86 an even richer portrait of a familiar type—the rake, whose progress brings him near to an excess even Lovelace himself would have forsworn. Inheritor of his father's substantial fortune, Agamus has lived a virtuous life for twenty years in London until passion for a chambermaid brings him to a seduction that produces a daughter. Providing for the mother, who subsequently dies of smallpox, and her daughter, Agamus congratulates himself for his "deliverence from an engagement which I had always considered as resembling in some degree the shackles of matrimony" (3:140). Thereafter, he resorts to the delights of Cuper's, Vauxhall, and Ranelagh. A few weeks after celebrating his sixtieth birthday he once again looks forward to an evening's pleasure with an especially beautiful young girl who possesses "a softness and modesty in her manner, which is quickly worn off by habitual prostitution." To his unspeakable agony, however, she turns out to be his abandoned daughter. "I was instantly struck with a sense of guilt with which I had not been familiar," he exclaims, "and, therefore, felt all its force. The poor wretch, whom I was about to hire for the gratification of a brutal appetite, perceived my disorder with surprize and concern" (3:141–42). The tale presents with considerable vividness a theme that Hawkesworth frequently illustrates: sin once indulged in is soon followed by more vice, which eventually produces disastrous consequences. Or, as he writes in *Adventurer* no. 140, summarizing the moral view that he attempted to convey in the periodical generally, "Vice is a gradual and easy descent, where it first deviates from the level of innocence: but the declivity at every pace become more steep, and those who descend, descend with greater rapidity" (4:241).

Hawkesworth may have intended to devote only one paper to the sad decline of Agamus, but he continued it in three more installments (nos.

134–36), focusing on the trials of his daughter, Nancy, after her father first rejects her. She survives the brutal care of a woman appointed her guardian by parish officers; later she prospers under the direction of a clergyman's widow, after whose death she becomes apprenticed to a mantua maker, a respectable but harsh station in life that she finds increasingly intolerable. Deserting her work—an act no less fatal than Clarissa's first flight from her family—Nancy is drawn to sin and prostitution. As Clarissa is befriended and seduced by Mrs. Sinclair in an evil sanctuary in Holborn, so a Mother Wellwood, whose business is also pleasure, tends to poor Nancy. Prostitution, arrest, and incarceration in the special hell of Bridewell and Newgate follow, and Nancy records with shock similar to Moll Flanders herself that her "ears were now violated every moment by oaths, execrations, and obscenity; the conversation of Mother Wellwood, her inmates, and her guests, was chaste and holy to that of the inhabitants of this place; and in comparison with their life, that to which I had been solicited was innocent" (4:219).

Suffering hunger, thirst, cold, and nakedness in her dungeon, Nancy returns to the lesser evil of the brothel, where she is miraculously rescued by the chance meeting with her father. She leaves the reader with the moral her sad story so clearly generated. "Let none, therefore, quit the post that is assigned them by providence," she asserts, "or venture out of the streight way; the bye-path, though it may invite them by its verdure, will inevitably lead them to a precipice; nor can it without folly and presumption, be pronounced of any, that their first deviation from rectitude will produce less evil than mine" (4:220–21).

The moral truths that Hawkesworth illustrates in his oriental and domestic tales, however they are enriched by details of scene and character, are simple; whether a reader is transported to a romantic world of sand, sultans, and seraglios or finds himself in the familiar interiors of country homes, fashionable parks, or (more terribly) dark brothels and damp prisons, he sees the value of faith, hope, and charity and the disasters that await those who fail to exercise these virtues. For all their separation by custom and geography, Amurath and Melissa are kindred spirits; both learn, though in different ways, that happiness is possible through ideas and ideals that admit of no local qualification but serve for all mankind to follow.

Hawkesworth's oriental and domestic tales helped establish his reputation as a moralist; the papers he devoted in the *Adventurer* to religious commentary confirmed it. Although the tone of these papers is obviously Christian, they are not explicitly sectarian, and they appealed to an age that welcomed general endorsements of the faith without incursions into the real complexities of its meaning and demands. In *Adventurer* no. 10, for example, Hawkesworth attacks the contemporary fondness for debating moral and theological topics in the marketplace, in taverns where "it is common to hear disputes concerning everlasting happiness and misery, the mysteries of religion and the attributes of God, intermingled with lewdness and blasphemy, or at least treated with wanton negligence and absurd merriment" (1:65–66). Nothing here and in other similar essays could displease the most orthodox reader save, perhaps, Hawkesworth's curious omission of references to the efficacy of Christ's intercession to save man from damnation.

Many must have found more troublesome *Adventurer* no. 91, entitled "No Universal rule of moral conduct, as it respects society. Story of Yamodin and Tamira." The title itself suggests something less than full commitment to a view that even a latitudinarian age found fundamental, and the text itself only confirms these darker suspicions. Though cast as an oriental tale, the paper's real intent is theological, and Hawkesworth takes upon himself an exploration of an exceedingly delicate issue—why, in fact, if Christianity is universally true, it has not been universally accepted.

"It is contended by those who reject CHRISTIANITY," Hawkesworth writes, "that if revelation had been necessary as a rule of life to mankind, it would have been universal; and they are, upon this principle, compelled to affirm that only to be a rule of life, which is universally known." Instead of engaging in vigorous refutation of this heresy, Hawkesworth tends more to become its apologist, arguing that "no rule of life is universally known, except the dictates of conscience." To Hawkesworth Christian revelation was hardly more than a lucky accident for part of mankind: "Those, by whom a system of moral truths was discovered through the gloom of paganism," he writes, "have been considered as prodigies, and regarded by successive ages with astonishment and admiration; and that which immortalized one among millions can scarce be thought possible to all" (3:176).

To illustrate the operation of conscience in a non-Christian milieu, Hawkesworth takes his reader to the kingdom of Golconda in the reign of Yamodin, a ruler whose people are threatened with depopulation by pestilence. To placate the gods Yamodin prepares to sacrifice his virgin daughter, Tamira, but is frustrated when she secretly marries the prince, her lover. Yamodin then executes the prince, and his daughter, according to custom, joins her husband on his fiery bier. Hawkesworth stresses that Yamodin acted according to conscience, and although he tempers his absolution of the monarch by citing the Christian's access to a higher morality through revelation, he virtually designates Christianity a local, not a universal, phenomenon: "If this sun is risen upon our hemisphere, let us not consider it only as the object of speculation and inquiry; let us rejoice in its influence, and walk by its light; regarding rather with contempt than indignation, those who are only sollicitous to discover, why its radiance is not farther diffused; and wilfully shut their eyes against it, because they see others stumble to whom it has been denied" (3:182).

William Duncombe, writing in 1755 to Dr. Thomas Herring, the archbishop of Canterbury, noted such "free remarks" as these seen in *Adventurer* no. 91, but found Hawkesworth a "good man and an excellent writer. He is undoubtedly possessed of a fine genius and a fertile imagination, which he happily employs to advance the cause of virtue and religion."[34] Years later, however, a similar theological rumination in his Cook's *Voyages* about the operation of Providence when Cook confronted almost certain disaster off the coast of Australia brought public outcry and charges of heresy. It is clear that this was no occasional lapse on Hawkesworth's part, no temporary philosophical blunder, no mischance induced by too free association with Lord Sandwich's circle. Hawkesworth's "Providential" heresy was the product of a lifetime's thinking, of the exposure as a young man to the deism of such figures as Chubb, Morgan, and Shaftesbury, and later, its most persuasive exponent, Benjamin Franklin himself. The *Adventurer*, for all that it established Hawkesworth's reputation as a writer and a moralist, provides as well the first solid clue to the disaster that awaited him in his final days.

There is good humor in many of Hawkesworth's essays, especially his polished facsimiles of Addison's commentaries on town life. In this mode his best is *Adventurer* no. 52, "Distresses of an author invited to read his play," which recalls *Rambler* no. 157, "The scholar's complaint of his own bashfulness," and the incident when John Gay was invited to read his tragedy, *The Captives*, before the princess of Wales.[35] Hawkesworth's hero, Dramaticus, is a playwright called by a great lady to share his tragedy with her and her friends at breakfast. Unwittingly admitted to her quarters with an enormous queue of brown paper which some brat had attached between the two locks of his periwig, his distress is compounded when he addresses a lady other than his patronness with a carefully prepared speech that cannot be repeated when she finally arrives. At that time, moreover, he overturns a large Indian screen with his profound bow, crippling a lapdog that thereafter receives as much attention as his play. Even with such unhappy occurrences as prologue, the reading progresses well, or appears to, until one of the company, a man of great quality, a professor of "Buckism," suddenly interrupts the playwright for fear that he might forget something if he does not immediately communicate it to his friend. "Then turning to his companion, 'Jack,' says he, 'there was sold in Smithfield no longer ago than last Saturday, the largest ox that ever I beheld in my life' " (2:116). Dramaticus, whose play was meant to show that "virtue had been sustained by her own dignity," and vice had been "betrayed into shame, perplexity, and confusion," soon withdraws to consider his humiliation (2:117).

Hawkesworth offered his readers much more than humorous essays tending mainly to amuse. In no. 47, for example, he considers the unhappy fact "that one man has been immortalized as a god, and another put to death as a felon, for actions which have the same motive and the same tendency, merely because they were circumstantially different" (2:76). To illustrate this truth, he compares Bagshot, a robber, with Alexander the Great. The former is both thief and murderer, and few would fail to applaud his capture. But violence on a larger scale—Alexander's kind—causes no such revulsion. "If Bagshot, then, is justly dragged to prison," he writes, "amidst the tumult of rage, menaces, and execrations; let Alexander, whom the lords of reason have extolled for ages, be no longer thought worthy of a triumph." And he continues his argument: "The wretches who compose the army of a tyrant, are associated by folly in the service of rapine and murder; and that men should imagine they were deserving honour by the massacre of each other, merely to flatter ambition with a new title, is, perhaps, as inscrutable a mystery as any that has perplexed reason, and as gross an absurdity as any that has disgraced it" (2:81).

This is a powerful essay, one that, temporarily, at least, causes sufficient shock to produce a new awareness of our values. One does not ordinarily consider the common criminal and the great military leader kindred spirits. Hawkesworth is even more ruthless in his assessment of the duration of military achievements. In his conclusion he examines an historical chart in which "the rise, the progress, the declension, and duration of empire" are represented by various colors—a chart that vividly testifies to the inability even of an Alexander to dominate. "And indeed, the question, whose name shall be connected with a particular country as its king is, to those who hazard life in the decision," Hawkesworth asserts, "as trifling, as whether a small spot in the chart shall be stained with red or yellow" (2:81–82). While the benevolent author of the *Adventurer* could hardly be charged with hating or detesting "that animal called man," this particular essay is charged with evident indignation and proves with vivid illustration "the falsity of that Definition *animal rationale*.[36] It is such a paper that gained Hawkesworth the reputation as a moralist and brought him not only the plaudits of the clergy, but the praise of the general population as well.

As a serial publication and later as a book the *Adventurer* was very popular. Serially it may have reached nearly three times more readers each week than the *Rambler* and only one-fifth fewer than the popular *World*. Arthur Murphy, a fellow laborer in periodical journalism, wrote, with a touch of envy, perhaps, about the paper's popularity in his *Gray's-Inn Journal* for October 20, 1753 (no. 53): "In the softer Climate of St. James's

Air, I was told that my Bays are likely to flourish, and I was particularly assured, by a Gentleman who frequents the *Cocoatree* in *Pallmall*, that *Ranger* has gained Admittance there notwithstanding their attachment to the *ADVENTURER*." It was such a reception as a serial paper (printed on six pages, folio sheet and a half, selling for two pence) that guaranteed similar success when the *Adventurer* was distributed as a book, first in folio (these were the folio sheets of the serial paper stitched and bound) and later in a second, revised edition, four volumes duodecimo, published simultaneously and in some quantity. In December 1755 John Payne sold one half-share of the copyright of the second edition to Dodsley for £120. After costs of producing two thousand sets were deducted, Payne netted a profit of some £422.[37]

A critical success, Hawkesworth's periodical had a great impact on English letters and beyond. Its wide readership in serial form was extended through reprinting in the *Gentleman's Magazine* and other publications; in book form it saw some ten London and four Dublin editions independent of its republication in various collections of essays; and it was translated three times into French and once into German. Long after Hawkesworth's death critics noted the special merit of his contributions, Nathan Drake observing that he "takes his station, indeed, after *Addison* and *Johnson*; and the *Adventurer*, which rose under his fostering care, need not fear a comparison with the *Rambler* and *Spectator*."[38]

While the matter of Hawkesworth's *Adventurer*'s essays recalled Addison's to many readers, their manner recalled Johnson's. So successfully did Hawkesworth mirror Johnson's prose that not only his contemporaries but readers to this day confuse his writing with Johnson's. "I discern Mr. Johnson through all the papers that are not marked A, as evidently as if I saw him through the keyhole with his pen in his hand," Miss Talbot wrote to Mrs. Carter on January 29, 1753; and John Courtenay summarized the consensus of an age in verse, observing, "Ingenious HAWKESWORTH to this school [Johnson's] we owe, / And scarce the pupil from the tutor know."[39] Four passages from the *Adventurer*, two each by Hawkesworth and Johnson, reveal the similarity of their literary styles:

1. I have, therefore, sometimes led them into the regions of fancy, and sometimes held up before them the mirror of life; I have concatenated events, rather than deduced consequences by logical reasoning; and have exhibited scenes of prosperity and distress, as more forcibly persuasive than the rhetoric of declamation. (4:241)

2. He has learned to no purpose, that is not able to teach; and he will always teach unsuccessfully, who cannot recommend his sentiments by his diction or address. (4:151)

3. There remains yet another set of recluses, whose intention entitles them to higher respect, and whose motives deserve a more serious consideration. These retire from the world, not merely to bask in ease, or gratify curiosity, but that being disengaged from common cares, they may employ more time in the duties of religion: that they may regulate their actions with stricter vigilance, and purify their thought by more frequent meditation. (4:152)

4. Let those who still delay that which yet they believe to be of eternal moment, remember, that their motives to effect it will still grow weaker; and the difficulty of the work perpetually increase; to neglect it now, therefore, is a pledge that it will be neglected forever: and if they are roused by this thought, let them instantly improve its influence; for even this thought when it returns, will return with less power; and though it should rouse them now, will perhaps rouse them no more. (4:178)

Most would agree that all four passages, selected almost at random, *sound* Johnsonian and would have difficulty determining that the first and fourth are Hawkesworth's (from *Adventurer* nos. 140, 130), the second and third Johnson's (from no. 126). Such similarity caused Boswell to observe that "Hawkesworth's imitations of Johnson are sometimes so happy, that it is extremely difficult to distinguish them, with certainty, from the compositions of his great archetype." The late R. W. Chapman remarked that he "once took the *Adventurer* on a day's outing—being then ignorant of the key furnished by initial signatures—and by the end of the day was at a loss to tell Hawksworth from Johnson."[40] The problem of distinguishing Hawkesworth's writing from Johnson's is no idle one, especially as one attempts to sort out their respective contributions to the *Gentleman's Magazine*. What is at stake is not only the definition of Hawkesworth's canon but that of Johnson's as well. While absolute distinctions between their literary styles may never be made, even with recourse to a computer, some larger principles should be kept in mind while finer discriminations are noted.

In one of the best appreciations of Johnson's prose style, James Sutherland writes:

The foreseen triumphs continually over the fortuitous; nothing is set down that is not the outcome of calm and mature deliberation. . . . The attraction of Johnson's prose lies to a large extent in the complete confidence which it induces; whether he launches himself upon a long or a short period one knows that his point will be made exactly as he means to make it, the emphasis always falling upon the right places, and the rhythm coming to a regular close with the completion of the thought.[41]

Sutherland's commentary might apply to the best of Hawkesworth's *Adventurer* prose, but there are differences between his style and Johnson's. His vocabulary is more limited, and he affects "hard" words less often; if some of his sentences display the qualities noted above, they are more occasions for the demonstration of stylistic power than part of a consistent fabric of his texts. Alexander Chalmers justly observes that Hawkesworth's style resembles Johnson's more "in the beginning of his essays, and in the concluding paragraphs, than in the body." Nathan Drake, in fact, sees differences in their styles, suggesting that Hawkesworth was not "a servile imitator" of Johnson, but that "his composition has more ease and sweetness." He notes further that Hawkesworth "has laid aside the *sesquipedalia verba*, and, in a great measure, the monotonous arrangement and the cumbrous splendour of his prototype, preserving, at the same time, much of his harmony of cadence and vigour of construction."[42]

Whatever the differences between their prose styles, the similarities at times are obvious. Hawkesworth's prose is clearly impregnated with the Johnsonian ether that he inhaled at meetings of the Ivy Lane Club On at least one occasion toward the end of his career he may have felt some embarrassment at so frank an emulation of his teacher. Boswell comments rather acidly that "Hawkesworth was [Johnson's] closest imitator, a circumstance of which that writer would once have been proud to be told; though, when he became elated by having risen into some degree of consequence, he, in a conversation with me, had the provoking effrontery to say he was not sensible of it."[43]

While the periodical paper is a modest genre without the scale and grandeur of the epic, the range and immediacy of the drama, or the amplitude and analysis of the novel, it played an important role in the development of eighteenth-century culture. Peter Gay, the distinguished historian of the Enlightenment, argues that the *Spectator* was instrumental in "constructing the tradition of modern civility," and C. S. Lewis suggests that Addison's and Steele's values lie so deeply embedded in the modern world that he wonders "whether the very degree of their success does not conceal from us the greatness of their undertaking."[44] In a variety of papers unmatched by any other contributor to the *Adventurer* Hawkesworth addressed those broad cultural environs that lie generally between the sanctions of the law and the chastisement of the pulpit, clarifying the ideals proper to that territory in which most of our lives are played out. His essays were periodical reminders to those who read them that life without moral commitment is not only unseemly but potentially disastrous. If a modern reader finds that Hawkesworth's *Adventurer* essays cloy at times in their moral fervency, he should recall that Hawkesworth wrote for a world better depicted by Hogarth than by Reynolds. In the reign of George II Hawkesworth continued the moral mission begun by Addison and Steele during the days of Queen Anne; the *Adventurer* announced that a new literary talent as well as a shaper of British culture had come upon the scene.

Hawkesworth gained both commercial and literary success from his publication and special recognition from the archbishop of Canterbury, who, Sir John Hawkins writes, "having perused his essays, and informed himself of his general character, made him an offer of a faculty that should raise him above the level of vulgar literati, and, almost without his being conscious of any such exaltation, created him a doctor of both laws, and the honour was accepted."[45] Both the fiat and the degree itself are preserved in the Lambeth Palace Library; the fiat, issued in December 1756 by the archbishop to "The Worshipful Dr. Topham Master of the Faculties," reads: "Having thought fit to Confer on John Hawkesworth Gentleman the Degree of Doctor of Laws, These are to Order and Require, that You issue forth Letters Testimonial of his Creation in the Faculty under Your Seal of Office, according to the usual and accustomed form in the like cases observed. And for your so doing, This shall be Your Warrant, Given at Croydon this 3ᵈ day of December 1756." The degree itself, a long document, refers to Hawkesworth's "Proficiency in the Study of Laws, Uprightness of Life and Purity of Morals."[46]

Although the archbishop had the power to grant such a degree, Hawkins's words about the honor are severe. "Among men of real learning," he charges, "there is but one opinion concerning what are called Lambeth degrees. . . . Degrees of this kind are often convenient for clergymen, as they are qualifications for a plurality of livings, but, as they imply nothing more than favour, convey little or no honour." Hawkesworth apparently welcomed the recognition, but it may have caused him some distress. He attempted, unsuccessfully, to use it to practice law in Doctors' Commons; even worse, it may have caused some cooling of his friendship with Johnson. Hawkesworth's success with the *Adventurer*, Hawkins notes, "wrought no good effects upon his mind and conduct; it elated him too much, and betrayed him into a forgetfulness of his origin, and a neglect of his early acquaintance; and on this I have heard Johnson remark, in terms that sufficently expressed a knowledge of his character, and a resentment of his behaviour." Not content with a recitation of what appears, at least, to be first-hand evidence, Hawkins engaged in a damaging speculation about Johnson's personal response to Hawkesworth: "It is probable that he might use the same language to Hawkesworth himself, and also reproach him with the acceptance of an academical honour to which he could have no pretensions, and, which Johnson, conceiving to be irregular, as many yet do, held in great contempt; thus [sic] much is certain; that soon after the attainment of it, the intimacy between them ceased."[47]

Although Hawkins is a valuable biographer of Johnson's early years, perhaps this passage needs modification. If, as he claims, the Lambeth degree was of so little value, then Hawkesworth, the author of a celebrated periodical, could hardly be accused of being pretentious in accepting it: Sir John can have it one way, but not both ways. It is interesting to note as well Boswell's comment that after Johnson gained his Dublin degree he appears "to have been seized with a temporary fit of ambition, for he had thoughts both of studying law and of engaging in politics." In other words, Hawkesworth was not alone in suffering illusions of self-importance—a common disease, perhaps, of recipients of honorary degrees. A recollection of Miss Reynolds, though, tends to corroborate Hawkins's view that the strong ties that once bound Hawkesworth and Johnson lessened at this time. Returning from a meadow in Johnson's company she writes, "I remember we met Sir John Hawkins, whom Dr. Johnson seemed much rejoiced to see. . . . On asking Dr. Johnson when he had seen Dr. Hawkesworth, he roared out with great vehemency, 'Hawkesworth is grown a coxcomb, and I have done with him.' "[48]

Yet Johnson's response here may signal momentary pique rather than any absolute rupture with Hawkesworth. Their friendship persisted, though on less intimate terms, for many years after the dissolution of the Ivy Lane Club in 1756, when, Hawkins writes, "Death had taken from us M'Ghie; Barker went to settle as a practising physician at Trowbridge; Dyer went abroad; Hawkesworth was busied in forming new connections."[49] Although Hawkesworth undoubtedly felt a strong obligation to Johnson, who had done much to insure his success in the literary world of the time, the publication of the *Adventurer* enabled him to stand on his own feet. While he had received valuable assistance from a wide literary community in the preparation of this work, it properly belong to him: he opened it, closed it, and provided for it a range of contributions unmatched by any other author. Through these essays he established himself as a leading moralist and a stylist comparable to the masters of English prose. Finally, his essays had been recognized by the archbishop of Canterbury, primate of all England. Through him, in fact, Mr. Hawkesworth became Dr. Hawkesworth, and a future of promise lay ahead.

III BIOGRAPHER AND EDITOR OF JONATHAN SWIFT

> An Account of Dr. Swift has already been collected, with such great diligence and acuteness, by Dr. Hawkesworth, according to a scheme which I laid before him in the intimacy of our friendship. I cannot, therefore, be expected to say much of a life concerning which I had long since communicated my thoughts to a man capable of dignifying his narration with so much elegance of language and force of sentiment.
>
> Samuel Johnson, "Swift," in *Lives of the English Poets*

Good fortune came to Hawkesworth during the 1750s. In contrast to the previous decade, when his life's course was by no means set, he now looked forward to a successful literary career. His *Adventurer* periodical brought him acclaim, flattering comparisons with Addison and Johnson, and the prospect of further successful literary ventures. While this decade would not provide Hawkesworth the more dramatic, though ultimately fatal, encounters that awaited him in the 1770s, the texture of his life was pleasingly complicated as he settled into a routine of writing and a life in letters, both in Bromley and in London. Although he actively pursued these activities in each locale, there was probably a difference in emphasis: in Bromley he apparently produced much of his creative work as well as the somewhat less demanding journalism that he wrote in such volume; in London he cultivated booksellers, projected future works, looked for new opportunities to display his talents (Garrick was soon to turn for him for revisions of plays), and generally maintained his varied connections with the city's literary community. St. John's Gate, though, remained central to his concerns in the capital, and he focused his energies there at month's end when he helped prepare the *Gentleman's Magazine* for publication.

In both country and city, however, there was frequent surcease from literary labor. At Bromley, Hawkesworth must have gladly interrupted the hours spent in composition to welcome the Garricks, the Strahans, and the Johnsons; in London, though the meetings of the Ivy Lane Club came to an end during the middle years of the decade, Hawkesworth's friendships with some of its members persisted, and he found himself a participant at many other assemblies that welcomed one of his prominence. Commitment to letters was obviously paramount for Hawkesworth at this time, a fact easily verified by a simple enumeration of the number of essays, reviews, and criticism that he produced during this period. In no way, though, is it made clearer than in his publication, only a year after his last *Adventurer* appeared, of a work that commemorated the life and writings of Jonathan Swift.

When Swift was buried in St. Patrick's Cathedral, Dublin, in October 1745, one of the true originals in the life and literature of Great Britain passed from the scene. He told his friend Pope that he aimed to "vex the world rather than divert it."[1] But this writer not only vexed but also diverted the world in brilliant works that teach and expose at the same time they delight. He touched an age as have few men, flashing angrily at the abuses of the clergy and corrupters of wit; he infuriated a queen yet served her administration with his powerful pen; he lacerated mankind generally but could form deep friendships and became the champion of a whole people on John Bull's other island; and he left in *Gulliver's Travels* one of the indisputable classics of the language. Among Hawkesworth's achievements, special note must be given to his involvement with this author; for in his life of the Dean as well as in his edition of Swift's writings and correspondence Hawkesworth made a significant contribution to the reputation and our understanding of one of the central figures in English literary history.

Hawkesworth's *Adventurer* came to an end in the spring of 1754. Slightly more than a year later, his life of Swift and his edition of Swift's works appeared, advertised for the first time in the *Public Advertiser* for Wednesday, May 7, 1755. Available "upon a large New Letter, and superfine Paper," either in six volumes quarto or twelve volumes large octavo, this new edition, issued by no fewer than eight London booksellers, including C. Bathurst in Fleet Street and the Dodsley brothers, was an ambitious undertaking, one meant to present the Dean and his various writings in the best format possible.[2] Johnson may have urged Hawkesworth to undertake this formidable task; certainly he and other members of the Ivy Lane Club gave Hawkesworth encouragement if not outright assistance. The various London booksellers engaged in the project must have been pleased to have included Hawkesworth in their enterprise. He was the successful author and editor of the *Adventurer* and a rising star in the *Gentleman's Magazine*, one who would soon receive recognition from the archbishop of Canterbury.

Hawkesworth's edition of Swift's works is prefaced by his *Life of Swift*, a study of some significance in the evolution of Swiftian biography, especially since it serves in part as a source for Johnson's more famous account of the writer. Hawkesworth's life is the first modern study of Swift's career—

not in its stress upon psychology, but in method. If Hawkesworth undertakes no real biographical research in the manner of young Boswell, who would run "half over London, in order to fix a date correctly," he does make judicious use of the fragment of Swift's *Autobiography* as well as the best published accounts of Swift's life, including Lord Orrery's *Remarks on the Life and Writings of Dr. Jonathan Swift* (1752), Patrick Delaney's *Observations upon Lord Orrery's Remarks on the Life and Writings of Dr. Jonathan Swift* (1754), and Deane Swift's *Essay upon the Life, Writings, and Character, of Dr. Jonathan Swift* (1755).[3] The first of these is generally uncomplimentary; the second and third, from which Hawkesworth derives much of the substance as well as the tone of his own biography, are more flattering. In his life of Swift, Hawkesworth aims not so much for Boswellian amplitude as for the conciseness in generality that marks Johnson's *Lives of the English Poets*. Hawkesworth states at the outset that he attempted to select such details from Swift's life "as will sufficiently distinguish the pecularities of his character and manners, and transmit a knowledge of him to posterity, of the same kind, if not in the same degree, as was obtained by those among his contemporaries, who were admitted to his conversation and friendship."[4]

To effect this end, Hawkesworth works closely with his principal sources, which he carefully notes in marginal citations. His biography, though, is no mere compilation, no simple derivative account based on the works of others, but a creative effort frequently marked by intelligent attempts to illuminate the terrain of a complex life. Hawkesworth is not meekly subservient to previous biographers, who had access to information he must take at second hand; if any err in judgment, he is quick to point it out. In censuring Lord Orrery's comment concerning Swift's failure to obtain the deanery of Derry, for example, Hawkesworth is unequivocal: "As *Swift* did not receive these livings [of Laracor and Rathbeggin] till after the deanery was given to another, his non-residence could not, as lord *Orrery* supposes, be the reason why it was not given to him" (Hawkesworth, *Swift*, 1:14n). Nor does he avoid the more puzzling contradictions implicit in his accounts, even one so confusing as Swift's reception when he left England for Ireland to take possession of his appointment at St. Patrick's in 1713. Of this event he writes:

> Upon his arrival to take possession of his deanery, and his return after the queen's death, he was received, according to the account of lord *Orrery* and Mr. *Deane Swift*, with every possible mark of contempt and indignation, especially by the populace, who not only reviled and cursed him, but pelted him with stones and dirt, as he passed along the streets. The author of the observations [Patrick Delany] on the contrary, affirms, that he was received by all ranks of men, not only with kindness, but honour, the tories being then in full power, as well in

> *Ireland* as in *England*, and *Swift's* service to the church and credit at court being well known. (1:29)

In this passage Hawkesworth draws upon three biographical accounts, two of which disagree with the third. Instead of letting the majority of his sources decide for him, as a less conscientious biographer might have done, Hawkesworth proposes a plausible interpretation that makes possible the truth of *both* versions of the same event. He continues:

> This [Swift's favorable reception] indeed was true, when he went to take possession; but, when he returned to his deanery, the power of the tories and the dean's credit at court were at an end; circumstances which might well cause the rabble at least to forget his services to the church; it is certain, that great clamour was then raised by the new men against the late ministry, with whom *Swift* had been closely connected; they were charged with a design to bring in the pretender, and the same design was consequently imputed to *Swift*, whom it was, therefore, considered by some as a qualification for preferment to revile and oppose: which party the mob took, whose fault it has never been to coincide implicitly with a court, posterity must judge for themselves; but it seems probable that these accounts, however contradictory, may both be true, and that *Swift* at this time might be the *Sacheverel* of *Ireland*, followed by the mob of one faction with execrations, and by the other with shouts of applause. (1:29–30)

While Hawkesworth may present no absolute truth about the question, at least his attempt to resolve it is laudable. Admittedly, it is not of great significance—it does not involve, for example, an assessment of a great man's character or state of mind so much as a mere event in a crowded life—but even a small event deserves accurate transmission to posterity, and it is clear that Hawkesworth took such an obligation seriously.

Although Hawkesworth's biography is factually derivative, it is rhetorically original, and the stylistic strength that Johnson noted is everywhere manifest, nowhere more vividly, perhaps, than when Hawkesworth temporarily suspends his account of the events of Swift's life to reflect on their meaning. Of Swift's removal to Ireland, for example, Hawkesworth observes:

> There is a time when every man is struck with a sense of his own mortality, and feels the force of a truth, to which he has consented merely from custom, without considering its certainty, or importance. This time seldom happens in the chearful simplicity of infancy, or in the first impatience of youth, when "the world is all before us," when every object has the force of novelty, and every desire of pleasure

> receives auxiliary strength from curiosity; but after the first heat of the
> race, when we stop to recover from our fatigue, we naturally consider the
> ground before us, and then perceive, that at the end of the course are
> clouds and darkness; that the grave will soon intercept our pursuit of
> temporal felicity; and that, if we cannot stretch to the goal that is beyond
> it, we run in vain, and spend our strength for nought. Great disappoint-
> ments which change our general plan, and make it necessary to enter the
> world, as it were, a second time, seldom fail to alarm us with the brevity
> of life, and repress our alacrity by precluding our hopes. (1:30–31)

This assessment is marked throughout by real artistic merit as Hawkesworth speaks not simply about the experience of a single life, however rich,
but the lesson it suggests for humanity at large: the particular impasse Swift
endured is eventually settled upon us all.

It is with such eloquence that Hawkesworth writes not only about
Swift himself but figures collateral to him, including Esther Johnson, the
famed Stella of the *Journal*, who is interwoven into Hawkesworth's biography as she was into Swift's life. At one point she becomes the subject of a
rich prose portrait:

> Beauty, which alone has been the object of universal admiration and
> desire, which alone has elevated the possessor from the lowest to the
> highest station, has given dominion to folly, and armed caprice with the
> power of life and death, was in *Stella* only the ornament of intellectual
> greatness; and wit, which has rendered deformity lovely, and conferred
> honour upon vice, was in her only the decoration of such virtue, as
> without either wit or beauty would have compelled, affection, esteem,
> and reverence. . . . Her virtue was founded upon humanity, and her
> religion upon reason; her morals were uniform, but not rigid; and her
> devotion was habitual, but not ostentatious. (1:45–46)

Although one is struck with the manner of Hawkesworth's presentation, as
clause flows into clause, and style and content are elegantly fused, he tends
to idealize Stella and eschews discussion here and later in his edition of the
Journal of a connection that has evoked generations of commentary. "Why
the Dean did not sooner marry this most excellent person," he writes, "why
he married her at all; why his marriage was so cautiously concealed, and
why he was never known to meet her but in the presence of a third person,
are inquiries which no man can answer, or has attempted to answer without
absurdity, and are therefore unprofitable objects of speculation" (1:46).[5]

Even though Hawkesworth is reticent to deal with certain sensitive
aspects of Swift's personal life, his general treatment is marked by modera-
tion, honesty, and restraint, and perhaps no one has summarized with such
powerful astringency Swift's terrible final years:

> Such was Dr. *Jonathan Swift*, whose writings either stimulate mankind
> to sustain their dignity as rational and moral beings, by shewing how
> low they stand in mere animal nature, or fright them from indecency,
> by holding up its picture before them in its native deformity: and whose
> life, with all the advantages of genius and learning, was a scale of
> infelicity gradually ascending till pain and anguish destroyed the facul-
> ties by which they were felt; while he was viewed at a distance with
> envy, he became a burden to himself; he was forsaken by his friends,
> and his memory has been loaded with unmerited reproach: his life,
> therefore, does not afford less instruction than his writings, since to the
> wise it may teach humility, and to the simple content. (1:70–71)

In a single sentence Hawkesworth surveys Swift's art and the example of
his life in such a way that addition or emendation would be superfluous.
Such commentary brought him warm praise from students of Swift's life
from his day to our own. Thomas Sheridan, one of Swift's best eighteenth-
century biographers, commented that Hawkesworth was "a man of clear
judgment, and great candour. He quickly discerned the truth from falsehood; wiped away many of the aspersions that had been thrown on Swift's
character; and placed it, so far as he went, in its proper light." A more recent
student concluded that Hawkesworth's life "ultimately presents a picture of
Swift which might well stand for the eighteenth century as the most
levelheaded and just description of the man."[6]

The sincerest compliment to Hawkesworth's *Life of Swift*, however,
came in the form of imitation from one of the century's greatest
biographers, Johnson himself, whose debt to Hawkesworth's biography in
the *Lives of the English Poets* has only recently been clarified. "An Account of
Dr. Swift has been already collected, with great diligence and acuteness, by
Dr. Hawkesworth," Johnson writes at the opening of his life of Swift,
"according to a scheme which I laid before him in the intimacy of our
friendship." And in one of the finest measures taken of Hawkesworth's
achievement Johnson observes, "I cannot, therefore, be expected to say
much of a life concerning which I had long since communicated my
thoughts to a man capable of dignifying his narration with so much elegance
of language and force of sentiment."[7] Curiously, although Johnson acknow-
ledges his use of such biographers of Swift as Patrick Delany and Lord
Orrery, this is the last reference to Hawkesworth himself, whose influence
on Johnson's composition apparently remained obscure even to Johnson's
distinguished editor, George Birkbeck Hill.

While Johnson makes use of several sources for his life, and in tone his
work more closely resembles the harsher assessment of the Dean provided
by Lord Orrery than the more favorable estimates given by Delany and
Deane Swift, a portion of his account is dependent upon Hawkesworth's

for both structure and detail, and in some cases for exact words and phrases. There is no question that Johnson possessed a copy of Hawkesworth's text: about 1780 he wrote to John Nichols requesting various volumes to prepare for the *Lives*, including "Swifts Works with Dr. Hawkesworths life," the edition that probably appears in *The Sale Catalogue of Samuel Johnson's Library*.[8] Parallels in the opening sections of Hawkesworth's and Johnson's lives of Swift are so clear, especially where the emphasis is on details of the Dean's life rather than critiques of his work, that the debt of the later to the earlier life is unmistakable. Consider, for example, their respective treatment of Swift's academic failure at the University of Dublin, his subsequent efforts to overcome it, and his eventual connection with Sir William Temple.

> But upon *Swift*, this punishment was not ineffectual, he dreaded the repetition of such disgrace as the last evil that could befal him, and therefore immediately set about to prevent it as the principal business of his life. During seven years from that time he studied eight hours a day; and by such an effort of such a mind, so long continued, great knowledge must necessarily have been acquired. He commenced these studies at the university in *Dublin*, where he continued them three years, and during this time he also drew the first sketch of his *Tale of a Tub*.
>
> In the year 1688, when he was about twenty-one, and had been seven years at college, his uncle *Godwin* was seized with a lethargy, and soon after totally deprived both of his speech and his memory; as by this accident *Swift* was left without support, he took a journey to *Leicester*, that he might consult with his mother what course of life to pursue. At this time sir *William Temple* was in high reputation, and honoured with the confidence and familiarity of king *William*. His father, sir *John Temple*, had been master of the *Rolls* in *Ireland*, and contracted an intimate friendship with *Godwin Swift*, which continued till his death, and sir *William*, who inherited his title and estate, had married a lady to whom Mrs. *Swift* was related; she therefore advised her son to communicate his situation to sir *William*, and sollicit his direction what to do; this advice, which perhaps only confirmed a resolution that *Swift* had secretly taken before he left *Ireland*, he immediately resolved to pursue.
>
> Sir *William* received him with great kindness. (Hawkesworth, *Swift*, 1:6–7)

Of this disgrace it may be easily supposed that he was much ashamed, and shame had its proper effect in producing reformation. He resolved from that time to study eight hours a-day, and continued his industry for seven years, with what improvement is sufficiently known. This part of his story well deserves to be remembered; it may afford useful admonition and powerful encouragement to men whose abilities have been made for a time useless by their passions or pleasures, and who, having lost one part of life in idleness, are tempted to throw away the remainder in despair.

In this course of daily application he continued three years longer at Dublin; and in this time, if the observation and memory of an old companion may be trusted, he drew the first sketch of his *Tale of a Tub*.

When he was about one-and-twenty (1688), being by the death of Godwin Swift his uncle, who had supported him, left without subsistence, he went to consult his mother, who then lived at Leicester, about the future course of his life, and by her direction solicited the advice and patronage of Sir William Temple, who had married one of Mrs. Swift's relations, and whose father, Sir John Temple, Master of the Rolls in Ireland, had lived in great familiarity of friendship with Godwin Swift, by whom Jonathan had been to that time maintained.

Temple received with sufficient kindness the nephew of his father's friend. (Johnson, "Swift," 3:2–4)

The resemblance between Johnson's and Hawkesworth's versions is unmistakable, and the parallels in structure, in detail, and in specific words and phrases indicate that Johnson worked closely with his friend's biography. The sequence of events in both versions is identical: both men refer to Swift's scholastic difficulties and the long hours of compensatory study, the composition of the *Tale of a Tub*, the death of his uncle Godwin, Swift's visit to his mother at Leicester, and his solicitation of and kind reception by Sir William Temple. The use of the word "disgrace" in paragraph 1 of both biographies, the phrase "drew the first sketch of his *Tale of a Tub*" in Hawkesworth's first and Johnson's second paragraph, and "consult" and "course of life" in paragraph 2 of Hawkesworth and paragraph 3 of Johnson show the latter's use of the earlier study; and it is obvious that the opening of the last paragraph in each case is virtually the same, though Johnson chooses the modifier "sufficient" instead of "great." In spite of such clear parallels as these, Dr. Hill provides no reference to Hawkesworth's life, though he cites Patrick Delany, Deane Swift, and other sources, thus giving the impression that Johnson drew exclusively upon texts other than his friend's biography.

The following paragraphs, involving Swift's quests for preferment, provide additional evidence of Johnson's use of Hawkesworth's biography.

Yet the employment to which he was invited would have been secure; but it happened, that, after he had acted as secretary during the whole journey to *Dublin*, one *Bush* found means to insinuate to lord *Berkeley*, that the post of secretary was not fit for a clergyman, and his lordship suffered himself to be so easily convinced of this impropriety, that, after making some apology to Mr. *Swift*, he appointed *Bush* secretary in his stead.

> This disappointment was soon after followed by another; it happened that the deanery of *Derry* became vacant, and it was the earl of *Berkeley's* turn to dispose of it; . . . [but Swift] received instead of it the two livings of *Laracor* and *Rathbeggin*, in the diocese of *Meath*, which together did not amount to half the value of the deanery. (Hawkesworth, *Swift*, 1:13–14)

> He was then invited by the Earl of Berkeley to accompany him into Ireland as his private secretary; but after having done the business till their arrival at Dublin, he then found that one Bush had persuaded the Earl that a Clergyman was not a proper secretary, and had obtained the office for himself. In a man like Swift such circumvention and inconstancy must have excited violent indignation.
>
> But he had yet more to suffer. . . . And Swift was dismissed with the livings of Laracor and Rathbeggin in the diocese of Meath, which together did not equal half the value of the deanery. (Johnson, "Swift," 3:8–9)

Again, the parallels in structure and detail in the two passages are striking; the repetition of the phrase "one Bush" and the concluding words concerning the deanery, which are virtually identical, again suggest that Johnson made close use of Hawkesworth's work.

Perhaps one final quotation will put the matter beyond dispute. Johnson, no less than Hawkesworth, had to contend with the apparent contradiction in Swift's reception in Ireland when he went to take possession of his deanery, and it is interesting to consider his words on the matter and compare them with Hawkesworth's conclusions, already quoted:

> The accounts of his reception in Ireland, given by Lord Orrery and Dr. Delany, are so different, that the credit of the writers, both undoubtedly veracious, cannot be saved but by supposing, what I think is true, that they speak of different times. When Delany says that he was received with respect, he means for the first fortnight, when he came to take legal possession; and when Lord Orrery tells that he was pelted by the populace, he is to be understood of the time when, after the Queen's death, he became a settled resident. (Johnson, "Swift," 3:26–27)

It seems almost inescapable here that Johnson silently draws upon Hawkesworth's unique clarification; Johnson's explanation of the curious discrepancies of his authorities concerning Swift's reception in Ireland is, in fact, a solution advanced by Hawkesworth himself.

Johnson's study is no mere imitation, however, and obvious parallels fade as Johnson moves from biographical material, which could be culled quite easily from existing sources such as Hawkesworth's, to critical assessment that called for original commentary, though the latter is surprisingly brief in this life compared to others. Even when Johnson relies on Hawkesworth's text, he does not follow it slavishly. In his somewhat astringent assessment of Stella (3:40–43), moreover, he even seems to take issue with Hawkesworth's more romanticized portrait. For all these qualifications, though, it is obvious that Hawkesworth's account of Swift served as an important source for Johnson, and this, coupled with the fact it stands as a literate and judicious assessment of the Dean, makes it worthy of scrutiny and its author deserving of attention.

Although highly praised for his biography of Swift, Hawkesworth was far less successful as an editor of Swift's works and correspondence, leaving few students of the Dean from his day to our own satisfied with his performance.[9] Even a brief summary of his involvement with Swift's most famous work, *Gulliver's Travels*, shows the magnitude of the problem that he faced in dealing with the complexities of the Swift canon.

Gulliver's Travels was first issued anonymously in October 1726 by Benjamin Motte, a London bookseller. Swift was dissatisfied with this edition, and through his friend, Charles Ford, he passed on a list of corrections that Motte incorporated in what he called his second edition, though actually it was his fourth or fifth. Swift was still displeased with the state of his text, however, and probably at his suggestion Ford prepared on an interleaved copy of the first edition a corrected text. These corrections were never incorporated in Motte's edition. In 1735 George Faulkner, the Dublin printer, issued Swift's works, including *Gulliver's Travels* in a version claiming to correct errors in the London and Dublin editions. Hawkesworth's edition, more particularly his Preface, concerns itself primarily with *Gulliver* and is at once a commendation of the excellence of Hawkesworth's own text and a condemnation of Faulkner's. In the Preface Hawkesworth seems intent on destroying the credibility of Faulkner's edition; he cites various errors and concludes indignantly that "*he who is not convinced by these, that the Dean could not thus alter to pervert his meaning, and overlook blunders that obscured it, would still doubt if all the rest had been brought together*" (Hawkesworth, *Swift*, 1:xii).

If Hawkesworth wished to thrust Faulkner's edition into obscurity with such an attack, he succeeded, for it was not until 1926 that Sir Harold Williams resurrected the Irish edition, which in his eyes had been unfairly denigrated. Hawkesworth's fervent declarations in his preface are seen to be contradictory, or, even worse, dishonest, when collation shows that he drew repeatedly on the very edition he castigates. In view of such contradiction, it is not surprising that Hawkesworth has earned the scorn of students of Swift's texts, though they tend to ignore that much of his prefatory rhetoric resulted from an editor's desire to tout the advantages of his edition over that of his chief rival.[10] It should be noted as well that Hawkesworth grappled throughout with editorial problems that have taxed the ablest students of Swift; the Faulkner edition, for all its merits, has failed to achieve universal acceptance by textual experts. Finally, though, all such arguments are beside the point, for Hawkesworth is far better remembered as a commentator on Swift's texts than as their editor. In a series of notes that he appended to *Gulliver* and to some of Swift's most controversial poetry, one sees a penetrating reading of a sensitive eighteenth-century man of letters worth review today.

Hawkesworth's notes to *Gulliver's Travels* are frequent, often elaborate, and taken together constitute an important dialogue with the text and its meaning. As one might expect, the *Adventurer's* author is especially struck by Swift's capacity to illuminate the human condition in moral terms given special force by the powerful imaginative fable of the first book. Here abstractions such as pride and justice are seen in brilliant tangibility. Lilliputian pride in the person of the emperor, which so obviously mirrors our own, causes Hawkesworth to observe:

> The masculine strength of features [of the Lilliputian emperor], which *Gulliver* could not see, till he laid his face upon the ground; and the awful superiority of stature in a being, whom he held in his hand; the helmet, the plume, and the sword, are a fine reproof of human pride; the objects of which are trifling distinctions, whether of person or rank; the ridiculous parade and ostentation of a pigmy; which derive not only their origin, but their use from the folly, weakness, and imperfection of ourselves and others. (Hawkesworth, *Swift*, 2:14)

And the injustice seen in the Lilliputians' decision to starve Gulliver to death causes Hawkesworth to reflect upon man's inability in the end to refuse the call of conscience.

> There is something so odious in whatever is wrong, that even those whom it does not subject to punishment, endeavour to colour it with an appearance of right; but the attempt is always unsuccessful, and only betrays a consciousness of deformity, by shewing a desire to hide it. Thus the *Lilliputian* court pretended a right to dispense with the strict letter of the law to put *Gulliver* to death, though by the strict letter of the law only he could be convicted of a crime; the intention of the statute not being to suffer the palace rather to be burnt than pissed upon. (2:58)

If in such annotation one sees more evidence of a heightened moral awareness than critical insight, Hawkesworth's discussion of a passage that has provided enduring, perhaps perverse, fascination—the eating habits of the Brobdingnagian queen—is more provoking. He writes:

> Among other dreadful and disgusting images which custom has rendered familiar are those which arise from eating animal food: he who has ever turned with abhorrence from the skelton of a beast which has been picked whole by birds or vermin, must confess that habit only could have enabled him to endure the sight of the mangled bones and flesh of a dead carcase which every day cover his table: and he who reflects on the number of lives that have been sacrificed to sustain his own, should enquire by what the account has been ballanced, and whether his life is become proportionably of more value by the exercise of virtue and piety, by the superior happiness which he has communicated to reasonable beings, and by the glory which his intellect has ascribed to God. (2:94)

For Hawkesworth, Gulliver's graphic depiction of the eating habits of the queen is no occasion to reflect upon Swift's possible loathing for the body and bodily functions, as a modern might in an age of psychology, but an opportunity for the self-assessment that Swift demands in asking whether our animal nature, our need to cannibalize on nature, is compensated for by a development of our virtue, piety, and reason. In his assessment of Gulliver's loathing he sees that what Swift illustrates is not a personal pathology of his hero but a universal condition of the race.

While Hawkesworth illuminates particular aspects of *Gulliver* with such commentaries as these, he shows no less ability to comment on the nature of whole books. His final assessment of the first two is especially perceptive and reflects not only the capacity to deal in meaningful generalization that characterized the age, but the special powers of the literary theorist and moralist of the *Adventurer*:

> From the whole of these two voyages to *Lilliput* and *Brobdingnag*, arises one general remark, which, however obvious, has been overlooked by those who consider them as little more than the sport of a wanton imagination. When human actions are ascribed to pigmies and giants, there are few that do not excite either contempt, disgust, or horror; to ascribe them therefore to such beings was perhaps the most probable method of engaging the mind to examine them with attention, and judge of them with impartiality, by suspending the fascination of habit, and exhibiting familiar objects in a new light. The use of the fable then is not less apparent than important and extensive; and that this use was intended by the author can be doubted only by those who are disposed to affirm, that order and regularity are the effects of chance. (2:142)

It is almost impossible here not to recall Johnson's comment about the same books, that "when once you have thought of big men and little men, it is very easy to do all the rest,"[11] and to suggest that Hawkesworth has converted his friend's strangely condescending and limiting assessment of Swift's genius into a critical appreciation that does full credit to the Dean and his masterpiece. Hawkesworth recognizes the inventive power of the first two books, how it results from brilliant calculation and not mere caprice; he sees that Swift had discovered what eludes all but the greatest writers—"the most probable method of engaging the mind . . . by suspending the fascination of habit, and exhibiting familiar objects in a new light."

This capacity to clarify frequently distinguishes Hawkesworth's notes to *Gulliver* even when he confronts that disgusting inhabitant of the fourth book, the Yahoo. To him the strange beast is yet another incentive to virtue within a text calling generally for the amendment of man's corrupt nature. "Whoever is disgusted with this picture of a *yahoo*," Hawkesworth writes, "would do well to reflect, that it becomes his own in exact proportion as he deviates from virtue, for virtue is the perfection of reason: the appetites of those abandoned to vice, are not less brutal and sordid, than that of a *yahoo* for asses flesh, nor is their life a state of less abject servility" (2:221). Such commentary has been properly termed "brilliant" by one of Swift's best modern critics, who laments that Hawkesworth "did not see fit, in his edition of Swift's *Works*, to give more of his own opinions,"[12] a view readily shared when one sees his capacity to judge not only the particulars of text and even whole books but the meaning of the masterpiece itself:

> To mortify pride, which indeed was not made for man, and produces not only the most ridiculous follies, but the most extensive calamity, appears to have been one general view of the author in every part of these travels. Personal strength and beauty, the wisdom and the virtue of mankind, become objects not of pride but of humility, in the diminutive stature and contemptible weakness of the *Lilliputians*; in the horrid deformity of the *Brobdingnagians*; in the learned folly of the *Laputians*; and in the parallel drawn between our manners and those of the *Houyhnhnms*. (2:292)

In spite of the generalizing power Hawkesworth displays here and in other notes, his reading of *Gulliver* is by no means complete—there is no indication, for example, that he appreciated Gulliver as a character independent of Swift or perceived the thrust of Swift's irony. Even with these reservations, though, for any who would seek a penetrating reading of the Dean's masterpiece by a near contemporary steeped in the moral assumptions underlying this great text, Hawkesworth remains an important resource, one who suggests that in literary history no less than in psychology one can find illumination of one of the most demanding classics of the language.

Perhaps even more engaging for a modern reader than Hawkesworth's notes to *Gulliver's Travels* are his responses to several of Swift's most controversial poems, including "The Lady's Dressing Room" (1730), "Strephon and Cloe" (1731), and "Cassinus and Peter" (1731). In the first, poor Strephon encounters a harsh reality in his surreptitious visit to Celia's dressing room:

> And, first, a dirty smock appear'd,
> Beneath the arm-pits well besmear'd;
> *Strephon*, the rogue, display'd it wide,
> And turn'd it round on ev'ry side:
> In such a case few words are best,
> And *Strephon* bids us guess the rest;
> But swears, how damnably the men lie
> In calling *Caelia* sweet and cleanly.
>
>   Now listen, while he next produces
> The various combs for various uses:
> Fill'd up with dirt so closely fixt,
> No brush could force a way betwixt;
> A paste of composition rare,
> Sweat, dandriff, powder, lead and hair.
> A fore-head cloth with oil upon't
> To smooth the wrinkles on her front:
> Here allum-flower, to stop the steams
> Exhal'd from sour unsav'ry streams;
> There night-gloves made of *tripsey*'s hide,
> Bequeath'd by *tripsey* when she dy'd;
> With puppy-water, beauty's help,
> Distill'd from *tripsey*'s darling-whelp.
> Here gally-pots and vials plac'd,
> Some fill'd with washes, some with paste;
> Some with pomatums, paints, and slops,
> And ointments good for scabby chops.
>   (Hawkesworth, *Swift*, 7:130–31)

While many readers would be scandalized by such verse, they would be even more horrified by the poem's progress, in which Swift unblushingly treats fecal matter, as Strephon finds awful proof that Celia's nature no less than his own is alimentarily defined. Unrelenting scatology is also seen in "Strephon and Chloe," where the hapless groom comes to similar knowledge after marriage. Although generations have read Alexander Pope's celebration of the female form divine in the lovely Belinda of *The Rape of the Lock*, the makers of popular school texts have spared students (and their teachers) Swift's ruthless inversion of Pope's sunny assessment of the fair sex. Numerous scholars, however, have found their way to these works, which, in combination with the offensive Yahoos, have produced some of the most ingenious, if possibly outlandish, criticism of this great eighteenth-century wit. Such poems held no terrors for Hawkesworth, and his defense of Swift against charges raised by some of his more delicate contemporaries anticipates the best of modern psychoanalytic criticism.

Of "The Lady's Dressing Room" Hawkesworth comments in an extended note:

> No charge has been more frequently brought against the dean, or indeed more generally admitted, than that of coarse indelicacy, of which this poem is always produced as an instance: here then it is but justice to remark, that, whenever he offends against delicacy, he teaches it; he stimulates the mind to sensibility, to correct the faults of habitual negligence; as physicians, to cure a lethargy, have recourse to a blister: and though it may reasonably be supposed, that few *English* ladies have such a dressing-room as *Caelia*'s, yet many may have given sufficient cause for reminding them, that, very soon after desire has been gratified, the utmost delicacy becomes necessary to prevent disgust. (Hawkesworth, *Swift*, 7:129–30)

A note he appends to "Strephon and Chloe" is similar in tone:

> This poem has, among others, been censured for indelicacy; but with no better reason than a medicine would be rejected for its ill taste. By attending to the marriage of *Strephon* and *Chloe*, the reader is necessarily led to consider the effect of gross familiarity in which, it is to be feared, many married persons think they have a right to indulge themselves. He who is disgusted at the picture feels the force of the precept, not to disgust another by his practice; and let it never be forgotten, that nothing quenches desire like indelicacy, and that, when desire has been thus quenched, kindness will inevitably grow cold. (7:169)

What is remarkable here is not that Hawkesworth avoids the false moral outrage typical of his contemporaries and of the following century, but that he sees the poems for what they are—depictions of the truth that in no relationship so much as the sexual do we recognize our divided being. In his first note above Hawkesworth recognizes the medicinal effect of Swift's verses—he does minister to our lethargy or, perhaps in more modern terms, to an anxiety produced by sublimation of the truth of our humanity—and Hawkesworth's use of the term "delicacy" in both notes reflects a critic in close harmony with his subject. "Delicacy" should not be read with its almost inevitable Victorian connotations as a squeamish withdrawal but as the mechanism of mind or will that makes possible acceptance of the apparently irreconcilable disharmonies of flesh and spirit, or, more graphically in Swift's poems, of brain and bowels. Delicacy is to Hawkesworth the balance struck in "A Lady's Dressing Room," where the poet, if not Strephon, reconciles himself to our divided being; delicacy is marriage itself, in "Strephon and Chloe," providing a permanent area in which one must struggle to preserve the equilibrium between illusion and disillusion, between fantasy and reality.

The measure of Hawkesworth's accomplishment here is highlighted when one realizes the great difficulty that many critics have had with Swift's scatology and the vigor with which they have assailed what Norman O. Brown has aptly termed "this tiger of English literature." Compare Hawkesworth on *Gulliver* or on the poems above, for example, with Thackeray's view that the moral of Swift's great satire is "horrible, shameful, unmanly, blasphemous," or, more recently, with George Orwell's contention that the "durability of *Gulliver's Travels* goes to show that if the force of belief is behind it, a world-view which only just passes the test of sanity is sufficient to produce a great work of art." On this subject even the best critics have indulged in wild exaggeration or shrunk from exploration. Aldous Huxley, who illuminated the excremental theme in Swift, claims that his greatness lies in the intensity, the almost insane violence, of that " 'hatred of the bowels' which is the essence of his misanthropy and which underlies the whole of his work"; and John Middleton Murry, who coined the memorable phrase "the excremental vision," sees Swift's scatology as a sign of disease rather than of health.[13] It might be argued, in fact, that for real assessment of the subject, Hawkesworth awaited Norman O. Brown; and it is only in *Life Against Death* one finds a critic once again able to assess the subject dispassionately, aided at the same time by the perspective of time and the resources of modern psychology.

In Hawkesworth we see a critic who finds in Swift not sickness, but truth, not disease, but wit; in *Gulliver* and in such poems as "Strephon and Chloe" he is not confused for a moment by Swift's scatology. He sees Swift's creations for what they are: an artist's vision of universal truths made vivid by the art and imagination of one of the most creative minds in the literature, giving us in *Gulliver* and seemingly outrageous poetry an expression of a true wit "whose truth convinced at sight we find, / That gives us back the image of our mind." In Hawkesworth, then, we find Swift before Mr. Bowdler and Mrs. Grundy—before, in fact, Victoria and Freud; through Hawkesworth we see a satirist as much interested in calling attention to man's special vulnerability as to his excesses, a writer who heals and clarifies as much as he is thought to wound and castigate.

With the publication of his life of Swift and edition of Swift's *Works* in 1755, Hawkesworth's principal connection with this famous writer came to an end. Some ten years later, however, in 1766, he joined in the production of a voluminous edition of Swift's correspondence. As Swift's biographer and editor he was a likely candidate for such an undertaking; indeed few would have been so qualified to illuminate those aspects of Swift's texts and world that had already begun to fade into obscurity. The letters Hawkesworth edited came from the Reverend John Lyon, who had made an inventory of Swift's books and papers at the deanery at St. Patrick's between 1742 and 1744. He in turn passed them on to Thomas Wilkes of Dublin, who transmitted them to the London booksellers sponsoring the work. They engaged Hawkesworth. With the assistance of the Reverend Thomas Birch, Hawkesworth produced an edition of Swift's correspondence that had real promise of commercial success. With some few exceptions even a modern editor would find little to fault in Hawkesworth's editing of much of Swift's correspondence—the alterations he makes are slight and usually involve only minor changes in capitalization, spelling, and punctuation—but in his work on that group of letters constituting the *Journal to Stella* he drew the censure not only of eighteenth- but also twentieth-century editors.[14]

The *Journal to Stella* is a series of letters Swift wrote in journal form between September 1710 and June 1713 to Esther Johnson (Stella) and her companion, Mrs. Rebecca Dingley, a period in his life when he was associated with the Harley cabinet as well as with some of the greatest figures in the nation. Although portions of some twenty-four of these letters first appeared in Deane Swift's *Essay upon the Life, Writings, and Character, of Dr. Jonathan Swift* (1755), Hawkesworth was the first to publish the initial as well as letters 41 to 65 of the *Journal*.

The letters Swift sent to Stella and her companion not only give a full account of his daily activities, but are also marked by an intimacy that finds chief focus in what has been called little, nursery, or baby language in combination with a variety of cryptic symbols. The former is seen in Swift's interchange of *l* and *r*, as in "nite deelest logues," and the latter in such combinations as "Ppt" ("poor pretty things"), "MD" or "Md" ("My dears"), and "Pdfr" (probably for "poor dear foolish rogue"), the last term referring to Swift himself. The little language has been variously explained as an imitation of a child's attempt to talk, lover's prattle, or a refuge from the formality and convention of Swift's busy life. Whatever its source, it must have come as a great surprise to Hawkesworth, who promptly decided to excise such matter, a practice he continued rigorously until letter 53, when he was willing to grant a slight concession to his originals. For this editorial judgment he was censured not only by John Nichols in the eighteenth century, but by Sir Harold Williams in the twentieth. Certainly in light of modern editorial practice Hawkesworth's decision to censor Swift is indefensible—we want our literary figures warts and all, and in some ways the more warts the better—but his probable motive has never been fully appreciated.

In Hawkesworth's edition, Swift's letters to Stella appear in sequence with the rest of his correspondence, not as a separate work we read today. In a sense, then, he had to deal with two different bodies of writing, one generally routine and conventional, the other highly personal and intimate. Obviously he feared that they could not exist in any harmony, and the dissonance caused by the little language appearing periodically within the larger correspondence could only have intensified doubts about the Dean's character, a subject that Hawkesworth wished to avoid. If he printed his originals as he found them, he would have to present readers an intolerable combination, or so he thought—sweet reason followed by such apparent blatherings as "and oo lost oo money at Cards & dice ze Givars device. So I'll go to bed. Nite my two deelest Logues," or "Nite deelest Sollahs; farwell dellest Rives; rove poopoopdfr farwell deelest richar Md, Md Md FW FW FW FW FW Me Me Lele, Me, lele lele richar Md." At least in Hawkesworth's eyes, such outbursts were unbecoming to the author of *Gulliver's Travels* and other distinguished literary creations, not to mention the Dean of St. Patrick's and intimate of Oxford and Bolingbroke and numerous other notables of the age. What Hawkesworth did not realize, of course, was that in suppressing this little language, he denied his readers clues to the very humanity of one who appeared to separate himself from the race in unkind and vitriolic tirade.[15]

Hawkesworth's edition of Swift's correspondence brought to an end his extensive and interesting connection with one of the central figures of English literary history. However flawed, Hawkesworth's work cannot be ignored by students of the Dean, and the merits of his biography of Swift as well as his commentary on such works as *Gulliver's Travels* have gained him increased respect during recent years.[16] In terms of his future career Hawkesworth's edition and life of Swift offer an obvious preview of the time when an even greater editorial task would present itself. Then he would contend not simply with imaginary travels of a fictional Lemuel Gulliver but with the real voyage of a real Englishman named James Cook, who sailed to places in the South Seas no less magical than Houyhnhmn-land itself. But all this was far in the future, and Hawkesworth was to turn to another phase of his career when he encountered at first hand the excitement of London's theatrical life and began a friendship with its greatest actor.

IV
JOHN HAWKESWORTH, DAVID GARRICK, AND THE EIGHTEENTH-CENTURY THEATER

I am almost kill'd with my fatigues—dead! dead— I cannot Enjoy a Day at Bromley till ye Burden of ye Benefits are off my shoulders— but I shall sing *old Rose & burn y^f bellows* & bid adieu to my Cares when I shall set out for my Friend in Kent—

David Garrick to John Hawkesworth,
March 20, 1759

While John Hawkesworth's youth and young manhood were enriched by the company of Samuel Johnson and the closing years of his life defined by his connection with Captain James Cook, his middle years were enlivened by a friendship with one of the age's most celebrated figures—David Garrick, the actor and manager of the Drury Lane Theater. Throughout the period no man offered more entertainment to the nation. As Johnson was later, Garrick was buried with pomp in Westminster Abbey with kings and queens; after the writer and moralist it is difficult to name one who so dominated the cultural life of England. Johnson left one of the finest memorials to the man, concluding that Garrick's death "eclipsed the gaiety of nations and impoverished the publick stock of harmless pleasure."[1]

Although Garrick's friendship with Johnson has been well charted by Boswell and others, his association with Hawkesworth has remained somewhat obscure. From the time of the first meeting (in the early 1740s, it appears, and possibly effected by Johnson) the two men enjoyed a friendship of considerable intimacy, one based on natural affinities of personality as well as those strong professional ties that bind lives together. In Hawkesworth, Garrick found not simply a social companion but a confidant, literary advisor, theatrical collaborator, and, finally, a staunch defender in those disputes into which one in his position was inevitably drawn. Theirs was a friendship marked by real equality and reciprocity (unlike Hawkesworth's long association with the magisterial Johnson). If Hawkesworth had good reason to enjoy the company of one who had come to the center of the English stage, so too did Garrick undoubtedly savor

65

connection with the member of Johnson's first club, author of the *Adventurer*, and principal literary and drama critic of the *Gentleman's Magazine*.

Although none of their considerable correspondence dates from the early years of their friendship, the first extant letter, written by Garrick around December 1755, indicates a friendship of some duration before this date. Garrick writes:

> You cannot imagine how Exactly We agree in our Sentiments of the *Duke de Foix*: Your Letter is a very agreeable Critique upon ye Performance, & might make a very good Letter in y^r Magazine: I shall preserve it with ye hopes that You'll do Something with it— I have sent You y^e *Orphan of China*, which You may keep, if ye other does not arrive, if it does, keep it for Me— Y^r Notion of Dialogue is ye truth, & what You must practise hereafter— put it in practice when you attack ye Orphan. If you have anything to communicate & sh^d come this way, I shall be at home till Nine, & drink Tea at Six. But I don't desire to See you, unless You have Nothing Else to do—
>
> Y^r Confidence in Me will not (I flatter Myself) be disappointed, I am sure You take my open plain friendly dealing with you, as it is meant.

Garrick asks in a postscript, "Is Mrs Hawkesworth in Town? pray Mrs Garrick's & my best compliments to her."[2]

This letter reveals a good deal about the social and business sides of Garrick and Hawkesworth's relationship: the tone is friendly, even conversational, and Garrick talks with the honest familiarity of one friend to another, though careful to avoid bluntness. He obviously values Hawkesworth's critical skills, is aware that the *Gentleman's Magazine*'s principal literary voice held a position of importance in the cultural world of his time, and sincerely flatters Hawkesworth in suggesting that his friend's comments on the *Duc de Foix* should see publication in his magazine. In addition, the letter points to the dramatic collaboration that enriched their friendship: Hawkesworth was at work on an adaptation of Voltaire's *L'Orphelin de la Chine*, first acted in Paris on August 22, 1755. He had apparently read the Thomas Francklin translation published in December of the same year, which he probably reviewed in the *Gentleman's Magazine*, also in December (25: 545–49). Hawkesworth's version never materialized, however, though Arthur Murphy's alteration of the play began a long run at Drury Lane on April 21, 1759.[3]

Certainly, Hawkesworth and Garrick were on close terms by 1756, as is seen in a letter Garrick wrote from Hampton on Wednesday, July 21, 1756, to John Payne, who issued the *Rambler* and the *Adventurer*: "I am disappointed going to Bromley by an unforeseen affair wch will detain me here till Saturday—so that I must (much against my will) delay my visit to our Worthy Friend, till my return from Staffordshire— & then Mrs Garrick, who is proud of Hawkesworth's regard, will go with Me." Garrick wrote to Hawkesworth himself on August 24, 1756: "I am return'd from Staffordshire & Shall be glad to meet You any Morning that You shall please to appoint this Week in London— You must breakfast With Me (if you please) & I will be in Southampton Street ready for You at Nine or ten o'Clock, as You shall Command Me."[4]

Garrick provides a link between Hawkesworth and Fulke Greville, the fashionable young aristocrat who matriculated at Brasenose College but left without a degree to lead a life of cultivated ease at his country home at Wilbury House in Wiltshire. In a letter of July 24, 1756, Garrick tells Hawkesworth, who apparently planned to visit Greville, "Pray my best respects to Mr Greville." At Wilbury House, if not in London itself, Hawkesworth may have met young Charles Burney, a man who served Greville personally and his household more generally in the late 1740s, one who would have an incalculable impact on Hawkesworth's literary career.[5] Garrick, in fact, had recommended that Hawkesworth assist Greville with a book he published in 1756 entitled *Maxims, Characters, and Reflections, Critical, Satyrical, and Moral.* It is, as the title suggests, a volume that a man of position would like to write, though not without the careful scrutiny of a professional man of letters; and few were more qualified than the author of the *Adventurer.* Just what help Hawkesworth gave is not clear, though he probably had a hand in the book's long and fluent preface, if not in the text itself. More important, perhaps, he defended the volume, at least by letter, against criticisms by Johnson, who had cast doubting eyes upon the *Maxims.* Writing to Greville on March 14, 1756, Hawkesworth commented:

> I enclose you Johnson's Letter it will cost you threepence but I dare Say you will think it worth twice the Money. It is an Original, and as I told you it would be expressed in general Terms without referring to particular passages as new, striking, delicate or recherché. You see in the first place that he has not read the Book through; he never reads any Book through: you see in the next place that he has had Ingenuity enough to find Something to blame in what he allows to be fine Thoughts finely expressed, which perhaps you would have thought included every possible Excellence of literary composition; but he found out that the *Names* of your Characters are ill formed or ill chosen, and that upon the whole it is too Gallick. Excellent indeed is that Book in which the Microscopic Eye of Johnson discovers no other blemishes than such Specks as these. take however his own Testimony in his own words, they are written indeed not in Letters but in pothooks, a kind of Character which will probably cost you some time to decypher, & perhaps at last you may not succeed.[6]

The efforts Hawkesworth expended on Greville's behalf were but a byway, however, for during 1756, at Garrick's request, he was at work recasting Dryden's *Amphitryon*. Besides his regular work for the *Gentleman's Magazine* he apparently had no other major project before him, and like Johnson, when he put his mind to a task, he quickly effected it. Hawkesworth's adaptation of *Amphitryon* is first mentioned in Garrick's letter of July 24, 1756. "I could wish for my Pleasure & Satisfaction," Garrick asserts, "that You would write to Me, what you had to Say Yesterday upon the Subject of Amphytrion & I will answer y^r Letter in a Post or two after." In October or November 1756, Garrick wrote: "I have receiv'd ye additions & like 'Em, they are spirited, humorous & Characteristic: I shall give them to Woodward & will answer for their pleasing him." And always with an eye to his audience, Garrick asked of Hawkesworth: "What think You of having a little Entertainm^t of Singing & Dancing at ye End of ye Play, instead of ye fourth Act? introduc'd by Jupiter for ye Amusem^t of ye Company— but that will be certainly ye best, wch strikes you ye most." In early December, all the details of composition and revision complete, Garrick wrote to Hawkesworth, "Amphytrion rehearsd to Morrow Morning."[7]

As a playwright—or, at least initially, as an adapter—Hawkesworth wrote for a stage influenced at mid-century by forces well known to students of the theatrical history of the period.[8] His audiences would no longer endorse the worlds seen in the striking comedies of Etherege, Wycherley, Congreve, and Farquhar, where silken dalliance frequently prevailed over love regularized by marriage, where "wit" triumphed over the less articulate emanations of heart and emotions. They sought purer dramatic models, preferring to the urbane satire of manners chaster entertainments and sentimental productions prizing tender emotions; they preferred, in short, *The Conscious Lovers* to *The Old Bachelor*. While some might argue that the eighteenth-century stage was dominated more by priest than playwright, it was, in fact, a time of great energy in the theater. During the early years of the century, rising attendance generated several new theaters whose audiences were entertained by the accomplished acting of Kitty Clive, Peg Woffington, Sarah Siddons, Robert Wilkes, John Kemble, Charles Macklin, and David Garrick. With generally short runs (even a popular play usually lasted no more than nine performances) there was a steady demand for material, and the rich dramatic legacy of the past was mined and adapted for contemporary use. Garrick himself turned frequently to adaptations of Shakespeare to cater to the taste of his age (even *Hamlet* fell victim to vigorous revision), and it was as much in a spirit of commerce as in any commitment to art that he asked Hawkesworth to render Dryden's *Amphitryon* suitable for the Drury Lane stage.

Hawkesworth's alteration of *Amphitryon* helps make tangible the shift in taste that took place between the late-seventeenth-century stage and eighteenth-century theater. His adaptation is a heavy bowdlerization of a tale which from its Plautine original through versions by such playwrights as Molière, Dryden himself, and, more recently, Jean Giraudoux gives a comic presentation of human frailties with particular emphasis on man's sexual nature. It was, however, precisely this latter aspect of the play that Hawkesworth aimed to obliterate, and his preface reflects the new morality that defined the chastened, mid-century stage. While he pays homage to Dryden's great literary abilities in his preface, Hawkesworth finds that his *Amphitryon* "is so tainted with the Profaneness and Immodesty of this Time in which he wrote, that the present Time, however selfish and corrupt, has too much Regard to external Decorum, to permit the Representation of it upon the Stage, without drawing a Veil, at least, over some Part of its Deformity." In his prologue he persists in his critique of Dryden's tainted world:

> The Scenes which PLAUTUS drew, To-night we shew
> Touch'd by MOLIERE, by DRYDEN taught to glow.
> DRYDEN!—in evil Days his Genius rose,
> When Wit and Decency were constant Foes:
> Wit then defil'd in Manners and in Mind,
> Whene'er he sought to please disgrac'd Mankind.
> Freed from his Faults, we bring him to the Fair;
> And urge once more his Claim to Beauty's Care.[9]

Although his preface and prologue indicate that Hawkesworth has subjected Dryden's play to a thorough moral cleansing, neither indicates the liberties he takes with his original. Dryden's *Amphitryon* is sexually bold, an unbuttoned comedy of the confusions resulting from various kinds of intercourse between gods and men, particularly between Jupiter and Amphitryon's lovely wife, Alcmena. Hawkesworth completely Platonizes this sexual motif, and there is roughly the same correlation between his version and Dryden's as between an unexpurgated *Gulliver's Travels* and a children's text purged of offensive Yahoos and other indelicacies. Such are Hawkesworth's excisions that his audience and Dryden's saw essentially different plays, a fact easily verified through a brief examination of the two dramas. First, though, a comment on the plot.

Jupiter desires, in Dryden's words, to "beget a future *Hercules*; Who shall redress the Wrongs of injur'd Mortals, Shall conquer Monsters, & reform the World" (p. 15). For the human half of his proposed divine union, he selects the beautiful Alcmena, wife of Amphitryon. To achieve this dubious goal disguise is employed: Jupiter becomes Amphitryon, and

Mercury, his slave, becomes Sosia, Amphitryon's slave. Conflict and comedy, primarily sexual, result from the mistaken identities, involving Jupiter, Amphitryon, and Alcmena in the main plot, and in the even more bawdy subplot, featuring Sosia, Mercury, and Sosia's shrewish wife, Bromia.

From the beginning Hawkesworth faces a formidable task, making Dryden's licentious text as sexually neutral as possible, though he appears equal to the challenge. While Dryden's Jupiter is libido and lust incarnate, Hawkesworth's is seen almost as a chaste medieval knight, whose real intentions are so disguised and moderated as to disappear practically from the scene. He takes great care to excise any passage that might cause disgust not only to the "Fair" but to common decency itself, and offending lines leap to the adapter's cautious eyes. Mercury's comment to Phoebus, after Jupiter has grandly announced that Alcmena has been chosen as his love's object, must assuredly go, and at mid-century Drury Lane's audience is spared such a crudity as "No more of your Grumbletonian Morals, Brother; there's Preferment coming, be advis'd, and pimp dutifully" (Dryden, p. 15). Jupiter's description to Night of his forthcoming union with Alcmena is denied to auditors of high moral sensibilities: "Now, I will have a Night for Love and me; A long luxurious Night, fit for a God to quench and empty his immortal Heat." Also sacrificed is Mercury's comment, "I'll lay on the Woman's side for all that; that she shall love longest to Night, in Spight of your Omnipotence" (Dryden, p. 16).

In Hawkesworth's version sentimental, fleshless love replaces carnality; offending passages are either removed or rewritten. Compare the following exchange between Jupiter and Mercury.

Dryden

JUPITER.   Dull God of Wit, thou Statue of thy self!
Thou must be *Sosia*, to keep out *Sosia*:
Who by his Entrance, might discover *Jove*,
Disturb my Pleasures, raise unruly Noise,
And so distract *Alcmena's* tender Soul,
She wou'd not meet my Warmth, when I
dissolve
Into her Lap, nor give down half her Love.
(Pp. 16–17)

Hawkesworth

JUPITER.   Dull God of Wit, thou Statue of thy self!
Thou must be *Sosia*, to keep put *Sosia*;

Whose Entrance well might raise unruly
    Noise;
And so distract *Alcmena's* tender Soul,
She wou'd not meet Warmth, my love.

                                (Pp. 16–17)

A longer passage better illustrates not only the specific changes Hawkesworth made in Dryden's text but how such emendations reflect the change in taste between the late seventeenth century and the Drury Lane audience.

Dryden

NIGHT.   Oh, my nimble Finger'd God of Theft, what make you here on Earth, at this unseasonable Hour? what Banker's Shop is to be broken open to Night? or what Clippers, and Coiners, and Conspirators, have been invoking your Deity for their Assistance?

MERC.   Faith none of those Enormities; and yet I am still in my Vocation: for you know I am Jack of all Trades: at a Word, *Jupiter* is indulging his Genius to Night, with a certain noble Sort of Recreation, call'd Wenching: The Truth on't is, Adultery is its proper Name.

NIGHT.   *Jupiter* wou'd do well to stick to his Wife, *Juno.*

MERC.   He has been marry'd to her above these Hundred Years; and that's long enough in Conscience to stick to one Woman.

NIGHT.   She's his Sister too, as well as his Wife; that's a double Tie of Affection to her.

MERC.   Nay, if he may bold with his own Flesh and Blood, 'tis likely he will not spare his Neighbours.

NIGHT.   If I were his Wife, I would raise a Rebellion against him, for the Violation of my Bed.

MERC.   Thou art mistaken *Old Night*: his Wife cou'd raise no Faction: all the Deities in Heaven would take the Part of the Cuckold-making God; for they are all given to the Flesh most damnably. Nay, the very Goddesses wou'd stickle in the cause of Love; 'tis the way to be popular to whore and love. For what dost

thou think old *Saturn* was depos'd, but that he
was cold and impotent; and made no Court to
the fair Ladies. *Pallas* and *Juno* themselves, as
chaste as they are, cry'd Shame on him. I say
unto thee, *Old Night*, Wo be to the Monarch
that has not the Women on his Side.

(Pp. 17–18)

Hawkesworth

NIGHT.	O, my industrious and Rhetorical Friend, is it you? What makes you here upon Earth at this unseasonable hour?
MERC.	Why I'll tell you presently, but first let me sit down for I'm confoundedly tired.
NIGHT.	Fye, Mercury! sure your Tongue runs before your Wit now, does it become a God, think you, to say that he's tired?
MERC.	Why do you think the Gods are made of Iron?
NIGHT.	No, but you shou'd always keep up the decorum of Divinity in your conversation, and leave to mankind the use of such vulgar Words as derogate from the dignity of Immortality.
MERC.	Ay 'tis fine talking, faith, in that easy Chariot of yours: you have a brace of fine Geldings before you, & have nothing to do, but to touch the Reins with your finger & thumb throw your self back in your seat, & enjoy your Ride wherever you please; but 'tis not so with me: I, who am the Messenger of the Gods, & traverse more ground both in Heav'n & in Earth than all of them put together am, thanks to Fate, the only one that is not furnish'd with a Vehicle.
NIGHT.	But if fate has denied you a Vehicle, she has bestow'd Wings upon your Feet.
MERC.	Yes, I thank her, that I might make the more hast, but does making more hast keep me from being tir'd d'ye think.
NIGHT.	Well, but to the Business; what have you to say to me?
MERC.	Why, as I told you, I have a Message from Jupiter; it is his will & pleasure, that you muffle up this part of the World in your dark

mantle somewhat longer than usual, at this
time of the Year.

NIGHT.   Why, what is to be done now?

MERC.   Done! Why, he is this night to be the
Progenitor of a Demi god, who shall destroy
Monsters, humble Tyrants, & redress the
Injur'd; Men are to become happy by his
Labours, & heroic by his Example.

(Pp. 17–18)

The profound changes in theatrical taste between the age of licentious
Charles II and the sober Georges could hardly be better illustrated.
Hawkesworth practically rewrites Dryden's text: nowhere in the revision is
there any trace of the ribald dialogue between Night and Mercury, no hint
that the proposed union between Jupiter and Alcmena is anything but a
selfless act performed for the benefit of mankind. If subsequent passages of
Dryden's play receive less severe revision, Hawkesworth continues his
attempts to appeal to the moral spirit of his times. Indelicacy of any kind is
banished. Bromia, Sosia's shrewish wife, for instance, is visibly moved by
the apparently happy reunion of Amphitryon (really Jupiter in disguise)
and Alcmena and comments in Dryden's version: "Good, my Lord what's
become of my poor Bedfellow, your Man *Sosia*? you keep such a Billing and
Colling here, to set one's Mouth watring; what I say, though I am a poor
Woman, I have a Husband as well as my Lady; and shou'd be as glad as she,
of a little honest Recreation" (p. 21). In Hawkesworth's rendition, though,
her statement is much chastened: "Good, my Lord, what's become of my
poor Bedfellow, your Man *Sosia*? what, I say, though I am a poor Woman, I
have a Husband as well as my Lady" (p. 21). On occasion Hawkesworth
even amends nonsexual matters: references to bribery and justice corrupted
involving a Judge Gripus are removed, and Jupiter's harmless lament about
the chattering of Bromia, Phaedra, and Alcmena is expunged: "A Man had
need be a God," he complains, "to stand the Fury of three talking Women! I
think in my conscience I made their Tongues of Thunder" (Dryden, p. 21).

Thus purified, *Amphitryon* was presented for the first time at Drury
Lane on Wednesday, December 15, 1756, with David Ross as Jupiter,
Henry Woodward as Sosia, Mrs. Yates as Alcmena, Mrs. Macklin as
Bromia, and William Havard as Amphitryon. It was performed on December 16, 17, 21, 22, and 23, several times again after the first of the year in
1757, and revived periodically throughout the century. Receipts were
substantial, and one of Hawkesworth's benefit nights grossed some £180,
from which house expenses of eighty guineas were deducted. With such
financial reward Hawkesworth had cause for pleasure in his first venture

into the theater and the attendant satisfaction that he had correctly gauged the moral temper of his times. The Reverend Dr. Warburton, an official custodian of morality, commented in a postscript in a letter written to Garrick on January 25, 1757: "I forgot to thank you for the entertainment "Amphitryon" afforded us. I think Dr. Hawkesworth has added, altered, and retrenched with judgment. The prologue is manly, lively, and worthy to usher in the honest purpose of washing the wit of the last age from its impurities." Bonnell Thornton, a fellow author, echoed Warburton's remarks in his comment about Hawkesworth's rendition: "From this play, Moliere and Dryden have each formed a drama, in which are many excellent additions, absolutely necessary for the modern taste. The former deserves to be admired on the French stage; and Dryden's, since it has been purged of its licentiousness by Dr. Hawkesworth, can never fail of meeting with approbation from an English audience."[10]

If Garrick rejoiced in the success of Hawkesworth's adaptation, he undoubtedly welcomed as well his support in his literary quarrels, one of which involved his rejection of John Home's play *Douglas*. This drama had been commended to Garrick by the earl of Bute himself (Home had been in his orbit and had become his private secretary in 1757), but even this powerful patron of Scottish letters proved unable to move Garrick to accept the production. He wrote Bute on July 10, 1756, to say that there were "insurmountable Objections, which in my Opinion, will ever make *Douglas* unfit for ye Stage." Later he adds that "a Friend of Mine has made some Slight Remarks upon ye Margin with his pencil." The friend was apparently Hawkesworth, who had reviewed the manuscript for Garrick. Around July 18, 1756, Garrick thanked Hawkesworth for his assistance: "I agree with You about Douglas—almost throughout— I have a doubt upon a few of Y^r Remarks— for them & Every thing Else, I am sincerely oblig'd."[11]

Garrick, though, could not prevent the successful presentation of *Douglas* at Covent Garden, where it opened on Monday, March 14, 1757. Some of the praise heaped upon the play was undoubtedly generated by the fact that its author was a North Briton who was contending for dramatic honor well south of the Tweed. A young Scot was heard to exclaim from the pit, "Weel, lads; what think you of Wully Shakespeare now?" and David Hume broke into hyperbole in speaking of a fellow countryman who possessed "the true theatric genius of *Shakespear* and *Otway*, refined from the unhappy barbarism of the one, and licentiousness of the other." Hawkesworth attacked such critical license and defended his friend Garrick at the same time in a pamphlet entitled *A Letter to Mr. David Hume, On The Tragedy Of Douglas: Its Analysis: And The Charge Against Mr. Garrick. By an English Critic*, printed for J. Scott in Paternoster-Row. It was published on April 1,

1757, shortly after *The Tragedy of Douglas Analyzed* itself appeared on March twenty-fifth.[12]

In seventeen pages Hawkesworth censures both the play and David Hume, citing numerous faults of the critic as well as the playwright. "How high were my expectations raised by your dedicatory commendation of *the tragedy of Douglas*," Hawkesworth writes, "but, alas! how fallen, from seeing its representation: nor has a perusal since won me over as an admirer of it." In the caustic tone of much of his criticism in the *Gentleman's Magazine* he continues, "I am sorry to inform you, Sir, that in consequence, your *national* judgment has been greatly run upon here, and your critical stocks reduced almost to bankruptcy." There is little indeed that Hawkesworth cannot blame in Hume's support of *Douglas*, which appeared in his dedication to the play and subsequently in a separate publication. "Not satisfied to have preluded to the assured triumph of this tragedy in your dedication," Hawkesworth charges, "an unprovoked and congenial enforcer of the extravagance of its merit, has been artfully diffused thro' the public under the title of *The Tragedy of Douglas analyzed*, a seeming attack, which the disappointed reader finds to be the second part of the same tune you had begun in your dedication."[13]

Hawkesworth's criticism of the play itself is severe; characteristically, he notes flaws in diction and makes some unkind comments on the Scottish origins of the piece. Of lines uttered by Lady Randolph—"For in your shades I deem some spirit dwells / Who from the *chiding* stream, or *groaning* oak, / Still *hears*, and *answers* to MATILDA's moan"—Hawkesworth demands, "Wherefore *chiding, groaning, hears, answers?* This may be founded on some tradition, or popular error of *Scotland*; but to English understandings, if not altogether nonsensical, is at least chimerical." Of another line, "The youthful warriour, is a *clod* of *clay*," Hawkesworth charges, "*Clod* and *clay* are not only mean words, but also cacophonous to the ear." Concerning the image in the lines "The hand that spins th' uneven thread of life, / May sooth the length that's yet to come of yours," he complains, "This may appear a pretty figure to those acquainted with the art of spinning, tho' it does not to me. The last line is monosyllabically harsh, a fault our author is often guilty of." Stronger assessment follows, and no apparent fault of poor Home is left unnoted. When Home writes, "*Persistive* wisdom is the *fate* of man," Hawkesworth asks, "I do not understand this line; and confess my ignorance of what *persistive* means." Concerning the lines "*Red* came the river down, and loud and oft / The angry spirit of the water shriek'd" he says bluntly, "The meaning of *red* here, and the *angry spirit of the water shrieking*, are unknown to us *South Britons*."[14]

Not only does Hawkesworth attack Hume and Home mercilessly, but he defends his friend Garrick with equal vigor:

> I now take leave of Douglas, this *aurora borealis* of tragedy, that had so
> long corruscated over us from the North, to execute the last part of my
> task, to wit, to defend Mr. *Garrick*, by disculpating him from a heavy
> charge, disseminated every where from the drawing-room in *St. James's*
> to the night-cellars; which is, that he had the impudence to refuse *The
> Tragedy of Douglas*, the best play ever acted, not only on the *English*
> stage, but on any other, ancient or modern. . . . This is the upshot of
> his crime. Has he then deserved all the foul-mouthed abuse that has
> been lavished on him? I think not, who am not partial to him.

Hawkesworth's last comment here is, of course, stuff and nonsense. Garrick had no stronger partisan in the city, one who happened to be conve-
niently situated in the editorial office of the most powerful review of the
age. "Corruscated"? "Disculpating"? This is heavy verbal artillery indeed
and only one example of a diction that some confused with Johnson's itself.
In his attack upon *Douglas* Hawkesworth may have exceeded even Garrick's
wildest dreams of defense, for the latter wrote to him early in 1757,
apparently in reference to this corrosive pamphlet: "Quare. are not y^r
Remarks upon Douglas rather too refin'd—& minute?"[15]

But such excesses could readily be forgiven, especially when they
occurred in the defense of a close friend and a fellow laborer in the theatrical
fields of the day. There is considerable evidence that the two men, and their
wives, were on close terms, especially during the 1750s. The Hawkesworths must have been frequent callers at 27 Southampton Street, Garrick's London residence until he moved in 1772 to the magnificent Adelphi
Terrace, as well as at his handsome Hampton villa, where they viewed
architecture by Robert Adam and grounds by Capability Brown. At this
estate, on the banks of the Thames, Garrick had constructed an octagonal
brick temple to Shakespeare, inside of which stood a life-sized statue of the
Bard made for him by Roubiliac.[16] One can imagine that Hawkesworth and
his wife were moved by a locale in which art and nature were brought to
such exquisite harmony, and it is clear that the Garricks looked to the
Hawkesworths' lovely Bromley home for a rejuvenation of spirit similar to
that they received in visits to Hampton.

"I will send you a Line when I shall have a Day to Enjoy myself at
Bromley," Garrick added in a postscript in a letter written to Hawkesworth
around July 18, 1756. To Garrick, harried constantly by the burdens of
profession, Bromley represented surcease from the pressures of the city. "I
am almost kill'd with my fatigues—dead! dead," he wrote to Hawkesworth
in great perturbation of spirit on March 20, 1759; "I cannot Enjoy a Day at
Bromley till ye Burden of ye Benefits are off my shoulders— but I shall sing
old Rose & burn y^f bellows & bid adieu to my Cares when I shall set out for my
Friend in Kent." A visit took place in the following month, Garrick writing

on Thursday, April 19: "I will see You next Sunday by ten o'Clock, if agreeable to You— Mrs Garrick & Mr Berenger will likewise partake of Y^r Beef & Pudding & will be with Mrs Hawkesworth & You before two— they will come after Me— so let not Mrs Hawkesworth lose her Church." Garrick, then, joined many of the age who found their way to Bromley over the years—Samuel and Tetty Johnson, William Strahan, Benjamin Franklin, and others who treasured their association with the man of letters and his agreeable wife.[17]

Garrick's friendship with Hawkesworth included those favors that intimates willingly do for one another. On September 17, 1757, for example, Garrick wrote to Hawkesworth about a place for one of David Henry's apprentices, telling him that "if the Lad wants a good Place & the best of Masters, He may have both at Hampton— If he is disEngag'd & will repair as soon as possible to this Town; He will be a very happy Boy; provided that he will answer ye Character You gave him." In obliging Hawkesworth in this instance Garrick had assisted a manager of the *Gentleman's Magazine*, Hawkesworth's employer, and it was not long before his friend reciprocated. In the spring of 1759, in fact, Garrick sent his young protégé Samuel Cautherly to Bromley, where Hawkesworth could oversee his education, though Cautherly would one day return to the London stage; he first played the role of George Barnwell in *The London Merchant* at Drury Lane on September 26, 1765, and remained a regular member of the company until 1775. Garrick apparently consulted Hawkesworth frequently on matters best handled by one of his literary capabilities. Sometime before December 17, 1757, for instance, Garrick sent his friend a short advertisement "intended to be put before a New Edition of y^e *Fatal Marriage*." Garrick continues that he "shall be much Oblig'd to you if You would read it over & correct what you don't like, or add if You please. These things should be always full, correct, short, Spirited & to ye Purpose— & I knew of no way of accomplishing this, but sending It to You."[18]

It was not only as a friend, confidant, and literary advisor that Hawkesworth served Garrick during the 1750s, but once again at decade's end as his defender, this time in the pages of the *Gentleman's Magazine*; in a quarrel resulting from Garrick's termination of John Hill's farce *The Rout* after only two performances. An angry Hill castigated Garrick in the papers, apparently citing specious reasons for the play's cancellation, including the face-saving claim in the *Public Advertiser* for Saturday, December 23, 1758, that it was "a trifle given to a public Charity, and written with no other Purpose." Hawkesworth would have none of Hill's rationalizations, which, he claimed in his review of the affair in the *Gentleman's Magazine* for January 1759 (29:37), falsified the facts of the case:

Who now, after all this, would imagine, that the *veritable* author of the
Rout is no other than Dr *Hill*; that it was written and offered for
presentation *before* the public charity was in view; that the representation of it was *not* interrupted by the indisposition of a performer, but by
the distaste of the public; that the primary view of it was *profit to the
author*; that the managers, who in the advertisement, are said to be
welcome to any advantage that might result from it, have been sollicited
for a gratification, even after the piece was set aside.

Garrick acknowledged Hawkesworth's defense rather profusely in a
letter written around January 1759: "I wrote to You Yesterday in such
haste, that perhaps (as Bayes says) I did not make myself very well understood. I did not mean that You sh^d mention Hill's rascally work, without
You had Y^rself intended it, & if so, that then you might back y^r Observations by my Intelligence." Garrick may have seen a manuscript version of
Hawkesworth's commentary on the affair or the account in the *Gentleman's
Magazine*. The letter continues in an almost apologetic tone: "And once for
all, my dear Friend, let Me assure You; that I never would desire so delicate
a Mind as Yours to do any thing in my behalf that does not immediatly
coincide with It's own rectitude & conviction. I am so Sensible of my own
Warm disposition, that I must desire You, by all our Friendship, to correct
my irregular Sallies, rather than Encourage them." Garrick, of course, was
well able to take care of himself in the matter of the devious Hill; of all the
insults Hill endured, perhaps none was more damning than Garrick's
epigram: "For Physick & Farces his Equal there scarce is / His Farces are
Physick, his Physick a Farce is."[19]
Hawkesworth continued to assist Garrick on the stage itself through
these years. Garrick's letter to Hawkesworth written April 19, 1759, refers
to two theatrical productions that Hawkesworth prepared for the Theatre
Royal at Drury Lane—an adaptation of Thomas Southerne's *Oroonoko* and
an original entertainment, *Edgar and Emmeline*. The production of the latter
will have to be postponed, Garrick notes, but asks Hawkesworth, "What
time sh^d You like best next Season for *Oroonoko*; I wish you would hint Y^r
Mind to me for on Saturday Night I must settle wth another Gentleman."[20]
Just when Hawkesworth began revising *Oroonoko* is not known, but he
completed his adaptation by the summer of 1759 and accepted Garrick's
revisions sent in a letter from Hampton on August 14 of that year. Sometime around November 30, 1759, Garrick raised questions about Hawkesworth's benefit night,[21] and the play soon saw production. Hawkesworth
may have had an adaptation of Southerne's play in mind for some years and
possibly wrote a lengthy critique of the drama in the *Gentleman's Magazine*
for April 1752. Criticisms of the play at that time anticipate the changes that

he made himself seven years later. In this review, for example, he notes particularly the weaknesses of mixed drama:

> Of all the inventions that ever came into a poet's teeming brain, the *tragi-comedy* may justly be deemed the most absurd and most unnatural. A man who should attempt to weave the adventures of *Ulysses* and *Don Quixote* together in one piece, might, perhaps, (from such an odd variety) catch little readers and afford them great entertainment; but surely all those of taste and judgment would exclaim against so wild a scheme. . . . With such a taste was Mr *Southerne* forced (much against his inclination) to comply, whose tragedy of OROONOKO, if stripped of all the low wit and dull obscenity, would be an excellent performance.[22]

In his adaptation Hawkesworth clearly attends to the faults revealed in the 1752 review, and his prologue reveals that, as in *Amphitryon*, he is principally concerned with a moral purgation of his original. If nothing else, he means to strip it "of all the low wit and dull obscenity" his age could no longer countenance.

> This Night your tributary Tears we claim,
> For Scenes that *Southern* drew; a fav'rite Name!
> He touch'd your Father's Hearts with gen'rous Woe,
> And taught your Mothers' youthful Eyes to flow;
> For this he claims hereditary Praise,
> From Wits and Beauties of our modern Days;
> Yet, Slave to Custom in a laughing Age,
> With ribbald Mirth he stain'd the sacred Page;
> While Virtue's Shrine he rear'd, taught Vice to mock,
> And join'd, in Sport, the Buskin and the Sock:
> O! haste to part them!—burst th' opprobrious Band!
> Thus *Art* and *Nature*, with one Voice, demand:
> O! haste to part them, blushing *Virtue* cries;—
> Thus urg'd, our Bard this Night to part them tries.—
> To mix with *Southern's* though his Verse aspire,
> He bows with Rev'rence to the hoary Sire:
> With honest Zeal, a Father's Shame he veils;
> Pleas'd to succeed, not blushing though he fails:
> Fearless, yet humble; for 'tis all his Aim
> That hence you go no worse than here you came:
> Let then his Purpose consecrate his Deed,
> And from your Virtue your Applause proceed.[23]

While Hawkesworth preserves with few modifications the play's tragic main plot—the pure, tender, but ultimately fatal love of Oroonoko (the son and heir of the king of Angola brought as a slave to Surinam in the West Indies) and Imoinda—he eliminates its comic subplot. The latter is often absurd, bawdy, and ludicrous, depicting as it does the scheming (complete with bed tricks) of fortune-hunters and husband-hunters, chiefly Charlotte Welldone, posing as a man, the Widow Lackit, and her son, Daniel. In dispensing with the subplot Hawkesworth effectively purifies his original, expunging the "ribbald Mirth that stained Southerne's sacred page." *Amphitryon*'s censor is zealous to "veil the father's shame," and Drury Lane's audience is spared the following exchange on husband-hunting between Charlotte Welldone and her sister, Lucy, which might offend those of more refined sensibility or, even worse, stimulate the prurient imagination.

> LUCY.   What will this come to? What can it end in? you have
>   persuaded me to leave dear England, and dearer Lon-
>   don, the place of the World most worthy living in, to fol-
>   low you a husband-hunting into America: I thought
>   Husbands grew in these plantations.
> CHARLOTTE.   Why so they do, as thick as oranges, ripening one under
>   another. Week after week they drop into some woman's
>   mouth: 'tis but a little patience, spreading your apron in
>   expectation, and one of 'em will fall into your Lap at
>   last.

Such a passage must go, double-entendre and all, and with it the comic subplot as a whole. Yet this, no less than the main story, where pathos replaces bawdry, illustrates the larger truth of the piece, which is not the exclusive domain of any of its constituent parts, comic or tragic, but seen in the play generally—that all men and women are slaves of economic and political forces that forcefully control their lives. At worst these can, in the case of an Oroonoko or an Imoinda, produce permanent separation through suicide; where comedy precludes such an extreme, they can lead to an undesirable uprooting from "the place of the World most worth living in."[24]

Thus altered, *Oroonoko* was first acted at Drury Lane on Saturday, December 1, 1759, with Garrick himself as Oroonoko and Mrs. Cibber as Imoinda. It was presented seven more times that month—on the twenty-eighth, by command of the prince of Wales. Not only were receipts substantial (Hawkesworth's first benefit night produced a gross of £190), but here, as in his adaptation of *Amphitryon*, Hawkesworth accurately judged the moral and critical temper of the times. While a modern student of the piece might legitimately claim that in Hawkesworth's obedience to propriety he obscured the real meaning of Southerne's drama, leaving his audience with a merely local and transitory definition of virtue, his contemporaries, including Johnson, would not have agreed. "The intermixture of the low, trivial, and loose comedy of the Widow Lackit and her son Daniel, with the addresses of Charlotte Weldon, in breeches, to the former," the *Biographia Dramatica* observes of the original, "are so greatly below, and indeed so much empoison the merit of, the other parts, that nothing but the corrupt taste of the period in which the author first imbibed his ideas of dramatic writing, can stand in any degree of excuse for his having thus enwrapped a mass of sterling ore in rags and filthiness." And the reviewer notes as well that in Hawkesworth's version Southerne's "Augaean stable is indeed cleansed, the comic parts being very properly omitted."[25]

Johnson himself provided one of the strongest appreciations of Hawkesworth's achievement; in the columns of the *Critical Review* for December 1759 (8:480–86) he generously repays some of the extensive critical support he received from his friend in the pages of the *Gentleman's Magazine*. "That it was necessary to alter it," Johnson asserts, "cannot be denied: the tragic action was interrupted, not only by comic scenes, but by scenes of the lowest buffoonery, and the grossest indecency." Writing with his characteristic stylistic force Johnson commends Hawkesworth while commenting on the problems faced by the adapter:

> If there be any who looks into this performance, with a desire of finding faults, let him first consider how few opportunities of excellence the reformation of a play affords. The characters are already settled; so that no great knowledge can be discovered of human nature, or of human life. The events of the play are fixed; for a play that wants amendment in the great events, is scarcely worthy to be reformed: even sentiments are very little in the reformer's power; for the necessary connection of the new scenes with the old, confines the writer to a certain line of transition, from which he cannot pass aside, whatever treasures of sentiment might reward his deviations. There is, likewise, a necessity of yet greater constraint, by conforming the diction and thoughts to those of the first author, that no apparent dissimilitude may discover what is original, and what is additional. These are obstructions, by which the strongest genius must be shackled and retarded, and the writer who can equal Southern under such difficulties, may be expected to excel greater authors, when he shall exert his natural powers without impediment, by adapting his own sentiments to his own plan.[26]

Although Hawkesworth must have been pleased with the successes of his adaptations of *Amphitryon* and *Oroonoko*, he revealed real dramatic talent only in 1761 in a wholly original production called *Edgar and Emmeline*, the first occasion that he had to adapt, in Johnson's words, "his own sentiments to his own plan." Yet revising other men's plays had not been a profitless use of time, for *Edgar and Emmeline* reflects a sense of character and dramatic action as well as a tightness of construction possible only from a playwright who had encountered the dramatic process at first hand in the theater.

The subject of the play is the matter of comedy itself—the love game, which finds exemplification in several characters: Edgar, the son of the earl of Kent; Emmeline, daughter to the earl of Northumberland; and a rakish courtier, Florimond. Destiny has decreed special terms for the final union of the young couple, described by Elfina, an old fairy:

> Thus their Destiny was Read,
> While the Sisters spun their Thread;
>   "This Youth a Maid, this Maid a Youth must find,
>   "The best, the fairest both in Form and Mind;
>   "Each, as a friend, must each esteem, admire,
>   "Yet catch no Spark of Amourous Desire:
>   "Till this be done no Chance shall bliss bestow,
>   "When this is Done, no Chance shall work them Woe.[27]

To fulfill the command of the fates, the fairies have commanded Edgar to disguise himself as a woman named Elfrida, and Emmeline is to assume a man's guise in the name of Gondibert. The duration of the transformation is a month, and it quickly works hardships on the two participants. Emmeline, as Gondibert, complains: "What a Situation am I in!—Is this Figure (looking at herself) really and truly Emmeline?—the beloved and only daughter of Great Northumberland? . . . Oh! how weary am I of this Dress! If I had known half that I should have suffer'd in it, all the Fairies in the World should not have persuaded me to put it on" (p. 3).

The reversal of roles provides not only the dramatic situation governing the play's action but, more important, its theme: an exploration, and an intelligently comic one, of the relationship of the sexes that suggests any valid union must be based on more than mere physical attraction. Change of costume brings about changes in custom, allowing Edgar and Emmeline, as they assume different sexual identities, to see the kind of sex-colored world the other inhabits. Hawkesworth skillfully rescues a conventional subject matter—the love game—and while he violates none of the moral conventions of his time, he avoids the platitudes that deadened so much of its genteel comedy. In *Edgar and Emmeline* one sees an essentially timeless and astringently comic assessment of the human condition.

Emmeline, as a man, gains insight into the male world, which, not surprisingly, brings some sense of shock and even an appreciation of Edgar's decency. Her eyes have been rudely opened: "O 'tis my Dress that exposes me to more than half that I suffer; when one of my Sex is in Company, I am comparatively happy, but how unfit for a woman's ear is the Conversation of Men, when it is not restrain'd by knowing she is present!" (p. 4). Edgar's discoveries are, naturally, of a different kind and comically heightened by the disparity of his dress. Hawkesworth's worried protagonist cries:

> Was ever Man in such ridiculous Distress! I'm sure I ne'er knew any thing like it, since I was Edgar the son of Kent: Here have I had a young tempting Girl fiddle faddling about me these two hours; to dress me forsooth—with an officious handiness so provoking that no Virtue under that of a Stockfish could endure it patiently. Yet an old Woman upon these occasions I cannot bear; and in short I can no longer bear a young one. . . . A fine girl indeed may be less likely to love me, but as to myself, it is high time for me to get into Breeches that I may get out of Temptation: Here they flock about me, one sits down just before me and without any Ceremony ties her Garter. Another gets me to adjust her Tucker: I'm the Witness of so many pranks, and the Confidant of so many Secrets that I might fancy myself an Eunuch in a Seraglio. (P. 9)

Through a reversal of sexual roles Edgar learns truths about himself, hitherto repressed: he discovers how men treat women—not as human beings, sadly, but as mere sexual objects. In female dress he, too, has hours of mortification: "I am tormented by a Swarm of Profligate Fops who try to debauch every Woman they See with as little Ceremony as they take Snuff; Wretches, who are as destitute of Love, as they are of Virtue, and have as little enjoyment, as they have understanding; and here I am oblig'd to mince, and Pish, and Fie,—and affect to blush,—'Sdeath when I'm bursting with Indignation, and long to knock them down—I'll bear it no longer" (p. 9).

Before their happy union is effected, Edgar and Emmeline's tribulations are caused chiefly by the courtier, Florimond, who flits from one to the other spreading lies. He numbers among his ancestors those legions of fops and simpering sissies who trod the stage for generations before Hawkesworth created his own mid-century version. Throughout the piece he is kept in comic justaposition to Edgar and Emmeline, always unaware of their disguises, his innate foolishness compounded by his addresses unsuitable to the real sex of those who receive them. The comic possibilities of this device are nowhere better realized than when Edgar, disguised as the maid Elfrida, forgets his feminine wiles and exhibits a strength uncharacteristic of the sex. "By the Heavens," Florimond cries, "she has the Gripe of

a Bum Bailiff" (p. 16). With the kind intervention of the fairies such
confusion and wickedness as there is in the little world of Edgar and
Emmeline is banished (even Florimond asks humbly to be kicked into some
dark corner), and Edgar, now a man in dress as well as in fact, asserts the
play's moral:

> Come then my Fair, whom Fate my Love ordains,
> By whom kind heaven Over pays my fears and pains,
> Chosen as thou art for Graces of the mind,
> Ere Gold could influence, or Desire could blind,
> Whose Charms unsought, unknown are Friendship's
>   Dower.
> Whose Love in Reason founds its lasting power.
> O might Each Fair thus work what Fate intends
> And None be Lovers but who first were friends.
>
> (P. 25)

Hawkesworth's entertainment was first presented on Saturday,
January 31, 1761, at Drury Lane with music by Thomas Arne. William
O'Brien played the part of Edgar, and Mrs. Yates, who spoke the epilogue,
written by Garrick himself, played Emmeline. So well crafted a piece was
bound to please, and Arthur Murphy, a fellow dramatist, writes in what
must have been general appreciation of Hawkesworth's accomplishment:
"Dr. Hawkesworth favoured the public with a whimsical, but beautiful
little piece, called *Edgar and Emmeline*. The machinery of fairies, who direct
every thing, is well managed, and by the addition of musical interludes the
piece afforded an elegant entertainment to a number of crowded audiences." Frequent performances did indeed follow the initial presentation,
one occurring as late as April 27, 1795.[28] If in his adaptations of *Oroonoko*
and *Amphitryon* Hawkesworth reveals a playwright shackled by the reformist tendencies of his age, in *Edgar and Emmeline* he proves his capacity to
transcend those tendencies in a production suggesting that in the wasteland
some see separating Farquhar from Goldsmith there was an occasional oasis
and some anticipation of the comic fertility to be seen in *She Stoops to
Conquer*.

In his review of *Oroonoko* Johnson illuminated the problems the adapter
faced in establishing any claim upon his sources; while Hawkesworth's
revisions of *Amphitryon* and *Oroonoko* offer little artistry to assess, they
provide useful material for the student of the theater as well as the cultural
historian. For the former they reveal the great changes that occurred
between the Restoration and the eighteenth-century stage, as the old mi-
metic comedy, satiric in nature, gave way to drama populated not with
jades, jilts, and fortune-hunters but with more idealized examples of human

conduct, drama seasoned not with wit so much as washed with tears. For the latter they show that the theater contributed to the reformist literature that surfaced at century's beginning in the *Tatler* and the *Spectator*. In his theatrical adaptations no less than in his celebrated *Adventurer* periodical Hawkesworth can be seen as an artist deeply committed to the reform of his age, which depended not simply on the power of law and religion to curb behavior but on art itself to amend it.

Although he left the theater as an active playwright with *Edgar and Emmeline*,[29] Hawkesworth's association with Garrick did not cease, and this friend and luminary would eventually help him secure the literary prize of the century (or so it seemed)—the contract to write the account of Cook's first Pacific voyage. Few men enriched Hawkesworth's life as long as Garrick, one who brought him to the center of the eighteenth-century theater. He made of him not only observer but practitioner of one of the most exhilarating artistic pursuits, giving him passport to the green room, to the intimacy of the acting community, and, beyond these, to rehearsal, to the smell of the greasepaint and the crowd's roar, finally to the satisfaction of solid gate receipts. Garrick himself profited from his connection with a distinguished man of letters, one who could advise on matters of literature and theater at the same time that he offered him defense in the press and release from the pressures of city and position at his Bromley home. Perhaps, though, the most important result of their friendship lies in the fact that it must have been Garrick who encouraged Hawkesworth's labors as literary editor of the *Gentleman's Magazine*. In this position Hawkesworth became an important commentator on eighteenth-century literature and British culture generally.

V HAWKESWORTH AND THE GENTLEMAN'S MAGAZINE, 1741–1773

> I Rejoice I have contributed to establish the work which is now your's, and I beg you would with all freedom determine what My assistance is worth to you for the time to come, and what the state of the Magazine will permit you chearfully to pay.

John Hawkesworth to David Henry, 1756

While the eighteenth century witnessed the rise of the novel in the masterworks of Defoe, Richardson, Fielding, and Sterne, the development of another prose form, the magazine, can be credited to one man, Edward Cave, the son of a cobbler born February 27, 1692, in the village of Newton, Warwickshire. Through his energy, his good business sense, and his ability to attract talented writers seeking commercial routes to success as literary patronage faded, Cave established the *Gentleman's Magazine* at St. John's Gate, Clerkenwell, a publication soon to reflect as few others the cultural, commercial, and political energies of a nation. No less than Addison, Cave "brought Philosophy out of Closets and Libraries, Schools and Colleges, to dwell in Clubs and Assemblies, at Tea-Tables, and in Coffee-Houses"; and the *Gentleman's* appealed even more than the *Spectator* to the intellectual eclecticism of the middle class.[1] The publication was marked at the outset by the catholicity of its contents—it was truly a magazine, or storehouse, of materials, including news summaries; lists of births, deaths, promotions, bankruptcies; stock and weather reports; historical, scientific and political articles; commentary on religion; and, increasingly, literature and literary criticism. A world of print awaited the purchaser, and it was scarcely in hyperbole that Cave wrote in the preface for 1741, after only a decade's publication:

> *The* GENTLEMAN'S MAGAZINE *is read as far as the English Language extends, and we see it reprinted from several Presses in Great Britain, Ireland, and the Plantations. Our Debates and Poetical Pieces are copied by some, our Foreign History by others, and the Lives which we have inserted of eminent Men, have been taken into Works of larger Size, and, with other Parts of our Book, been translated into foreign Languages.*[2]

The *Gentleman's* enjoyed rapid growth in circulation, survived challenges from imitators and competitors (though the *Critical Review* and *Monthly Review* achieved success), and St. John's Gate lured talents great and small. Mark Akenside, Elizabeth Carter, Richard Savage, Christopher Smart, Thomas Percy, Charles Burney, James Boswell, Joseph and Thomas Warton, and Arthur Murphy attest to Cave's power to attract writers of ability. But none played a more crucial role in the periodical during its formative years than Johnson himself.

Johnson offered his services to Cave as early as November 25, 1734, though it was several years later, probably in 1737, that the two men met and formed a mutually beneficial relationship: in Johnson, Cave secured the talents of one destined to become the brightest literary star of the age, the Ursa Major of the third quarter of the eighteenth century; Johnson, in turn, found in Cave no encumbering patron but a practical man who offered financial remuneration, a means of focusing vast energies so easily dissipated, and most important, an opportunity to test his literary abilities against marketplace realities. It was from Cave, perhaps, that Johnson learned that "no man but a blockhead ever wrote, except for money."[3]

If blessed with Johnson's assistance at the outset, Cave was twice fortunate in finding in Hawkesworth another worthy coadjutor. Hawkesworth's involvement in the *Gentleman's Magazine* has remained one of the best concealed aspects of his varied literary career, one, however, that can be illuminated by a substantial body of internal and external evidence. Shadows persist, but the outline and many specifics of his work for Cave and Cave's successors are clear.

Hawkesworth's first recorded connection with the periodical occurred in a poem published in June 1741 but submitted a year earlier, when he was still nineteen. From this time to his death in 1773 his service to the magazine was matched by few others. Through the 1740s he contributed many poems to the publication, emerging in the later years of the decade as one who not only supervised the poetry columns of the publication but also helped direct the magazine as a whole. Up to Cave's death in 1754, in fact, he apparently served, in Johnson's absence, as an unofficial literary editor of the publication; in 1756 he assumed a position that might fairly be called that of literary editor of the *Gentleman's Magazine*, though without the power such a post would carry today. During the middle decades of the century Hawkesworth enriched the columns of the *Gentleman's* with numerous prose contributions—parliamentary "debates," translations from the French, original essays, and fictional pieces reminiscent of his oriental and domestic tales in his *Adventurer*. Most important, Hawkesworth helped make the *Gentleman's Magazine* a vehicle for the discussion of literature, and he emerged as one of the prime critics of the drama of the age and of the mass of works that flowed from both national and foreign presses. In this popular periodical, then, Hawkesworth served no less than Johnson as a "literary dictator" of his age. It is best to speak of Hawkesworth's poetry first since it constitutes an initial and somewhat independent phase of his work for the *Gentleman's Magazine.*[4]

Although a chief storehouse of eighteenth-century prose, the *Gentleman's Magazine* published quantities of poetry, much of it of dubious worth and some, no doubt, inspired as much by the fifty-pound prizes that Edward Cave offered in a series of poetry contests as by the call of the muse. The magazine's poetry columns often featured the works of the anonymous and the obscure, sometimes the productions of such limited talents as Moses Browne, and occasionally the work of poets of stature—Mark Akenside, Elizabeth Carter, Christopher Smart, and Johnson, for example. Hawkesworth contributed a number of poems to the publication during the 1740s. The first, in June 1741, is his first extant published work. Entitled "The Fop, Cock and Diamond," it is a long moral statement in the form of an animal fable: in substance it reflects his probable reading in Gay and La Fontaine; in verse it is a sustained study of Alexander Pope, a natural enough model for a beginning poet to emulate in the 1740s. If Hawkesworth lacks Pope's skill, he is an able versifier, a competent manipulator of the couplet, which he handles with economy, generally avoiding the monotony that afflicts this rhyme scheme. The subject of this poem, a commonplace of the time, is the luxury that produces the beau or fop, encumbered by artifice, out of touch with nature. Cato is all decoration and finery, a kindred spirit of such fops as the dainty, pirouetting Bellarmine in *Joseph Andrews*, one who "Straight on his Coat . . . clap'd gold lace, / And next with washes spoil'd his face" (GM 11:327). Cato loses his prized ring, the final sham repository of his hopes of dazzling the *beau monde*, the gem resting finally on a dunghill, where it calls forth the reflections of a philosophical cock, a bird of small brain but larger moral values than corrupted man.

The young attorney's clerk must have been delighted to see his literary effort in print and equally so with a note that declared, "*The following* Fable *was put into our Hands about this time last Year, and mislaid many months; we shall be glad to hear from the Author*" (11:327). Hawkesworth's response to this call was prompt, and Cave was obviously pleased with the fables he submitted, which were published the same year with such titles as "The Danger of trusting Individuals with exorbitant Power" (July), "The Patriot Prince" (August), and "The Pleasure-Seekers; or, The Way to Happiness" (September). All are animal fables, cautionary tales urging moral reform made palatable through the easy versification seen in the conclusion to the last poem mentioned above, which is perhaps an imitation of Pope's celebrated Alps passage in the *Essay on Criticism* (2. 225–32):

> No joys of sense, like conscious goodness please,
> More bright than glory, and more soft than ease;
> In prospect *those* enchant the treach'rous eye,
> Yet when approach'd illusive fleet and dye.
> Still others spring, still please and cheat the same,
> While hop'd for——mountains, when possess'd——
> ——a name——
> So charms a cloud with ev'ry colour gay,
> When from afar it breaks the sev'n-fold ray,
> But if we reach it, we discern no more
> The flatt'ring vapour so admir'd before.
> 'Tis virtue, reigning in the gen'rous heart,
> Alone, can true substantial bliss impart. (GM 11:492)

Cave published four more fables by Hawkesworth during 1742. A slight variation in format is seen in "The Miserable Glutton" (February) and its sequel, "The Unhappy Debauchee" (April), both of which make a moral commentary without recourse to animals. They are poetic equivalents of *Adventurer* papers that Hawkesworth was soon to write: in one a squire learns that happiness is secured through control of appetite; in the other a debauchee discovers that sexual bliss is possible only through married love. Apparently Hawkesworth ceased to contribute poetry to the *Gentleman's* from May 1742 to January 1746, when he began writing with regularity, abandoning animal and moral fables for more direct commentary in such poems as "Lines address'd to the Reverend Mr Warburton" (January 1746), "Some Lines occasion'd by a Series of Theological Enquiries" (April), "The Devil-Painter" (May), "The Smart; or, High Taste in High Life" and "A Thought from Marcus Antonius" (June), "The Close-Stool," a translation from the French (August), "Burlesque Epistle to the King of Prussia," another French translation (September), and "To Mr Layng, on his Sermon" (October).[5]

Although inclined towards didactic verse, Hawkesworth was at his best in lighter contexts, and many readers must have appreciated his "Devil-Painter. For the Petit Maitres, and Beaux Esprits," published in May 1746. More with the gentle attack of a Gay than with savage Swiftian assaults Hawkesworth chastises pretenders to art, specifically:

> One dunce I knew, whom no restraint
> Cou'd keep from pencil and from paint.
> Him *Hogarth's* praise had so bewitch'd,
> That ev'ry rival finger itch'd.
> He'd chalk and dawb, and stink and smear
> From morn to night, from year to year.

> But still, with some unlucky touch,
> Gave here too little, there too much.

Frustration ends, however, in discovering his innate talent—devil drawing—and from his creations

> Children ran screaming from the sight,
> And women shriek'd and swoon'd with fright.
> Our artist now, elate with pride,
> Looks big, and moves with stately stride;
> Contracts his brow severe and awing,
> A first-rate hand—at devil-drawing.
>
> (*GM* 16:265)

Johnson, however, preferred a more serious effort by Hawkesworth entitled, "Life. An Ode," which appeared in the July 1747 issue of the *Gentleman's Magazine*. Although Hawkesworth apparently controlled the poetry section of the magazine at the time, he still solicited Johnson's advice on literary matters, especially where his own composition was concerned. William Cooke writes that Hawkesworth took his poem to retouch at a friend's house in the country where Johnson was visiting. Johnson demanded two readings of the ode, after which he "read it himself, approved of it very highly, and returned it." The next morning at breakfast Johnson once again commended Hawkesworth's poetic effort but doubted its originality. Hawkesworth, deeply alarmed at this charge, demanded proof from his friend, who immediately repeated the whole of the poem with few omissions. An astonished Hawkesworth could only answer: "I shall never repeat any thing I write before you again, for you have a memory that would convict any author of plagiarism in any court of literature in the world."[6]

The poem that Johnson commended and practically memorized charts in sixty-eight lines man's brief time on earth as he moves from the gaiety and frivolousness of childhood and youth through maturity to old age and death. The concluding lines are:

> AGE—my future self—I trace
> Moving slow with feeble pace,
> Bending with disease and cares,
> All the load of life he bears;
> White his locks, his visage wan,
> Strength, and ease, and hope are gone.
> Death, the shadowy form I know!

Death o'ertakes him, dreadful foe!
Swift, they vanish—mournful sight,
Night succeeds, impervious night!
What these dreadful glooms conceal
Fancy's glass can ne'er reveal;
When shall time the veil remove?
When shall light the scene improve?
What shall truth my doubts dispel!
Awful period!—who can tell?

(*GM* 17:337)

It is not difficult to see why the author of *London* and one soon to write *The Vanity of Human Wishes* admired such elevated verses on the awful certainties of the human condition. A modern reader, however, might respond more favorably to the less sententious commentary seen in Hawkesworth's "The Death of Arachne," his longest poem, which appeared in the August 1747 issue of the *Gentleman's*. "An Heroi-Comi-Tragic-Poem," "Arachne" is a humorous narrative featuring a scholarly sage, Philo, his wife, Cloe, and her excited response to a spider. A fair copy of the poem in the British Library contains the comment that "the above poem was addrest by the Doctor to Mrs Hawkesworth who from infancy was terrified at the sight of a spider."[7] Philo and Cloe undoubtedly resemble John and Mary Hawkesworth; though Hawkesworth idealizes her and depicts himself in a self-deprecatory manner, the poem reflects their happy married state revealed in other material. Some readers of "Arachne" might need reminding that the common English spider can be a huge, loathsome creature. Of Philo, Hawkesworth writes:

Philo, tho' young, to musing much inclin'd,
A shameless sloven, in his gown had din'd,
From table sneaking with a sheepish face,
Before the circle was dismiss'd with *grace,*
And smoking now, his desk with books o'erspread,
Thick clouds of incense roll around his head;
His head, which save a quarter's growth of hair,
His woollen cap long since scratch'd off, was bare;
His beard three days had grown, of golden hue,
Black was his shirt, uncomely to the view;
Cross-legg'd he was and his ungarter'd hose
Of each lean limb half hide, and half expose;
His cheek he lean'd upon his hand, below
His nut-brown slipper hung his toe.

(*GM* 17:394)

Philo addresses airy and philosophical subjects: "Does *soul* in ought subsist, or *all* in soul? / Is *space, extension* nothing but a name, / And mere *idea* nature's mighty frame? / All *pow'r*, all *forms*, to intellect confin'd; / Place, agent, subject, instrument combin'd?" (p. 394). Although good humor prevails here, some might see in the hapless sage an anticipation of the mature Hawkesworth, who indulged, perhaps fatally, in metaphysical speculations about the operation of divine Providence during Captain Cook's celebrated voyage to the South Seas. The poem, though, is no more than a sustained *jeu d'esprit*, its subject no larger than Cloe's insistence that Philo kill the spider that frightened her. After much rumination and hesitation he capitulates, and the deed, to echoes of *The Rape of the Lock*, is effected with a shoe:

> Crush'd falls the foe, one complicated wound,
> And the smote shelf returns a jarring sound.
>   On *Ida's* top thus *Venus* erst prevail'd,
> When all the sapience of *Minerva* fail'd;
> Thus to like arts a prey, as poets tell,
> By *Juno* lov'd in vain, great *Dido* fell.
> And thus forever Beauty shall controul
> The saint's the sage's, and the heroe's soul.
>   (P. 395)

For more than ten years Hawkesworth submitted such verse to the poetry section of the *Gentleman's Magazine*; quantitatively, at least, he was among its major contributors. If his poetry has failed to survive his time, it evidently pleased his contemporaries. Mrs. John Duncombe, the wife of the clergyman responsible for identifying a number of his poems in the periodical, writes that "his fugitive poetical pieces that have been published, must enroll his name among the best of English poets, and the morality, true taste, wit and humour of his 'Arachne,' with the graver moral of the 'Ode on Life,' will mark his poetical abilities as long as poetry and sense united can charm the candid reader." Johnson's praise of the "Ode" has already been noted, and it is to Hawkesworth's credit that Johnson not only commenced an edition of his works but suggested that the poetry showed evidence "of a very powerful Mind." Both assessments of Hawkesworth's poetry are probably excessive, the one determined by close friendship, the other conditioned perhaps by Johnson's realization that Hawkesworth endured intolerable abuse over his edition of Cook's *Voyages* while supposed friends remained silent. Yet even a modern student of the *Gentleman's Magazine*, C. Lennart Carlson, finds that Hawkesworth's poetry "is some of the sprightliest in the magazine. Though it lacks the verve of La Fontaine, some of whose poems he imitated, it is far above the level of the contributions of Elizabeth Carter and other poetesses whose work was published there." With that evaluation few could disagree.[8]

But it was in his prose submissions, a more natural medium of expression for both the writer and the periodical, that Hawkesworth made the greatest impact upon the first magazine. For over twenty-five years, from the mid-1740s to his death in 1773, Hawkesworth not only contributed parliamentary "debates," translations, fiction, essays, and, principally, dramatic and book reviews to the *Gentleman's Magazine*, but he also served as the literary editor of the publication, succeeding Johnson as Cave's chief coadjutor in this area and emerging as the official literary editor in 1756. The difficulty in identifying specific pieces he submitted to the magazine, not to mention the larger dimensions of his editorial activity, results from Hawkesworth's anonymous contributions or, at best, contributions by initials. With recourse to memoirs, commentary by friends, his correspondence, and internal, stylistic evidence, however, it is possible to establish that Hawkesworth was a principal force in the *Gentleman's* during the later eighteenth century, one who defined one of the most important publications of the time.[9]

Although Johnson noted in his comments on *The Two Gentlemen of Verona* that "by the internal marks of a composition we may discover the authour with probability, though seldom with certainty," stylistic evidence first established Hawkesworth's role in the *Gentleman's Magazine*. It was, in fact, when scholars compared known Hawkesworth reviews of books and plays in the *Monthly Review* (published from December 1768 to August 1771) with those submitted by "X" to the *Gentleman's Magazine* (from April 1767 to March 1773), a signature appearing over 275 times, that his involvement first became clear. Verbal parallels, sometimes in reviews of the same book or play, confirm that Hawkesworth and X were the same man.[10] Compare the following examples from Hawkesworth's and X's reviews of Thomas King's *Wit's Last Stake*. I italicize verbal echoes.

> An old fellow whom infirmity and disease have brought to the brink of the grave, suddenly *takes it into his head*, instead of making a will, to marry a young lady engaged to his nephew; and instead of giving him a fortune, resolves to take away his mistress: he falls into a fit however *in the mean time*, and for fear he should die intestate, the nephew's valet, an arch fellow, *undertakes to personate him*, and *make a will in his stead*.
>
> *The mirth* of these scenes *arises* from the situation of the nephew when the uncle declares his intention to marry, and when his valet takes advantage of the situation he is suffered to assume with a view to leave

the old man's fortune to his master, to bequeath a very considerable legacy to himself, and to the girl he is going to marry. (*Monthly Review* 40 [Feb. 1769]:158)

A rich covetous old fellow,.supposed to be dying, *takes it into his head* to marry; he has promised to make his nephew his heir, but it is feared that he has not actually made a will. He is taken with a fit, and *in the mean time*, the nephew's valet *undertakes to personate the uncle*, and *make a will in his stead; the mirth arises* from the bequests of this valet to himself, and a girl he is to marry, which the master, though present, does not dare to contradict, for fear of a discovery, which could have cut off his hope of the rest. (*GM* 39 [April 1769]:199)

Both Hawkesworth and X reviewed Charlotte Lennox's *The Sister* in remarkably similar language. Compare the following:

Mrs. Lennox is already *well known* as the writer of Shakespeare illustrated, the Female Quixote, and several other performances, which make any compliment either to her judgment or imagination unnecessary.

This comedy is taken from a little novel which she published some years ago, *entitled Henrietta*; it was *exhibited* only one night at the theatre in Covent-garden; the audience *expressed* great *disapprobation*, and would not *suffer* it to be given out for another *exhibition*. . . .

It seems to have been written upon a supposition common to all who have not *a familiar acquaintance with the stage* as well as with the Drama; that the *exhibition* of a story will please, in proportion to the number of events, and intricacy of the plot. (*Monthly Review* 40 [March 1769]: 245)

This is the performance of Mrs. Charlotte Lenox, an ingenious lady, *well known* in the literary world by her excellent writings, particularly the Female-Quixote, and Shakespeare illustrated

She has taken the fable from one of her own novels, *intitled, Henrietta*, which renders an account of the story unnecessary. . . . It wants an intermixture of light scenes, such as *a familiar acquaintance with the stage* might have furnished, without the abilities of Mrs Lenox, and which, if her abilities had been still greater, could not, perhaps, have been furnished without *a familiar acquaintance with the stage*.

The audience *expressed* their *disapprobation* of it with so much clamour and appearance of prejudice, that she would not *suffer* an attempt to *exhibit* it a second time. (*GM* 39 [April 1769]: 199)

The parallels in approach and language seen above are not sporadic but constant; to argue that Hawkesworth and X were not the same reviewer would be to insist on a number of stylistic coincidences. Further evidence suggests, moreover, that Hawkesworth reviewed drama for the *Gentleman's Magazine* long before he used the X signature—as early, in fact, as 1747, when Cave published the periodical's first dramatic review.[11] Parallels in style and approach to drama are no less obvious between X (Hawkesworth) and his predecessor in the *Gentleman's* than they are between Hawkesworth in *Monthly* reviews and X in Cave's periodical from April 1767 to March 1773. Both are preoccupied with dramatic probability and consistency in development of plot and character; both are romantic rather than neoclassical in their criticism, more interested in a play's effect than in judging it by objective, Aristotelian principles; both comment frequently on a play's moral vision, share a fondness for sentimental drama and poetic justice, and digress on the sanctity of marriage; both scrutinize the play's language and frequently cite such stylistic inelegancies as mixed metaphors, flaws in diction, and appropriateness of speech to social condition; both compare plays on the stage with those read in the closet; both castigate characters who violate taste, decency, and morality.

If such general similarities help establish common authorship, there are more specific ones as well. For example, the reviewer of Dr. Benjamin Hoadley's *Suspicious Husband* argued in March 1747, in the magazine's first dramatic review, that a young rake named Ranger, who dominates the production, should have reformed at play's end (*GM* 17:140). Twenty-four years later, in March 1771, X (Hawkesworth) reviewed Richard Cumberland's *The West Indian*, which featured another rake named Belcour, about whom he writes that the "moral objections to the character of Belcour, are such as we made long ago to that of Ranger, in our account of the *Suspicious Husband*" (*GM* 41:126), and he refers his readers to the review, citing volume and page number. To argue here that the "we" is simply editorial is again to insist on a large coincidence—that X recalled a play from the past whose only real connection with *The West Indian* is the character of a rake. It is more likely that the moralist of the *Adventurer* wrote both reviews, and there is considerable stylistic evidence to suggest that X, one Hawkesworth, and his predecessor writing dramatic criticism before 1767 are the same man. Excerpts soon cloy but note the following criticism written by and before X.

The *Gentleman's* featured the celebrated Samuel Foote in reviews appearing in July 1760 and June 1765 (before X) and August 1770 and January 1772 (both by X), which contain verbal echoes indicating common authorship. In January 1772 X argues in a review of *The Theatres* by the pseudononymous "Sir Nicholas Nipclose, Baronet" that Foote's

excellency consists in throwing hastily together some *sprightly scenes*, *peculiarly adapted* to his *own peculiar powers* of diverting the public. He has, probably, never taxed himself with the production of a regular piece, in which connection of scenes, probability of events, and propriety of conduct were maintained. (*GM* 42:29)

In a review of Foote's *The Lame Lovers* in August 1770 X concludes that

upon the whole, the *humour* of this piece may well *attone* for its want of plot and regularity. (40:381)

Commenting on Foote's *The Minor* and *The Commissary* in July 1760 and June 1765, respectively, the reviewer writes,

As it [*The Minor*] is by the author *adapted* to his own *peculiar abilities*, it is . . . (30:325)

and

This piece [*The Commissary*] is to be considered rather as a collection of *glowing scenes*. . . . However, what Mr. *Foote* wants in conduct, he has . . . amply *atoned* for in *humour*. (35:254)

There is a striking unity of language and idea in the dramatic criticism from 1747 to 1773, not simply in reference to a single author such as Samuel Foote, but in a variety of plays reviewed before and after X. Of Charlotte Lennox's *The Sister* (already noted above) X writes that

the *dialogue is natural, lively and elegant*, the *incidents* are uncommon, yet within the pale of dramatic probability, and the *sentiments* are just and refined. (*GM* 39:199)

And in May 1770 X commends Hugh Kelly's *A Word to the Wise*, a sentimental comedy, noting that

the piece abounds in *sentiments* of virtue, generosity, delicacy, and honour; contains many useful lessons to young people, and is in every respect worthy of a better fate than it received. (40:227)

Of Richard Cumberland's *The West Indian* X writes in March 1771 that "it is full of *sentiment* and character," and he praises it for having parts "exceeding comic and many very *tender*" (41:126).

These brief passages can be profitably compared with excerpts from reviews before X. Consider, for example, how the critic of Edward Moore's *The Foundling*, in March 1748, reflects X's attitudes towards drama. He writes:

> As to the manner in which the author has conducted his *scene*, . . . it must be confessed, to his honour, that there is no double entendre introduced, no mirth at the expence of modesty, none of the low wit usually play'd off with great applause between favourite footmen and chambermaids. (*GM* 18:116)

A single sentence in a review of William Whitehead's *School for Lovers* in April 1762 repeats a number of X's favorite words and phrases:

> The characters are extremely well drawn, and sustained; the *dialogue is natural and spirited*; the *sentiments* are chaste and *elegant*, and some of the situations are *touching* and *tender* in the highest degree. (32:161)

Finally, in March 1767, a month before X appears, George Colman's *The English Merchant* draws words of praise reminiscent of X himself for

> great merit of every kind; the dialect is easy and *natural*, the *sentiments* noble, the *incidents tender* and *touching* and the characters well imagined and sustained. (37:129–30)

The above samples suggest, at least, what a sustained reading of the dramatic criticism in the *Gentleman's Magazine* supports—that the reviews of drama from 1747 to 1773 are united by common attitudes and a common critical vocabulary. However one might argue that these are commonplaces of the time, the property of no single author, the parallels between X's reviews and those that precede him are striking and made all the more so when other peculiarities of style common to both reviewers are noted, even briefly. Both use—abuse, really—the word *that*, which occurs frequently in the first review of *The Suspicious Husband* in March 1747 (*GM* 17:133–140) and often thereafter. Both resort to words and phrases (not cited above) so often they become virtual signatures—*to appear*, meaning "to seem"; *suppose*, used as a verb, as an adjective (*the supposed*), and in its cognate forms as nouns (*suppositions* and *presuppositions*); *in the mean time*, used habitually in plot recapitulations; *hastes* in preference to *hastens*; *attone* as a frequent substitute for *atone*. Both regularly employ such phrases as "agony of . . ." and "transport of . . . ," adding two or three words, as in an "agony of tenderness and grief" and "transports of astonishment, joy, and tenderness."[12]

It is such internal evidence, brief to be sure, that suggests the possibility of a common author for the dramatic criticism in the *Gentleman's Magazine*, John Hawkesworth, reviewing with and without the signature of X. He was probably involved with nondramatic reviewing as well, though stylistic evidence is less convincing. The review section of the *Gentleman's* went through a number of changes during the century's middle years: in the beginning Cave merely provided a brief list of books published in London; in March 1736 he added "Books published abroad" with some critical commentary, though it was not until mid-1748 that English books were discussed at any length; by December 1750 expansion of the review section is obvious, and by May 1752 specific attention is called to the critical nature of the section with the title, "Books publish'd . . . with Remarks"; by 1756 considerable expansion is seen, and by 1765 the *Gentleman's Magazine* had evolved into a major review organ. Dramatic and nondramatic material were often reviewed together, increasing the likelihood that Hawkesworth served as a general critic of literature and did not confine himself to drama alone; and important plays and books were featured outside of the review section proper—a long survey of Hogarth's *Analysis of Beauty*, an important critical document of the time, commenced the January 1754 issue.

Only in the longer reviews of the 1760s and 1770s does any discernible style and attitude emerge, and these are somewhat blurred by the eclectic nature of the books assessed: the *Gentleman's* universe included many constellations whose masses for the moment, at least, were held to be equivalent, and a volume detailing a new paste for piles was likely to gain as serious a hearing as the latest volume of *Tristram Shandy*. Indeed, the tone of the book reviews before and after X is almost always serious, tough, and astringent, and in the case of truly pathetic productions—the feeble poetry of feebler wits—it could be scathing and cruel. Both qualities of the review section—its seriousness and astringency of tone—were referred to by Hawkesworth (if only indirectly) and by Sir John Hawkins. In a letter to Ralph Griffiths, editor of the *Monthly Review*, written on March 3, 1769, Hawkesworth testified to his high regard for the book review as a significant art form, commenting that "perhaps there is no work so important as a Review honestly and ably executed," and Hawkins states in his *Life of Johnson* that Hawkesworth was thought to exercise his post as reviewer in the *Gentleman's Magazine* "with some asperity."[13] Both comments anticipate external evidence to come but serve as a convenient frame within which one might judge several quotations to follow from reviews by X (referred to hereafter as Hawkesworth) and his supposed predecessor, who sound much like the same man.

In June 1767, commenting on a study of Rousseau, Hawkesworth writes that "this is one of the dullest and yet the most extravagant rhapsodies that ever appeared: It is neither praise nor censure, narrative nor argument, and answering the definition of nonsense, it is neither false nor true" (*GM* 37:318). Hawkesworth was particularly fussy about grammatical violations, so that even when he found much to praise in a July 1767 review of a book about infant diseases, he noted "that in more places than one, it gives countenance to a barbarism that seems unaccountably to be gaining ground in our language; the substitution of *lay* for *lie*, the preterit for the present" (37:365). He routinely denounced texts in the bluntest of language. In assessing a travel book in September 1767 he comments that "it is, on every account, to be regretted, that in this book there is not one event, description or remark, worth recording" (37:458); a few months later, in December 1767, he castigates a writer on a classical theme, observing: "There is some reason to conclude, that if the writer of these pieces had succeeded in other pursuits, he would not have become an author; a criticism on his performance is therefore neither suitable to our plan nor inclination" (37:596). Even though Hawkesworth, like Samuel Richardson, was an acknowledged favorite of the ladies, their productions also risked censure. "Notwithstanding we are always tender in censuring the productions of the fair sex," he writes in a review of *The Brother*, "By a Lady," in May 1771, "yet we must declare, that it is a pity this Lady has misspent so much time in scribbling, when she would have been better employed in darning her ruffles, or working of cat-gut" (41:229). Clearly there is foundation for Hawkins' observation, and the "asperity" of tone is hardly less evident in reviews before X.

In February 1751, for example, the reviewer writes of *The Adventures of Lady Frail*: "This is yet unread by us, and by the account same gives of it, ever will be" (*GM* 21:95). Of a recent work by Bolingbroke the *Gentleman's* concludes in March 1752 that "these letters contain little more than some objections to revelation, which are almost as old as christianity, and upon the whole are so trite and superficial, that the name of the author, who has by some means acquired a popular reputation, much superior to his apparent abilities as a writer, will not be able to impose them upon mankind, as an exhibition of the discoveries of genius, or the acquisitions, of learning" (22:145). Responding to a negative commentary on Richard Glover's tragedy *Boadicia* (favorably reviewed in the *Gentleman's* in December 1753), the reviewer writes in January 1754 that "this is a verbose criticism on dramatic poetry in barbarous language, and even false grammar, of which the following extract is a proof, and therefore a sufficient specimen of the performance" (24:51). In July 1754 a pamphlet is characterized as "nothing more than one of those excrescences, which naturally grow upon every popular book: It is always hoped that some, at least, will take notice of the fungus, among the multitude who examine the tree, to which if it had not adhered, they know it must have been spurned to the dunghill or trodden under foot" (24:342). Finally, in March 1755, another poor pretender to literature is demolished: "If the author of this performance is mad," the reviewer states, "it is pity that he is not in Bedlam; if he is not mad, it is a pity he is not in Bridewell" (25:143).

One can see clearly from this evidence that the reviews in the *Gentle-*

man's were marked by a critical astringency long before Hawkesworth reviewed as X in 1767. These few examples tend to illustrate what a sustained reading of the dramatic and nondramatic criticism in the magazine from the 1740s to the 1770s reveals—that for all the divergence of subject matter, the criticism of works both belletristic and pragmatic is marked by an unmistakable unity of approach and language: from the larger assumptions about genres, to particulars of approach, to specific expressions and verbal preferences, all of which have been noted above, one perceives the work of a single man. While he was not in total control of the review columns of the *Gentleman's Magazine*, he worked with such frequency and ranged so widely in his reviews of the writing of his time that they bear his unmistakable imprint. On internal evidence alone, then, one could argue persuasively for Hawkesworth's participation in the magazine long before 1767, when he undoubtedly reviewed as X. But even a prolonged replication of the evidence already presented might fail to convince the skeptical; for them external evidence exists in abundance—in memoirs, in testimony of Hawkesworth's friends and others, and in his correspondence—which makes it possible to define his service to the magazine not only with probability but with certainty.

The Osborn sketch of Hawkesworth's life specifically links him with the publication in the early 1740s, noting first that he secured "pocket money" from the editor for his poetry contributions and, later, a small stipend for a somewhat greater involvement in the poetry section. The *Universal Magazine* memoir of Hawkesworth's life provides one of the most detailed descriptions of his work for the periodical. It records:

> He wrote both in poetry and in prose. His poetical pieces were in general but short copies of verses, rather grave than airy, and though pregnant with meaning, yet not unadorned with some of the lighter graces. In prose, his favourite attempts were to recommend ethical truth, by arraying it in those guises of fancy, which were then most popular in the elegant literature of England. He translated many pieces from the French. He selected extracts from some new books, and made abridgements of others. The Parliamentary Debates written for that Magazine from July 1736 to November 1740, by William Guthrie, the historian; and from that period till March 1743, by Dr. Samuel Johnson; were also from this date, for some time, either composed or corrected, in continuance of the same series, by Mr. Hawkesworth. He had, likewise, to examine the communications of correspondents, and to compile the details of political and private history.[14]

This is clear proof of Hawkesworth's multifaceted involvement in the

Gentleman's Magazine, and his own letter to David Henry in 1756 confirms it. Only recently discovered, it deserves extensive quotation.

> Dear Sir,
>
> Your favor dated 6th appears by the Post Mark not to have been forwarded to me from the office till the 9th and as I was then in town it did not come to my hands till yesterday. I am greatly obliged by the contents, but your candid declaration that my terms with respect to the Magazine will never be objected to, is the very reason why I cannot name any; for if you should think my demand overrates my services, it will be so very like my having taken advantage of your generosity to gratify myself at your Expense, that I would rather continue my Labor without any reward then suffer such an imputation but for a day. You will be astonished, and I very think not without some degree of indignation, when I tell you that the whole accumulated profit which I derived from my connection with the late Mr. Cave was less than £30 pounds a year, and that except a set of his Magazines, I never received from him in gratuities of any kind the value of forty shillings; such however was his unaccountable and injurious caprice, that after I had afforded him such assistance as he knew he could not procure from another, during ten years; he invited Mr Daniel whose pieces I had almost constantly new written, at the yearly salary of sixty pounds, and all the necessaries of Board & Lodging; this in a great degree cut off all my hopes of future advantage; yet to comfort him in the anguish of Mind which I saw him suffer, I told him, I would not forsake him, and stiffled my own resentment by reflecting that as I had never made any agreement with him, he violated no contract, and I could only reproach him with the want of kindness a sort of negative fault for which it was still in his power to attone, and for which I was determined to forgive him, if he did not; and at last he put my Charity to the Trial. Thus My dear Sir, it has stood with me, and thus it now stands. I do not expect you to atone for these deficiencies, I Rejoice I have contributed to establish the work which is now your's, and I beg you would with all freedom determine what My assistance is worth to you for the time to come, and what the state of the Magazine will permit you chearfully to pay; if I think it not equal to the present value of my time, I will honestly tell you; and if I do, I will apply to it with all my powers & engage in nothing that will lead my thoughts from that as their principal object.[15]

This letter, evidently part of negotiations between Hawkesworth and the magazine's editor, David Henry, Cave's brother-in-law, establishes his past associations with the publication and, by inference, his future ones. The letter confirms that he worked for the *Gentleman's* in 1756—the office cited is surely St. John's Gate—and indicates as well that he had served the publication "during ten years," a significant figure when one recalls that the first dramatic review appeared in 1747, and nondramatic reviews soon thereafter. Clearly, Hawkesworth could have been their author. Hawkesworth's description of his past employment with Cave is obviously designed to secure more favorable terms from Henry, and echoes Johnson's view that Cave "was a penurious pay-master; he would contract for lines by the hundred, and expect the long hundred." Yet Hawkesworth, no less than Johnson, admired the founder of the first magazine and probably would have agreed with the rest of Johnson's statement, that Cave "was a good man, and always delighted to have his friends at his table."[16]

Henry was ready, however, to offer more attractive terms to a man who had "helped establish the work" now his, and Hawkesworth probably assumed at this time, with more proper emoluments, the office of literary editor of the *Gentleman's Magazine*, which he had occupied unofficially for a decade. "About this time [the mid-1750s]," the Osborn Sketch records, "a considerable change took place in his conduct. Although he felt his employment in the Gentleman's Magazine rather beneath him, yet he applied to it with much earnestness, was late and even early in his study, became a man of the world in his dress, and punctual to his appointments which grew more numerous as his abilities were more known, till his company was universally sought for."[17] Such dedication to this post was well warranted, and for all that Hawkesworth might have lamented inevitable drains upon his creative energies, he found himself, as literary editor of the *Gentleman's*, at the center of the literary-journalistic-theatrical worlds of his time, able, as few men, to influence the taste and mind of an age.

If memoirs and Hawkesworth's own words give a general picture of his connection with the *Gentleman's Magazine*, John Gough Nichols provides a valuable specific account of his activities, including the fact that Hawkesworth helped establish Johnson's literary reputation in the pages of the periodical. Next to Johnson, Nichols comments, Hawkesworth "was one of my ablest coadjutors" whose "assistance was continued, more or less, over a period extending from five-and-twenty to thirty years; and I may readily acknowledge that it was considerable." Nichols states that Hawkesworth "conducted the Review department," cites him as the author of the preface to the 1754 volume, afterwards other prefaces "and very frequently reviews," and attributes to him commentary on Johnson's *Irene* in 1749 and on the *Dictionary* in 1755.[18] Such information removes all doubt about Hawkesworth's participation in the magazine before he appeared as X in 1767.

Hawkesworth reviewed Johnson's play in the February 1749 issue, signing himself, Nichols notes, "H.H., the first and last letters of his name."[19] It is one of the major contributions of the month. Although plot summary dominates, the critical evaluation that marks Hawkesworth's later reviews is clear: "Such is the plot of *Irene*," he writes, "wrought up within a space of time little more than that of the representation, with all the elegance of wit, and all the accuracy of judgment. . . . To instance every moral which is inculcated in this performance would be to transcribe the whole" (19:79).

Hawkesworth's review of Johnson's *Dictionary* is marked by an eloquence commensurate with the dignity of the work assessed and its author's genius. "The intent of this work," Hawkesworth begins his commentary, which commences the April 1755 issue of the magazine, "is to fix the pronunciation, facilitate the attainment, preserve the purity, ascertain the use, and lengthen the duration of the *English* language." He further observes that "the *English* language, while it was employed in the cultivation of every species of literature, has itself been hitherto neglected, suffered to spread under the direction of chance into wild exuberance, resigned to the tyranny of time and fashion, and exposed to the corruptions of ignorance, and the caprices of innovation" (25:147). In his concluding remarks Hawkesworth enunciates a viewpoint to which generations have subscribed:

> It is evident that such a work will in many particulars admit improvement from a mind utterly unequal to the whole performance; but let not any of those, who by long poring over minute parts, have discovered what was necessarily overlooked by an eye that could comprehend the whole, assume an air of superiority, or hope to escape the indignation of genius and learning, which, in the language of *Milton*, can *burn after them* for ever, if in the malignity of their folly they depreciate, for trivial imperfections, a work, in which perfection was not possible to man; or attempt to withhold the honour which is due to him, who alone has effected in seven years, what the joint labour of forty academicians could not produce to a neighbouring nation in less than half a century. (P. 150)

Although Nichols assigns no other reviews of Johnson's works to Hawkesworth, William Kenrick—a forgotten figure today but a perceptive student of Shakespeare in his own time, and perhaps unfairly characterized by Johnson as "one of the many who have made themselves *publick*, without making themselves *known*"—implies that there were others. He demands, in fact, in his *Defense of Mr. Kenrick's Review of Dr. Johnson's "Shakespeare,"* "Whether the Drs. J. and H. have not been long in a secret and partial combination to applaud the writings, and enhance the literary reputation of each other?" "Whether the Gentleman's Magazine hath not, for many years past, been notoriously prostituted to this purpose?" and finally, "Whether the Rambler and the Adventurer, in their journey to the temple of Fame, were not obliged, like travellers that had but one horse between them, to ride and tie, from month to month occasionally?"[20] Kenrick might be referring to the reviews cited above, perhaps the *Gentleman's* commentary on Johnson's edition of Sir Thomas Browne's *Christian Morals* in April 1756, or his *Rasselas* in April 1759. The latter is marked by that special eloquence that Hawkesworth brought to so many reviews in the magazine. He writes:

> By what means *Rasselas* escaped from this luxurious prison, which art and nature seemed to have exhausted their powers to secure; how he obtained companions of his flight; the several adventures that befel them; and the general result of their enquiries; are told in the subsequent chapters, to which the reader is referred, and which abound with the most elegant and striking pictures of life and nature, the most acute disquisitions, and the happiest illustrations of the most important truths. (*GM* 29:186)

If not these reviews, then certainly the acclaim that the *Gentleman's* accorded Johnson's *Shakespeare* infuriated Kenrick, and Hawkesworth's pointed defense of his friend and his great work could have produced the outburst noted above. Hawkesworth undoubtedly generated the excerpts from the *Shakespeare* and the commentary on the text that filled seven columns in the October 1765 issue and eight more in November and December. Johnson's achievement is celebrated—"Of this work all commendation is precluded by the just celebrity of the author, and rapid sale of the impression which has already made a second necessary, though it has not been published a month" (35:479)—no less than Kenrick's *Review of Dr. Johnson's new edition of Shakespeare* is attacked in November 1765, probably by Hawkesworth. "This piece is written with a malignity," the reviewer comments in a tone reminiscent of so much of Hawkesworth's biting criticism, "for which it is very difficult to account, as the authour declares that he is a stranger to Dr *Johnson*, and never received any offence from him." He observes, with further sarcasm, that "if his ill will arises from envy of the literary honour Dr *Johnson* has acquired, or the mark of distinction he has received from his sovereign, he is too much an object of pity to move any other passion in the breast either of Dr *Johnson*, or his friends" (35:529). Hawkesworth undoubtedly reviewed Johnson's *False Alarm* as X in the January 1770 issue of the magazine. "As this article consists of extracts from the pamphlet itself," he writes, "a character of it is unnecessary; the reader will see at once a strain of masculine eloquence in it, that has seldom been equalled, never exceeded, in our language" (40:36).[21]

In the columns of the *Gentleman's*, Hawkesworth supported not only Johnson's works but also one of Johnson's most controversial actions—his acceptance of a pension in 1762. The word pension itself received unhappy illumination in the *Dictionary*—"In England it is generally understood to mean pay given to a state hireling for treason to his country"—and the act seemed to mar a life hitherto unblemished by moral and political compromise. One need only read Boswell's anxious thoughts about the episode in the *Life* to sense the dimensions of the event, which elicited a good deal of commentary, in a couple of instances involving the *Gentleman's Magazine* and Hawkesworth himself.[22]

Thomas Birch, writing to Lord Hardwicke on September 4, 1762, observed:

> Hawksworth, in the last Gentleman's Magazine, is angry, your Ldp sees, with the *North Briton*, for animadverting upon the giving a pension to Sam. Johnson, which the candid & modest Superintendent of that Magazine stiles *encouraging literary Merit without regard to party principles*; a gentle Expression for furious Jacobitism. A Friend of Johnson's told me, that when he mention'd to him the Design of giving him a pension, he answer'd with a supercilious Air, "If they offer me a small Matter, I will not accept of it."

Several days later, on September 7, 1762, Lord Hardwicke responded to Birch:

> I took notice of Hawksworth's most indecent Remark on the Pension given to his fellow Labourer in Declamatory Impertinence Johnson; & I presume from several symptoms in his Collection that he flatters himself with the honor of standing next Oars in ye literary list. Both He & Smollet have changed their Livery lately, & Let them Wear Whose They will, I shall have a most sovereign Contempt for such Hackney Sycophants & Scriblers.[23]

These are harsh words indeed and generated, it appears, only by Hawkesworth's brief comment on the *North Briton* no. 12 in the August issue of the magazine in a section entitled "Account of Political Papers." Here he writes that this publication "has thought fit to insult and vilify the highest characters, for encouraging literary merit without regard to party principles" (*GM* 32:379). That such a statement could produce the heated asseverations of Thomas Birch and Lord Hardwicke is a partial indication of the intensity of the issue of Johnson's pension. More important here, though, is that both men testify to Hawkesworth's principal role in the *Gentleman's Magazine*, one apparently well known at the time. For all his massive self-confidence Johnson undoubtedly welcomed the support of his friend Hawkesworth, who as literary editor of one of the most powerful reviews of his age spoke forcefully and persuasively in his defense.[24]

Such evidence, then, establishes Hawkesworth's primary position in the *Gentleman's Magazine*. Nichols suggests that he was hardly less central to the magazine's development than Johnson himself. The rise of the magazine was commemorated in 1747, Nichols comments, by an emblematical frontispiece of a vision of Fame, attended by the Muses, giving audience to Sylvanus Urban and his coadjutors, a scene explained in a poem entitled "The Vision." Hawkesworth, Nichols notes, wrote the "very smooth and forcible verses" explaining the frontispiece; and the print, he observes, is the more worthy of attention from its presenting "an excellent whole-length portrait of Cave, attended by Hawksworth, Johnson, and others of his friends."[25] This frontispiece, then, is as emblematical of Hawkesworth's important role in the magazine as it is of the rise of the periodical itself, revealing that in 1747, a decade before he assumed an official position in the publication and two decades before he reviewed as X, that he and Johnson were among Cave's chief coadjutors. While one could not ask for better evidence of Hawkesworth's participation in the *Gentleman's Magazine*, commentary by such friends as Garrick, Sir James Caldwell, and Benjamin Franklin offers valuable corroboration.

Hawkesworth's long and intimate friendship with David Garrick has already been discussed. Here it might be recalled how the great actor's correspondence not only describes but specifically dates Hawkesworth's involvement in the *Gentleman's Magazine*—years before he reviewed as X. In a letter written around December 1755, Garrick commended Hawkesworth's critique of the *Duc de Foix*, suggesting that it "might make a very good Letter in y^r Magazine"; on July 24, 1756, Garrick addressed a letter "To Mr Hawkesworth at St John's Gate," the home of the *Gentleman's*, an address repeated in a letter dated August 24; sometime before December 6, 1756, Garrick wrote to "Mr Hawkesworth at Mr Henry's, Clerkenwell" and on Saturday, September 17, 1757, to Hawkesworth at Bromley about placement at Hampton of "Mr Henry's Boy," these two references obviously to David Henry, Edward Cave's successor. Hawkesworth's defense of Garrick in the *Gentleman's* over the furor caused by John Hill's *The Rout* (29:37) has previously been noted. Two letters written in 1759 further highlight Hawkesworth's involvement in the magazine. Around July 12, 1759, Garrick wrote expressing the hope of seeing Hawkesworth "when you come next to Town for y^r Monthly operations," an undoubted allusion to the magazine; in a letter written before July 31, 1759, he suggested that Hawkesworth had asked him to prepare a review of Oliver Goldsmith's *An Enquiry into the Present State of Polite Learning in Europe* for publication in the *Gentleman's*.[26] Garrick's correspondence proves that Hawkesworth was extensively involved in the magazine during the 1750s; it is this evidence that makes likely Hawkesworth's authorship of such reviews as that of Johnson's *Rasselas*, quoted above.

Hawkesworth's correspondence with another close friend, Sir James Caldwell, also illuminates his connection with the *Gentleman's* and clarifies Garrick's reference to "Y[r] Monthly operations." Writing to Sir James on January 11, 1767, Hawkesworth commented, "Your favour is this moment come to hand & it is with pleasure that I acquaint you your Trunks directed to M[r]. Cave will as Certainly bring y[r]. Papers to my Hand as if he was alive." On January 19, 1767, he noted, "Your favour coming to London when I was at Bromley, was not forwarded but put under my Door, here it lay till Saturday when I came to London to finish the Supplement; except you are sure that your Letters will arrive here during the last week of the Month it is better they should be directed to me in Kent."[27]

Another dear friend, Benjamin Franklin, again confirms Hawkesworth's central role in the *Gentleman's*, and connects specific works with him. Writing from Philadelphia on March 25, 1763, to Mary Stevenson, the daughter of his London housekeeper, Franklin observed that "already some of our young Geniuses begin to lisp Attempts at Painting, Poetry and Musick. . . . Some Specimens of our Poetry I send you, which if Dr. Hawkesworth's fine Taste cannot approve, his good Heart will at least excuse." Franklin explains that "the Manuscript Piece is by a young Friend of mine, and was occasion'd by the Loss of one of his Friends, who lately made a Voyage to Antigua to settle some Affairs previous to an intended Marriage with an amiable Lady here; but unfortunately died there."[28] The poem, "An Elegy, sacred to the Memory of Joshia Martin, Esq; jun. who died in the Island of Antigua, in June 1762," appeared in the August 1763 issue of the magazine (*GM* 33:407), no doubt at Hawkesworth's direction. Franklin's own narrative of an unfortunate massacre of friendly Indians in Lancaster County, Pennsylvania, was sent transparently from "J. H." in Bromley, Kent, for inclusion in the *Gentleman's* for April 1764 with the approving comment: "It is, indeed, so strongly marked, that by those who know him it could not be mistaken; it has all the Plainness and Force, all the Quietness and Philanthropy of the Author's Mind and Manner, which equally characterise and recommend it" (34:173).

In another letter to Mary Stevenson, written on January 9, 1765, Franklin proves that Hawkesworth contributed creative material to the magazine. "Your good Mama and myself are both of Opinion that the Christmas Gambols at Bromley last a great deal too long," he complains good-humoredly. "We expected you three Days ago," and adding his compliments to Dr. Hawkesworth, Franklin continues, "Tell him I have read three or four times, and every time with great Pleasure, *his* Dialogue in the Magazine between Mr. Sellaway and Friends in the Club. I call the Dialogue *his*, being sure nobody else could write it: '*Because why? The Thing speaks for itself.*' "[29] The piece that Franklin attributes to Hawkesworth appeared in the December 1764 issue, entitled "The Folly of useless Words exposed" (34:559–62). It is, though Franklin does not say so, a sequel to a November essay, "Rules for Writing and Speaking correctly," submitted to Mr. Urban from a correspondent signed "J.H." (34:519–20). In both Hawkesworth argues for correct usage, a common concern of his literary and dramatic reviews, especially the elimination of "because why," one of a hundred cant phrases "which folly coined, and custom has made current" (34:560). Franklin, then, confirms, as do others, Hawkesworth's prime role in the *Gentleman's Magazine*.

A brief comment is needed about Hawkesworth's book reviewing, for as a reviewer of works both aesthetic and practical he made a significant contribution to the publication and showed himself to be among the more able practitioners of this genre during the century. While he conformed to the contemporary practice of abstracting and excerpting from works he reviewed, he also engaged in criticism itself.[30] Although Hawkesworth lacked Johnson's powerful mind, he shared similar stylistic powers and the ability in reading a book "through" (in the Johnsonian sense of the term) to produce the trenchant summary, the meaningful observation, and often the scathing denunciation. It is to Hawkesworth's credit that he unerringly championed genuine literary ability, praising those works that have endured at the same time that he relegated less worthy efforts to the wastes of literary history. Many writers besides Johnson received Hawkesworth's critical endorsement—Hogarth, for example, whose *Some Account of the Principles of Beauty* . . . is proclaimed in January 1754 as "a book, by which the author has discovered such superiority . . . [that] there is no question but that the name of the author will descend to posterity with that honour which competitors only can wish to withhold" (24:15).[31] Hawkesworth endorsed Boswell's *An Account of Corsica* in the *Gentleman's* for April 1768, noting that "except a few grammatical inaccuracies which may perhaps be errors of the press, and some expressions peculiar to the author's dialect as a North Briton, the book is well written; it contains much observation and much thought, and every where glows with a spirit of liberty, virtue and religion" (38:177); in July 1770 he warmly praised Joseph Baretti's *A Journey from London to Genoa, through England, Portugal, Spain, and France* (40:323–24); in May 1771 he applauded a classic produced by a dear friend—Charles Burney's *The Present State of Musick in France and Italy* (41:222–24).

Hawkesworth lauded Goldsmith scarcely less than Johnson himself. In a comment affixed to an extract of Goldsmith's *The Traveller* published in the *Gentleman's* in December 1764, it is certainly Hawkesworth who writes:

> We congratulate our poetical readers on the appearance of a new author
> so able to afford refined pleasure to true taste as the writer of the
> *Traveller*. After the crude and virulent rhapsodies upon which caprice
> and faction have lavished an unbounded praise, that if known to any
> future time will disgrace the present, it is hoped this poem will come
> with some advantage, and that a general encouragement of real merit
> will shew, that we have not totally lost power to distinguish it. (34:594).

In February 1768, Hawkesworth commended Goldsmith's *The Good
Natur'd Man* (38:78–80), and in June 1770 he wrote a penetrating review of
one of the masterpieces of the age, *The Deserted Village*, not only discussing
its intellectual framework—questions of commerce, luxury, and depopulation—but also assessing its poetic worth:

> In the first place we cannot but congratulate the public upon an attempt
> to revive a true taste for this kind of composition, at a time when our
> fashionable poetical dialect is degenerating into a kind of cant; in which
> obsolete words and phrases are revived, new, quaint, and affected
> terms introduced, and an unnatural sense forced upon others; where
> the prosody of our early versifiers is adopted, with an affected relish of
> all the faults and imperfections which have since been corrected, both
> by precept and example; epithets multipled without advantage either to
> sense or sound, and a metaphorical language introduced, which like the
> nethermost abyss, teems with "all monstrous all prodigious things."

In Hawkesworth's view, *The Deserted Village* is notably free from such poetic
excrescences, and in celebration of this work he observes: "We shall not
multiply extracts, because we would rather increase than lessen the desire
of the reader to see the whole; in which, if he has not vitiated his taste, till,
like a sick girl, he prefers ashes and chalk to beef and mutton, we can
promise him more pleasure than he has received from poetry since the days
of Pope" (40:272–73).

Two famous novels, *Tristram Shandy* and *Humphry Clinker*, tested
Hawkesworth's critical powers in reviews in the *Gentleman's Magazine* for
February 1767 and July 1771, respectively. His comments on volume 9 of
Tristram Shandy deserve extensive quotation, for they show how one astute
student of literature struggled to assess a work that both perplexed and
amused. *Tristram Shandy*, says Hawkesworth,

> has been charged with gross indecency, and the charge is certainly true;
> but indecency does no mischief, at least such indecency as is found in
> *Tristram Shandy*; it will disgust a delicate mind, but it will not sully a
> chaste one: It tends as little to inflame the passions as *Culpepper's Family
> Physician*; on the contrary, as nastiness is the strongest antidote to

desire, many parts of the work in question, that have been most severely treated by moralists and divines, are less likely to do ill than good, as far as Chastity is immediately concerned. How far he is a friend to society, who lessens the power of the most important of all passions, by connecting disgustful images with its gratifications, is another question: Perhaps he will be found to deserve the thanks of virtue no better than he, who, to prevent gluttony, should prohibit the sale of any food till it had acquired a taste and smell that would substitute nausea for appetite.

He that would keep his relish of pleasure high, should not represent its objects in a ludicrous, much less in a disgusting light; whatever is made lightly familiar to the mind, insensibly loses its power over it, for the same reason that nakedness allures less in *Africa*, than apparel in *Europe*. He therefore that understands pleasure, will, in this respect, keep his conversation as pure as the Philosopher or Saint, which all dablers in bawdry and nastiness would do well to consider. (37:75–76)

These are obviously the comments of the moralist of the *Adventurer*, a member of Samuel Richardson's school more at ease with the delicacies and solid virtues of *Clarissa* than the unrestrained bawdry of Sterne; yet Hawkesworth, in applying rather rigidly the moral principles of this school, not to mention the ethical profundities of Johnson's tenth *Rambler*, resists outright condemnation of *Tristram Shandy* and the Great Cham's erroneous conclusion that "nothing odd will do long." Hawkesworth's criticism of another comic masterpiece, *Humphry Clinker*, is generally both perceptive and even-tempered.

This work is by no means a novel or romance, of which Humphry Clinker is the hero; Humphry makes almost as inconsiderable a figure in this work as the dog does in the history of Tobit: nor is it indeed principally a narrative of events, but rather a miscellany containing dissertations on various subjects, exhibitions of character, and descriptions of places. Many of the characters are drawn with a free but a masterly hand; in some particulars perhaps they are exaggerated, but are not therefore the less entertaining or instructive: Some appear to be pictures of particular persons, but others of human nature, represented indeed in individuals peculiarly distinguished, but drawn rather from imagination than life. . . .

In this part of the work consists its principal excellence, and its principal defect is the want of events. The whole story might be told in a few pages, and the author has been so parsimonious of his invention, that he has twice overturned a coach, and twice introduced a fire, to exhibit a scene of ridiculous distress, by setting women on their heads, and making some of his dramatic characters descend from a window by a ladder, as they rose out of bed.

It is by no means deficient in sentiment, and it abounds with satire that is equally sprightly and just. It has, however, blemishes, which would be less regretted where there was less to commend. (41:317)

It is with such pieces that Hawkesworth enlivened the *Gentleman's Magazine*. From the early 1740s to his death in 1773 he enriched the magazine with poems, translations, parliamentary "debates," prefaces, creative works, and chiefly, book and drama reviews. But while recognizing Hawkesworth's role in the magazine during this period, I do not wish to suggest that this publication revolved around the work of a single figure. While he served in fact as the periodical's literary editor, he apparently did so with less than the official force that such a post would now entail; his editorial position in the magazine might best be seen as advisory and at no time, perhaps, purely managerial. Yet, in merely listing the material he is known to have contributed to the magazine, and adding to this other items that could fairly be attributed to him, one begins to recognize what his contemporaries knew—that Hawkesworth was a major force in the *Gentleman's Magazine* during the middle years of the century.[32]

Any historical period is defined by a host of forces, by the ebb and flow of events seemingly beyond the control of any one man, by the special pushes of government through legislation, by the more subtle ones of culture. Any review of culture in the eighteenth century must take into account that belles lettres gradually gave way to more popular forms of discourse that appealed to new kinds of literacy. For all that Addison and Steele and Fielding reverenced a classical past, for all that Johnson himself stood preeminent as the age's greatest classicist, these authors addressed their age in the vernacular—in the periodical essay, in the novel, in journalism generally. These forms reflect the intellectual spirit of the time, and there were others—the *Encyclopaedia Britannica*, for example. Perhaps, though, the energies of the period are nowhere better reflected than in the pages of the *Gentleman's Magazine*, a document so rich that a fair reconstruction of the period could be made from its files alone. In historic retrospect one may regard this work with something of Johnson's reverence when he first viewed St. John's Gate.[33]

While Edward Cave was present at the conception of this remarkable publication, while Johnson nurtured it in youth, Hawkesworth guided it to maturity. His name is already secure in English literary history as Johnson's friend and imitator and as a principal creator of the legend of Captain Cook. To these must be added an achievement no less signal, for as literary editor of the *Gentleman's Magazine*, Hawkesworth was, as were few other men of his time, both purveyor and arbiter of British culture.

VI THE 1760s: WORKS, FRIENDS, AND ASSOCIATES

> Remember me in the same manner to your and my good
> Doctor and Mrs. Hawkesworth. You have lately, you tell
> me, had the Pleasure of spending three Days with them at
> Mr. Stanley's. It was a sweet Society!
>
> Benjamin Franklin to Polly Stevenson
> March 25, 1763

In 1760 a new king ascended the British throne—George III, the first native-born and educated Hanoverian. He was to rule till 1820, almost to the death of one of the greatest Romantics, John Keats. Although his reign has long been connected with a peculiar form of madness and with such political disasters as the loss of the American colonies, he might also be remembered for his support of the explorations of Captain James Cook. The world of letters received his attention as well. Not only did Samuel Johnson gain a pension from the crown but an interview with the king himself, which took place in February 1767 in the library at the queen's house. In his account of this meeting Boswell shows a sovereign capable of intelligent discourse about the kingdom's libraries, the merits of various literary journals, recent scholarly disputes, and of course, Johnson's writing—he hoped, in fact, that Johnson would execute a literary biography of the country. Johnson was clearly impressed and at the conclusion of the meeting told Mr. Barnard, the librarian, "Sir, they may talk of the King as they will; but he is the finest gentleman I have ever seen." Afterwards he told Mr. Langton, "Sir, his manners are those of as fine a gentleman as we may suppose Lewis the Fourteenth or Charles the Second."[1]

While 1760 ushered in a new king to guide the nation in the maturing years of the century, it brought Hawkesworth to middle age and a decade of his life filled with activity and literary productivity. As the 1750s had been marked by the publication of the *Adventurer*, substantial work on Swift, and considerable involvement in the London theater, the 1760s would see the appearance of a much-admired oriental tale and a highly praised translation from the French, and Hawkesworth would continue to influence the cultural life of the nation as literary editor of the *Gentleman's Magazine*. In matters of friendship he was not so much a man seeking acquaintances as a man sought after by some of the more important figures of the time. These included Benjamin Franklin, whose contemporary reputation Hawkesworth enhanced in the pages of his own magazine, and the Irish baronet Sir James Caldwell, who made of him not only an intimate but a literary and political advisor and introduced him to levels of English society he probably never dreamed of entering. Hawkesworth's friends also included those connected closely with the world of letters, such as Robert and James Dodsley, Ralph Griffiths, William Strahan, and Christopher Smart. Although Hawkesworth's intimacy with Johnson had ceased by the 1760s, Johnson's literary career may have continued to inspire him. It is possible that when he published his oriental tale, *Almoran and Hamet*, in 1761, he hoped to equal his mentor's success in *Rasselas*, a work Hawkesworth had praised in the *Gentleman's Magazine*.

The author of the *Universal Magazine* memoir of Hawkesworth's life argues, in fact, that he was "intoxicated to such a degree by the popularity of his writings, that he no longer esteemed Johnson to be, in native talents, at all superior to himself." *Rasselas*, he suggests, "had been read with the utmost eagerness by the public. Hawkesworth would try whether he might not excel Johnson in this species of composition."[2]

Although *Rasselas* influenced the composition of *Almoran and Hamet* in its final, published form, Mary Hawkesworth suggests in a letter to Mrs. John Duncombe in December 1781 that Johnson's tale did not initially inspire it. "The original story was written for the stage in three acts," she notes, "but the transformations and machinery staggered Mr. Garrick, who had just lost 3000£. in scenes and decorations for the Chinese Festival, which was not suffered to be exhibited on account of some French dancers, it being the beginning of a French war." Although Drury Lane's manager could not risk elaborate production costs in light of his recent trouble, *Almoran and Hamet* did not perish in this unhappy episode. Mary Hawkesworth writes, in fact, that her husband "thought the sentiments peculiarly adapted for the use of a young monarch, and was tempted to give it in another garb to the public."[3] Hawkesworth's oriental tale, then, owes its genesis to his theatrical career, his awareness of Johnson's success with *Rasselas*, and the ascension of a young monarch who might, like the Abyssinian prince, profit from the instruction of another Imlac. And it should be noted that in writing *Almoran and Hamet* he merely attempted at somewhat greater length what he had already perfected in many *Adventurer* papers.

For a modern student *Almoran and Hamet* invites comparisons with the greatest example of the genre, *Rasselas*, and it is interesting to observe that in its original play form Johnson (along with Garrick) added marginal notes to the copy Mrs. Hawkesworth alludes to in her letter above. Although both tales share Middle Eastern locales (Johnson's set in Abyssinia and Egypt, and Hawkesworth's in Persia) and similar themes (both are philosophical investigations of the choices life offers and the means by which happiness can be achieved), contrasts in treatment and effect are readily apparent. Johnson's story is framed by a physical pilgrimage mirroring his protagonist's intellectual and moral growth; Hawkesworth's is a more static assessment of Hamet's struggle to adhere to defined virtue. Hawkesworth, far more than Johnson, inflects his tale with the required oriental machinery—charms, magic, scrolls, sulphur-burning lamps, poisoned potions, a genius, mysterious voices, a seraglio, mysterious visitations, and miraculous transformations—and his story is defined by them, whereas *Rasselas* quickly transcends the few conventions Johnson embraces. Thus *Rasselas*, in contrast to *Almoran and Hamet*, is rhetorically and philosophically more complex, as Johnson engages his reader in varied quests for happiness vividly illustrated in various episodes and characters.

One need only to examine the opening lines of both tales to see the difference between a literary masterpiece and a skillful illustration of a once popular genre that offered moral instruction rendered palatable and delightful through a pleasing exoticism. Johnson begins: "Ye who listen with credulity to the whispers of fancy, and pursue with eagerness the phantoms of hope; who expect that age will perform the promises of youth, and that the deficiencies of the present day will be supplied by the morrow; attend to the history of Rasselas prince of Abissinia." Hawkesworth, in contrast, writes:

> Who is he among the children of the earth, that repines at the power of the wicked? and who is he, that would change the lot of the righteous? He, who has appointed to each his portion, is God; the Omniscient and the Almighty, who fills eternity, and whose existence is from Himself! but he who murmurs, is man; who yesterday was not, and who to-morrow shall be forgotten: let him listen in silence to the voice of knowledge, and hide the blushes of confusions in the dust.[4]

In their dignified moral tone the openings seem to resemble each other. Yet Johnson's invocation is cautionary rather than promising and heralds a somber tale in which exit from the Happy Valley produces only painful clarifications about life, while Hawkesworth's introduction is more self-confident and assumes a world where a Hamet, as long as he righteously perseveres, will find much can be concluded about routes to happiness and the relationship of man to God.

For all that *Rasselas* may have inspired the composition of *Almoran and Hamet* in its final form, a more immediate source is *Adventurer* nos. 20, 21, and 22, whose title is a virtual outline of Hawkesworth's longer oriental fiction: "Imperceptible deviation to vice. Moral use of punishment. Remonstrances of conscience universal. Amurath, an eastern story." In this popular tale Amurath resists the wise counsel of the genius Syndarac and strays from virtue's path to depravity and transformation into a beast before his final redemption. In *Almoran and Hamet* Hawkesworth simply recasts the lessons embodied in "Amurath" with focus upon two characters and more variety of scene and complication of incident.

Almoran and Hamet are the twin sons of "Solyman, the mighty and the wise, who in the one hundred and second year of the Hegyra, sat upon the throne of Persia" (*Almoran and Hamet*, 1:2). Although Almoran is slightly older, Solyman treats them equally and decrees they shall rule the kingdom between them. From the outset Almoran and Hamet are juxtaposed as radically different characters. Almoran seeks only pleasure and power: "If I must perish," he utters at a moment of crisis in the story, "I will at least perish unsubdued: I will quench no wish that nature kindles in my bosom; nor shall my lips utter any prayer, but for new powers to feed the flame" (1:109). Hamet, by contrast, adheres to paths of virtue no matter how tortured and achieves the peace, happiness, and tranquility the Almighty awards to those who so persevere.

While the contest between Almoran and Hamet gives his text dramatic energy, at one point Hawkesworth obscures their story to digress on the nature of good government. There is no doubt that he designed such commentary for the young monarch who had just ascended the British throne; he had, in fact, dedicated his work to George III, securing permission to do so from his friend and advisor, the earl of Bute. "I think myself happy to be permitted to put my Manuscript into your Lordship's hands," Hawkesworth wrote from London on March 2, 1761, "because though it encreases my Anxiety and my Fears, yet it will at least secure me from what I should think a far greater Misfortune, than any other that can attend my performance, the Danger of addressing to the King, any Sentiment, allusion, or opinion, that would make such an address improper."[5] Hawkesworth's felicitous dedication shows that he hoped the new monarch would benefit from the lessons of his text:

> As some part of my subject led me to consider the advantages of our
> excellent constitution in comparisons of others; my thoughts were
> naturally turned to YOUR MAJESTY, as its warmest friend and most
> powerful protector: and as the whole is intended, to recommend the
> practice of virtue, as the means of happiness; to whom could I address it
> with so much propriety, as to a PRINCE, who illustrates and enforces the
> precepts of the moralist by his life. (1:vi–viii)

Hawkesworth ostensibly embodies his views on politics in an extended dramatic confrontation between his principal characters, but at times he speaks with the directness of his strongest *Adventurer* essays:

> A supercilious attention to minute formalities, is a certain indication of a little mind, conscious to the want of innate dignity, and solicitous to derive from others what it cannot supply to itself: as the scrupulous exaction of every trifling tribute discovers the weakness of the tyrant, who fears his claim should be disputed; while the prince, who is conscious of superior and indisputable power, and knows that the states he has subjugated do not dare to revolt, scarce enquires whether such testimonies of allegiance are given or not. (1:31)

It is, of course, Almoran, a trifling absolutist despotically caught up in the details of state who is best described by Hawkesworth's comment above, not Hamet. The latter will become a strong monarch working through a system of laws, seeking "the government of a nation as a whole, the regulation and extent of its trade, the establishment of manufactories, the encouragement of genius, the application of the revenues, and whatever can improve the arts of peace, and secure superiority in war" (1:42). Hamet, the *Universal Magazine* memoir of Hawkesworth's life observes, appears to represent young George III himself, with "the mild, yet steady, and not inert virtues, by which our sovereign was expected to reign in the hearts of his people."[6]

Almoran's political failure, Hawkesworth eventually makes clear, is part of a larger moral failure, and this, not the debate on kingship, is the principal subject of his work. He was only temporarily a member of the school of Locke, and only in the most commonplace terms, but always a disciple of Samuel Richardson. The real subject of *Almoran and Hamet* is the need to regulate appetite, especially sexual appetite. Unlike *Rasselas*, whose complications remain philosophically generalized though temporarily rendered tangible in character, action, and episode, *Almoran and Hamet* receives its structure and direction from the twins' infatuation for Almeida, the lovely daughter of Abdallah, an ambassador from Circassia to Solyman's court. Through their relationships Hawkesworth presents not simply a general contest between vice and virtue, but the specific point that harmony between the sexes is a necessary precondition for society's stability. Just as a monarch must avoid political despotism through adherence to laws, so the individual must avoid bestiality through observation of moral dictates. King and commoner, and society at large, will flourish through checks upon their appetites, however natural they might be.

Almoran, turning his back on the wise counsel of his brother and Omar (the story's Imlac), pursues pleasures wherever he finds them. He sees the lovely Almeida merely an object of lust. But not Hamet. However great her physical beauty—and he, no less than his twin, is moved by her charms—he sees it as "the decorations only of a mind, capable of mixing with his own in the most exquisite delight, of reciprocating all his ideas, and catching new pleasure from his pleasure" (1:80–81). In Hamet desire ends, not in appetite, but in imagination and reason: "It included remembrance of the past, and anticipation of the future; and its object was not the sex, but ALMEIDA" (1:81). It is to Hawkesworth's credit that even though he gives his story a conventionally happy ending—the virtuous Hamet and Almeida are left to reign in peace, and corrupt Almoran is metamorphosed into a rock—he seems to avoid the febrile Platonism so often invoked to soothe the eternally troublesome relations between the sexes. He steers, in fact, an imaginative course between the extremes that another custodian of morality presents in *Pamela*, where sexual virtue is vulgarly compromised, and in *Clarissa*, where it is tragically defined.

For a time at least, *Almoran and Hamet* enjoyed great favor, and Owen Ruffhead, writing in the *Monthly Review*, saw it standing in moral counterpoint to no less a text than *Tristram Shandy*, though Sterne's bawdy masterpiece is nowhere specifically named. "The Genius of Romance seems to have been long since drooping among us," he complains, "and has, of late, been generally displayed only for the basest purposes; either to raise the grin of Ideotism by its buffoonry, or stimulate the prurience of Sensuality by its obscenity." In *Almoran and Hamet*, Ruffhead notes, one is spared a veritable catalogue of moral indiscretions, and readers will find "no winding up of Clocks,—no wanton double entendres,—no asterisms pregnant with gross ideas,—no lambent pupilability.—In short every thing here is chaste, elegant and moral." Leigh Hunt, who included Hawkesworth's popular tale in his *Classic Tales* in the following century (it was frequently reprinted), credits him with purifying and simplifying the style of the genre itself, which had become debased, he argues, in the hands of bad imitators of *Rasselas*. A more recent student, Martha Pike Conant, is severe in her commentary on Hawkesworth's text, charging that the "oriental colouring is thin and the characterization feeble," an observation of less value, perhaps, than her suggestion that it might have served as a source for William Beckford's *Vathek*. The most curious response to *Almoran and Hamet* came from Johnson, who when asked if he had read the book answered, "No! I like the man too well to read his book." The anonymous donor of this anecdote suggests, with some plausibility, that "if it be true, that men of genius are prone to censure each other, it is also inevitable, that it should be so; since they feel each other's defects with a sensibility much more poignant than that of other men." Out of feeling for a friend, then, Johnson resisted the reading of a text that might have drawn his censure.[7]

Of *Rasselas* Boswell sagely commented that the "fund of thinking which this work contains is such, that almost every sentence of it may furnish a subject of long meditation. I am not satisfied if a year passes without my having read it through." Such commendation would be excessive for *Almoran and Hamet*, though Hawkesworth's tale has some of the qualities he himself ascribed to *Rasselas*—"the most elegant and striking pictures of life and nature, the most acute disquisitions, and the happiest illustrations of the most important truths."[8] Hawkesworth's extended incursion into orientalism is a testimony to a refined literary sensibility; the fact that it can still serve as an index to the greatness of Johnson's classic remains a measure of its worth.

Not simply a maker of literary and critical texts, Hawkesworth always took pleasure in an active social life, especially during the 1760s, when he had achieved public prominence. Although his friends and associates included a range of illustrious figures from all walks of English life, he enjoyed one of his warmest friendships with Benjamin Franklin. A founding father not only of a nation but of electrical theory, an inventor, diplomat, author, signer of the Declaration of Independence, peace negotiator, and delegate to the Constitutional Convention, no man more than Franklin so fully embodied the spirit of the Enlightenment. His character is enhanced by private and by public actions: it was Franklin, for example, who refused an offer from the governor of Pennsylvania of an exclusive right to sell his Franklin stove, Franklin who in 1779, during the American Revolutionary War, ordered American naval commanders not to intercept Captain Cook and his crew, then returning from his third voyage of exploration (Cook's tragic death in Hawaii had not yet been reported).[9]

The time and place of Franklin's first meeting with Hawkesworth can only be conjectured. It may have occurred as early as 1757, when Franklin came to England to serve as an agent of the Pennsylvania assembly, then in dispute with the Penn family, the colony's proprietors. A probable locale is St. John's Gate, Clerkenwell, home of the *Gentleman's Magazine*, for by this time Franklin had enjoyed some exposure in the publication. As early as 1731 it had reported as an actual trial Franklin's celebrated hoax, "A Witch Trial at Mount Holly," an American tall tale describing tests by Bible and by water imposed upon several men and women who stood accused of causing their neighbors' sheep to dance and their hogs to speak and sing psalms. Far more important, the *Gentleman's Magazine* had brought Franklin's pioneering work on electricity to public attention, and Cave himself issued Franklin's *Experiments and Observations in Electricity* in 1751. Franklin, then, had received important recognition from a popular miscellany before the Royal Society awarded him the Copley Medal in late 1753, and it is likely that he quickly sought out the publication that gave him so much attention.[10]

If Hawkesworth and Franklin did not meet at St. John's Gate, it is possible that Mary Stevenson, the daughter of Margaret Stevenson, Franklin's London housekeeper, brought the two men together. Mary Stevenson—or Polly, as she was called—was an intimate of the Hawkesworths and visited Bromley often to see them and her cousins Dorothea (Dolly) and Catherine Blunt, two young ladies of good family who stayed with the Hawkesworths. Franklin joined this group, which included the printer William Strahan and John Stanley, the musician. His visits to Bromley must have helped lessen the misery of being separated from a family and a native land more than three thousand miles away.[11] Although not yet the revolutionary, founding father, and world statesman that would make of him a household name in several countries, Franklin's achievements by the late 1750s were considerable: he had already established the Library Company of Philadelphia, the first subscription library in North America; he had become one of the founders of the American Philosophical Society; and, perhaps most important, he had performed the famous kite experiment that turned a humble, self-educated Quaker into a modern Prometheus. Around the time that he met Hawkesworth, in fact, Franklin had been honored by Harvard, Yale, and William and Mary colleges and had received an honorary doctoral degree from the University of St. Andrews and membership in the Royal Society.

Hawkesworth, too, had much to offer. In him Franklin found an important overseer of letters and culture, one who, like himself, had gained position, not through birth or privilege, but through wit and industry. The dimensions of their friendship are seen in Mary Stevenson's correspondence to both men and in the few surviving letters they exchanged themselves. The earliest, written from Craven Street by Franklin on July 7, 1761, to Polly at Bromley included news of an impending visit:

> This is just to acquaint my dear Polly, that her good Mama, Mr. and Mrs. Strahan, and her Friend Franklin, purpose to be at Bromley on Tuesday Morning next, to have the Pleasure of seeing Dr. and Mrs. Hawkesworth and the agreable Miss Blunt's, dining there and returning in the Evening. They carry down with them Miss Peggy Strahan, and leave her there instead of Miss Stevenson who is to come to Town with them. This is the Scheme; but all this in case it will be agreable to our Friends at Bromley, of which you are to let us know. Mr. Strahan is here with us, and we all join in drinking your Health with that of our Bromley Friends.

The warmth of Franklin's tone indicates that his friendship with the Hawkesworths was already of some duration. Polly answered him on the eighth of July, obviously delighted by his communication and the promise of a visit. "Soon after my Eyes were open this Morning," she comments, "they were blest with a Letter from my dear and honour'd Friend. Mrs. Hawkesworth (for I have not seen the Doctor, but they seem to have both one Soul) bids me tell you they approve all your Scheme except that part of it which relates to me; and they shall expect to see all their Friends, who design them that Pleasure next Tuesday."[12]

Polly's letters give evidence not only about Hawkesworth's friendship with Franklin but also about aspects of his character detailed by no other observer. Writing to her cousin from Wanstead on December 17, 1761, she noted:

> I spent Sometime last Summer at D.ʳ Hawkesworth's. He is a most charming Man, and has done me great Honour by taking particular Notice of me. He has a high Understanding which he has improved with Learning, and his Condescension is as great as his Capacity. I receiv'd great Improvement from him. I must not omit the highest Parts of his Character, which are that he is a Pious Christian and a Benevolent Man. I never saw any Person more freely devout in the Offices of Religion, or more tenderly compassionate in all his Actions to every Creature. He has so quick a Sensibility that he cannot bear to hurt the vilest Insect. His Disposition is such that he is beloved by all who know him. He has a very amiable Woman for his Wife, who he is extremely fond of, and you may be sure she cannot fail to return an equal Affection to so deserving a Husband.[13]

Polly provides a singular portrait of Hawkesworth, good to recall when a few years later he fell victim to general censure and ridicule. She suggests that his commitment to virtue and decency was no convenient guise devised to please his readers but that his compositions very much reflected the man within.

Although Franklin's friendship with the Hawkesworths persisted through the 1760s and beyond, they were separated when he returned to America, and it was from America, in a letter written to Polly from Philadelphia on March 25, 1763, that he commented with real emotion about his Bromley friends. "Remember me in the same manner to your and my good Doctor and Mrs. Hawkesworth," he urges Polly. "You have lately, you tell me, had the Pleasure of spending three Days with them at Mr. Stanley's. It was a sweet Society! . . . I too, once partook of that same Pleasure, and can therefore feel what you must have felt." One suspects the Hawkesworths were among those who helped generate his deep attachment to England seen in the same letter when he writes: "Of all the enviable Things England has, I envy it most its People. Why should that petty Island, which compar'd to America is but like a stepping Stone in a Brook, scarce enough of it above Water to Keep one's Shoes dry; why, I say, should that little Island, enjoy in almost every Neighbourhood, more sensible, virtuous and elegant Minds, than we can collect in ranging 100 Leagues of our vast Forests."[14]

Hawkesworth, in Franklin's eyes, certainly possessed one of those "virtuous and elegant Minds," and Franklin had frequent cause to value his friendship with the literary editor of the *Gentleman's Magazine*, one as willing to transmit the poetry of Franklin's friends to the magazine as Franklin's own compositions (see Chapter V). And Franklin must have taken special pleasure in reading Hawkesworth's elegant review in the periodical for July 1767 of *The Examination of Doctor Benjamin Franklin relative to the Repeal of the American Stamp Act in 1767*. Franklin had been called before the House of Commons sitting as a committee of the whole to testify about the Stamp Act, which had so inflamed the colonies. In a presentation that Edmund Burke likened to a classroom in which the pupils questioned the schoolmaster, Franklin answered 174 questions to the universal admiration of all present. Hawkesworth wrote of the occasion: "The questions in general are put with great subtilty and judgment, and they are answered with such deep and familiar knowledge of the subject, such precision and perspicuity, such temper and yet such spirit, as do the greatest honour to Dr. *Franklin*, and justify the general opinion of his character and abilities."[15]

Hawkesworth's friendship with Franklin gained him entry into the circle of friends that the great American frequented, particularly men of science. Among these were Richard Price and John Canton, who had with Franklin assisted Joseph Priestley with his *History and Present State of Electricity*. Such connections are of interest when it is recalled that in a few years Hawkesworth would compile the history of the first great voyage dedicated to scientific exploration. Although some doubted the qualifications of a mere man of letters for such a complex task, they ignored the background that he had gained from his eclectic reviewing for the *Gentleman's Magazine* (often on technical, medical, or scientific subjects) and his frequent association with those interested in the natural world. Like Johnson, Hawkesworth's interests ranged well beyond belle-lettres. On March 31, 1761, for example, he was elected to membership in the Society for the Encouragement of Arts, Manufactures, and Commerce, an assembly dedicated to scientific and technological as well as cultural concerns. Although there is no record of his participation at this institution, he could have met there not only such friends as Franklin and Johnson but many from the scientific community, including Joseph Banks. Banks was to accompany Cook on the *Endeavour*, bringing back a brilliant botanical record of the South Seas as well as a journal that would greatly enrich the text soon to be known as Hawkesworth's *Voyages*.[16]

While it is interesting to speculate how much Hawkesworth's ties with one of the age's leading deists influenced his composition of his controversial preface to Cook's *Voyages*, it is a fact that Franklin helped school him in the larger scientific environment in which Cook's epic journey took place. In Hawkesworth's surviving correspondence with Franklin, in fact, one sees not simply the record of a friendship, but a writer's fascination with a man of science who demonstrated to him at first hand powers ranging from the merely pragmatic almost to magic itself.

On Wednesday night, November 6, 1769, for instance, Hawkesworth wrote from Bromley to Franklin at his residence on Craven Street, asking about an invention the season of the year made especially attractive. "These few Lines come hopping that you may not forget your promise of putting me in the way of getting a pensylvanian Stove," he comments, "time enough to enjoy the benefit of it this Winter." (With the possible exception of bifocals one can hardly point to an invention by Franklin prized more by his contemporaries and subsequent generations than his efficient stove.) Hawkesworth remained interested in Franklin's scientific prowess almost to his death. Early in May 1772 Hawkesworth, along with Garrick, Colonel Barré, and the Abbé Morellet, joined Franklin at High Wycombe, the estate of the earl of Shelburne, where Franklin performed the "magical" trick of calming the waves on a pond by ejecting oil from his cane; on May 8, 1772, Franklin wrote, in one of the last surviving exchanges between the two men, about the curative powers of "Fix'd air" and the process by which it is made.[17]

Hawkesworth's friendship with Franklin, then, was of obvious depth and duration, sustained for many years by common interests. Once again Hawkesworth was blessed by an association that must have had a great impact upon his mind and character—few men of the time could claim friendship and instruction from both Johnson and Franklin. If the former had prepared him for a life of letters at the Ivy Lane Club and in evening rambles thereafter, the latter must have taught him well in the ways of the new science, which would flower in Captain Cook's first voyage. With Johnson and Franklin as tutors, Hawkesworth had prepared himself better than most men could, regardless of advantages of birth, position, and education, for the great undertaking soon to come.

While it is not possible to document fully Hawkesworth's friendship with another famous man of the age, the poet Christopher Smart, he was apparently on close terms with Smart, one of the most colorful and creative, if most distressed, figures of the time. With Smart one leaves the sunshine of Franklin's enlightened world to enter the dark interiors of eighteenth-century madhouses. Two men, in fact, could hardly stand in starker contrast; the distance between the *Autobiography*, the sage man's reflection in balanced prose of a lifetime's accomplishment through reason, and the *Jubilate Agno*, the poetic record of a soul's torment, is immense. For Smart there were no thirteen points to guide one to a virtuous life. He faced instead a struggle against powerful compulsions, including his resistless urge to pray publicly and to enjoin others, even with a certain amount of force, to pray with him. Although Johnson stoutly maintained that his "infirmities were not noxious to society" and commented he would "as lief pray with Kit Smart as any one else," his charitable attitude was not shared by those called to devotions from dinners, beds, or places of amusement. This behavior, coupled with the charge that he did not like clean linen (Johnson confessed no passion for it either in his defense of Smart), led to Smart's incarceration, first for private treatment, later in St. Luke's Hospital, and finally for four years (from 1759 to 1763) in George Potter's madhouse at Bethnal Green.[18] This time of trial undoubtedly contributed to the creation of Smart's most inspired poem, his *Jubilate Agno*. Although this fertile document admits of many interpretations, it must be seen, its best student argues, as "a spiritual and historical journal of four years in the life of its composer, mirroring his moods, telling of his daily activities, revealing his suffering and gradual reconciliation to his lot, chronicling his illnesses, and giving his reaction to trivial and domestic events as well as to the more momentous and public ones that were taking place outside of his restricted world."[19]

Hawkesworth must have known Smart long before this painful period in his life. It is possible that Charles Burney brought them together in the mid-1740s. Smart at this time had not yet left Cambridge but certainly visited London on occasion, running up tailors' bills, among other excesses, while seeking at the same time the literary connections that only the metropolis afforded. Once again, St. John's Gate, the home of the *Gentleman's Magazine*, proved a lure to a promising talent, and it appears that Smart joins those who saw their literary reputation boosted in this publication, largely through the efforts of Hawkesworth. He probably transmitted Smart's poem "To Idleness" to the poetry columns of the May 1745 issue and saw that his other productions appeared frequently in the magazine thereafter.

While Hawkesworth thus helped bring public acclaim to one of the age's significant literary figures, he left in private correspondence a remarkable description of the man during a critical period in his life, shortly after his release from Potter's madhouse. In the fall of 1764 Hawkesworth visited Smart's sister, Margaret Hunter, at Margate. They undoubtedly discussed the sad condition of one who had suffered the debilitating effects of mental instability and worse, certainly, the incarceration that followed. Upon his release in 1763 Smart had taken quarters with a Mrs. Barwell in

the region around St. James's Park, Westminster. Here he had lived as a
bachelor and had importuned strangers to pray with him, drawing their
scorn and possibly the sharper rebuke of the nightwatch's stick. During his
visit to Margate, Hawkesworth promised Mrs. Hunter that he would see
the poet and write to her about his condition. Although Hawkesworth had
difficulty meeting Smart, he finally did so, probably during late October
1764, though a precise date is impossible to fix. His report to Mrs. Hunter,
dated October 1764, is a sufficiently strong sample of his writing, especially
given the subject matter, to deserve full quotation.

Dear Madam,
    I am afraid that you have before now secretly accused me, and I
confess that appearances are against me; I did not, however, delay to
call upon Mr. Smart, but I was unfortunate enough twice to miss him. I
was, the third day of my being in town, seized with a fever that was
then epidemic, from which I am but just recovered. I have, since my
being in town this second time, called on my old friend, and seen him;
he received me with an ardour of kindness natural to the sensibility of
his temper, and we were soon seated together by his fire-side. I perceived upon his table a quarto book in which he had been writing, a
prayer-book, and a Horace. After the first compliments I said I had
been at Margate, and had seen his mother and his sister, who expressed
great kindness for him and made me promise to come and see him. To
this he made no reply, nor did he make any inquiry after those I
mentioned; he did not even mention the place, nor ask me any questions
about it or what carried me thither. After some pause and some
indifferent chat, I returned to the subject, and said that Mr. Hunter
and you would be very glad to see him in Kent. To this he replied very
quick, 'I cannot afford to be idle.' I said he might employ his mind as
well in the town as in the country; at which he only shook his head, and
I entirely changed the subject. Upon my asking him when he should
print the Psalms, he said they were going to press immediately. As to
his other undertakings, I found he had completed a translation of
Phaedrus in verse for Dodsley at a certain price; and that he is now busy
in translating all Horace into verse, which he sometimes thinks of
publishing on his own account, and sometimes of contracting for it with
a bookseller; I advised him to the latter plan, and he then told me he was
in treaty about it, and believed it would be a bargain. He told me his
principal motive for translating Horace into verse was to supersede the
prose translation which he did for Newbery, which he said would hurt
his memory. He intends, however, to review that translation, and to
print it at the foot of the page in his poetical version, which he proposes
to print in quarto with the Latin, both in verse and prose, on the
opposite page. He told me he once had thoughts of printing it by
subscription; but, as he had troubled his friends already, he was

unwilling to do it again, and had been persuaded to publish it in numbers, which, though I had rather dissuaded him, seemed at last to be the prevailing bent of his mind. He read me some of it; it is very close, and his own poetical fire sparkles in it very frequently; yet, upon the whole, it will scarcely take place of Francis's, and therefore, if it is not adopted as a school-book, which perhaps may be the case, it will turn to little account. Upon mentioning his prose translation I saw his countenance kindle, and snatching up the book, 'What,' says he, 'do you think I had for this?' I said, I could not tell; 'Why,' says he, with great indignation, 'thirteen pounds!' I expressed very great astonishment, which he seemed to think he should increase by adding, 'But, Sir, I gave a receipt for a hundred.' My astonishment, however was now over, and I found that he received only thirteen pounds, because the rest had been advanced for his family; this was a tender point, and I found means immediately to divert him from it.

He is with very decent people, in a house most delightfully situated, with a terrace that overlooks St. James's Park and has a door into it. He was going to dine with an old friend of my own, Mr. Richard Dalton, who has an appointment in the King's library, and if I had not been particularly engaged I would have dined with him. He had lately received a very genteel letter from Dr. Lowth; and is by no means considered in any light that makes his company as a gentleman, a scholar, and a genius, less desirable. I have been very particular, dear Madam, in relating all the particulars of this conference, that you may draw any inference that I could draw from it yourself.

I should incur my own censure, which is less tolerable than all others, if I did not express my sense of the civilities I received from you and Mr. Hunter while I was at Margate. I have Mrs. Hawkesworth's express request, in a letter now before me, to do the same on her part. If you, or any of the family come into our part of the country, we shall be very glad to accommodate you with a table and a bed; you will find a cheerful fire-side and a hearty welcome. If in the mean time I can do you any service or pleasure here, you will the more oblige as you the more freely command me.

Our best compliments attend you, Mr. Hunter, your young gentleman, and Mrs. Smart, not forgetting the ladies we met at your house, particularly one who I think is daughter to Mrs. Holmes. I am, Madam, your obedient humble servant,

John Hawkesworth[20]

Mrs. Hunter could hardly have been more satisfied with Hawkesworth's letter than subsequent students of Smart's life, providing as he does, with the essayist's attention to meaningful detail and the biographer's regard for nuances of character, information about Smart's state of mind, his living quarters, his current literary interests, and those friends who still sought the company of this talented man. Mrs. Hunter must have been pleased that her brother saw and corresponded with men of scholarship—that he had an engagement to dine with Richard Dalton, keeper of the pictures and antiquarian to His Majesty, and had received a "genteel letter" from Dr. Lowth, whose lectures on Hebrew poetry Smart so much admired. Such positive news tended to compensate for Hawkesworth's frank conveyance of the poet's fury about a family that he considered had abused both his person and his pocketbook. Hawkesworth's sketch reflects as well his role as a man of letters; in highlighting Smart's varied literary activity he not only shows the improved condition of the poet, but reveals himself in the familiar role of literary advisor, suggesting the best way for his "old friend" to publish his works. One suspects that it was not the first nor the last such counsel he gave Smart, and it is not surprising to see Hawkesworth similarly engaged with others in the literary world, such as the Dodsley brothers.

James Dodsley (1724–97) was for many years a bookseller in Pall Mall, remembered, among other things, for contributing material about Johnson to Boswell for the *Life*, including the apparent genesis of the *Dictionary*.[21] In Robert's career (1703–64) one sees the dramatic rise of a one-time footman to a successful bookseller, author of an esteemed play, and friend generally to many writers of the time. For some years he published Johnson's works, including such famous texts as *Irene*, *London*, *Rasselas*, and the *Vanity of Human Wishes*. Hawkesworth had considerable involvement with both brothers: they were among those who issued his biography and edition of Swift in 1755; James participated in the publication of his edition of Swift's letters in 1766; and Hawkesworth served them both as a literary advisor and participated in their literary projects, none so controversial, perhaps, as Robert Dodsley's play *Cleone*, which emerged as the *cause célèbre* of the 1758–59 theatrical season.

With his *Cleone* Dodsley aligned not only Covent Garden against Drury Lane, but himself and his supporters against Drury Lane's manager, David Garrick, who had refused to accept this passionate domestic tragedy based upon Sir William Lower's translation of a French version of the story of St. Genevieve by Father René de Ceriziers. What has become an obscurity of eighteenth-century theatrical history once created a controversy in which virtual armies of loyalists followed Dodsley and Garrick into battle: with the former footman-turned-dramatist stood such luminaries as Lord Lyttelton and the earl of Chesterfield; with Garrick stood William Warburton, Dr. John Hill, and Mrs. Theophilus Cibber. Johnson himself enlisted in Dodsley's camp, and though at first hearing, he suggested that the play had "more blood than brains," he was quite unrestrained in his eventual verdict, observing that "if Otway had written this play, no other of his pieces would have been remembered." In the end, Covent Garden audiences gave generously of their applause.[22]

In gauging the sensibilities of his times well, Dodsley owed some thanks to Hawkesworth, who had been called upon to read the play in manuscript. In a letter to Dodsley dated September 14, 1756, it was no casual friend who commented at length about the play's characters, their motivation, and aspects of the plot, but the drama critic of the *Gentleman's Magazine* himself. Dodsley must have been pleased with his careful assessment as well as with Mary Hawkesworth's reaction to his text. "Mrs Hawkesworth was so interested that none of these objections occurred to her, except the want of business for Isabella," Hawkesworth writes, "& paid you the tribute of more tears than, considering her Indisposition, I thought she could afford." Although he apparently never saw a production of the play, Hawkesworth remained interested in it. On December 10, 1759, he wrote again to Dodsley: "Many thanks for your agreeable Present of Cleone which I have again read and think most if not all the objections I made upon reading the first MS judiciously removed; sure the Effect upon the Audience in the 4.th & 5.th Act must have been very great."[23]

Further indications of Hawkesworth's connections with the Dodsley brothers occurred just a few days before the letter above. On December 6, 1759, he, the Dodsleys, an Ann Smith, and Alexander Galley were signatories to an agreement stating that Galley was to compile a "new work to be intitled *A Compendium of the geography Natural History and Antiquities of England* from such material as are now or shall hereafter be put into his hands by the said James Dodsley with his best care and Judgment and according to a Plan and Specimen put into hands by the said John Hawkesworth." Hawkesworth was to superintend and revise the text in question, receiving a £105 for a first edition and an additional £52 10s. for a second. Although this volume was never completed, Hawkesworth assisted James Dodsley several years later, in 1766, by contributing essays on painting and taste to a short-lived periodical called the *Spendthrift*, and he wrote some five reviews for the *Annual Register* for 1766. To his known reviews for the *Gentleman's Magazine* and the *Monthly Review* can be added this work for Dodsley's publication, all of which suggests that in assessment of a variety of literary and nonliterary material few reviewers had a greater impact on the age.[24]

While Hawkesworth's friendship with Benjamin Franklin was cemented by a number of mutual interests, while his association with Christopher Smart and the Dodsley brothers was generated by a literary man's deep interest in the world of letters, his relationship with Sir James Caldwell was sustained by mutual favors and services.[25] Sir James Caldwell was the eldest son of the third baronet, Sir John, and his wife, Anne, the daughter of John Trench, dean of Raphoe. Educated at Dundalk and Trinity College, Dublin, Caldwell traveled abroad and not only acquainted himself with the languages and constitutions of different states, but performed military and diplomatic services for Maria Theresa, who created Caldwell count of Milan in March 1749. Although offered the post of lord chamberlain to the empress, Caldwell declined because an oath of allegiance was necessary. After some six years abroad, he returned to London in May 1749, confining his travels thereafter mainly between Ireland and England, principally Dublin and London. Committing his energies to Irish affairs especially, he wrote many pamphlets on trade, agriculture, and manufacturing, and is, perhaps, best known for his English and Irish *Debates*. In 1752 he became deputy governor of his own county, Fermanagh, and colonel of a regiment of militia there. Elected a Fellow of the Royal Society in 1753, he became colonel commandant of the Twentieth Dragoons (the Enniskillen Light Horse) in 1760, and in 1762 he was appointed a Gentleman of the Privy Chamber. Like Franklin, Caldwell followed many interests—political, social, military, economic, and literary—and was especially well connected in his time. Actively engaged in the social life of such centers as Dublin, London, and Bath, his friends and associates included Lady Mary Wortley Montagu; David Garrick; Arthur Young, the agriculturist and social economist; George Faulkner, the Dublin printer; and, most notably for students of literature, Samuel Johnson and John Hawkesworth. Only recently has it come to light, in fact, that Hawkesworth served Caldwell as a literary and personal advisor for a number of years, assisting him in his personal and public writings.

In one of the earliest surviving letters the two men exchanged, written on June 25, 1759, Caldwell asked Hawkesworth's advice about soliciting a diplomatic post from the crown. "I have for some time past omitted doing myself the pleasure of writing to you," Caldwell admits, "as I feared your keeping up a Correspondence with me might take up too much of that time which you otherwise so usefully employ in performances not less entertaining to yourself than beneficial to mankind." By this time, it is clear, their friendship was already of some duration, for Caldwell continues: "As I have formerly experienced your Friendship I take the liberty of writing you this letter to Intreat your assistance in a Solicitation that I am advised to make by a friend of mine." Hawkesworth was not only willing to give counsel, but he became directly involved in the writing or editing of a variety of materials for the baronet. Shortly after August 1762, for example, he composed the draft of a letter Caldwell sent to Lady Bute in an attempt to recover one thousand guineas that he had entrusted to her mother, Lady Mary Wortley Montagu, to help him secure an Irish peerage.

On November 2, 1763, Hawkesworth wrote another letter for Caldwell to be sent to William Pitt, but not without registering his opposition to the scheme. He was no amanuensis. "I have new written the Letter to M^r. Pitt," he tells Caldwell, "though both my Feeling and my Judgment disapprove the Measure: it is paying Court with too minute an Attention, and I would not myself stoop to gratify any man's self love by a Letter to which at the same time I omitted to subscribe my Name to save him the trouble of an Answer." Some years later, in December 1772, Caldwell wrote to Lord Townshend seeking his aid in securing an Irish peerage. Although the draft is in his hand, the whole is heavily amended by Hawkesworth and practically rewritten by him—he cancels whole passages with which he disapproves and obviously had Caldwell's permission to attend to substantive as well as stylistic matters. Similarly, Caldwell called upon Hawkesworth in drafting two memorials to the king, one by Caldwell himself concerning his claim for a peerage, and the other by Mrs. Bagshawe, his sister, who describes the services rendered by her late husband, Colonel Samuel Bagshawe. The latter piece is entirely in Hawkesworth's hand.[26]

Hawkesworth's involvement in Caldwell's political writings is of even greater interest than the editorial assistance that he gave in his personal correspondence. Caldwell's *Account of the Speeches in Both Houses of Parliament, at the Opening of the Session in 1762* is, for example, represented by two surviving manuscripts, both of which are in Hawkesworth's hand. Although Caldwell read them through and doubtless provided the material, Hawkesworth must be given credit for their composition. One involves Bedford's motion to end the German war, a manuscript of over ten pages, which Caldwell scarcely amended. It is interesting to recall here that although conclusive evidence is lacking, Hawkesworth is seen as Johnson's successor in compiling the popular parliamentary "debates" in the *Gentleman's Magazine*. The fact that he composed a fluent debate for Caldwell supports this idea.[27]

Hawkesworth's letter to Caldwell dated January 11, 1763, reflects the nature of his collaboration with Sir James and the difficulties that they faced working at some distance from each other. Hawkesworth writes:

> By the last Post I sent you my own original, of which I now enclose you the Copy which I procured to be made. I believe in this Copy there are a few trivial Improvements which you will discover & adopt upon comparing it with the original. I also enclose (as I did in my last) an account of the Reasons on which severel [*sic*] deviations from your own Instructions are founded. It is a great disadvantage on these occasions not to have a personal Conferrence [*sic*] however, being obliged to make my own Judgment the Standard I have taxed it to the utmost.

Hawkesworth must have written such letters to Caldwell frequently, assisting as he did with many species of composition. He apparently helped him, for example, with papers Caldwell intended to read before the Dublin Society. There is an extant four-page draft in Hawkesworth's hand, somewhat amended by Caldwell, of a plan that he proposed to the society in 1764 for encouraging the Dublin fish trade. Hawkesworth even wrote a hymn and prayers for special occasions for Sir James; the hymn was to be set to music by Hawkesworth's good friend, Charles Burney—"a very able and Ingenious man now rising into High Reputation," he wrote to Caldwell on April 2, 1769—and the prayers were designed to reform pilferers in Caldwell's employment. Unfortunately, there is no surviving record of the latter's efficacy.[28]

Although in placing his pen at a friend's disposal, if not exactly for hire, Hawkesworth joined a list of distinguished eighteenth-century writers, among them Addison and Steele, Defoe, Swift, and Johnson, he worried that such labors would become public knowledge. On December 11, 1761, he told Caldwell with apparent uneasiness that "the inclosed perhaps may go to George Just as it is but I beg you would keep my Secret and not let it be known that I have Endeavoured to oblige you in a Species of Composition that I never should have produced on any other Account." Hawkesworth's reticence is probably explained less by a writer's feeling that certain compositions were beneath him than by his awareness of the tenuous relationship existing at the time between letters and politics. He certainly recalled the sad occasion when Cave had been called before the House of Lords on April 30, 1747, for having printed in his magazine an account of the trial of Lord Lovat and the fine that resulted from this breach of privilege. In spite of any reservations, however, Hawkesworth served Sir James extensively and saw such assistance amply recompensed: Caldwell lobbied to secure subscribers for Hawkesworth's translation of *Telemachus* and later became involved in a projected edition of his works; he apparently promised to include Hawkesworth in his will at one time; in 1771, by writing to Tisdal, the attorney general for Ireland, and another friend at law, he endeavored to protect Hawkesworth's edition of Cook's *Voyages* in Ireland; finally, it was through Caldwell that Hawkesworth reached levels of society ordinarily closed to a writer.[29]

Hawkesworth's association with Caldwell, though, was not crudely based on favors rendered and returned; they had interests and friends in common, the latter including Johnson. George Faulkner, the Dublin printer, sent his best wishes to both Hawkesworth and Johnson in a letter to Caldwell on July 14, 1763; about the same time Caldwell invited both men to visit him in Ireland, though both Johnson, then in Hawkesworth's company, and Hawkesworth declined. Such correspondence lays to rest any arguments for a permanent breach between Johnson and Hawkes-worth. Similar material establishes the depth of his friendship with Cald-well. The baronet, in fact, entrusted the supervision of his sons' education (John, his heir, and Fitzmaurice) to Hawkesworth at Bromley, where they had been placed with a tutor probably recommended by the writer himself, who was ready to assist a man close to his heart. Hawkesworth wrote on December 11, 1767, in words that clearly reveal his feeling for Caldwell: "I miss you, my dear Sir James, like the friend of my heart; though we have long known each other we never associated till now, I regret your absence, and my mind follows you with affection and Solicitude. I hope you will come again in the spring for I shall feel very forlorne in London without you."[30]

Hawkesworth's correspondence with Sir James also reveals the wider world in which he moved at the time and the connections his friend had made possible. Mrs. M. Bernard, for instance, wrote to Lady Caldwell on April 7, 1768, that she had given Hawkesworth "some hours, if not days, employment by putting into his hands many letters of my late Uncles Hugh Bethell, the celebrated friend of M^r. Pope." Hawkesworth had long been interested in the poet and may have contemplated using these letters in some study of his career. Other figures of the Caldwell circle offer com-ments on Hawkesworth's character. Writing to Lady Caldwell on February 5, 1768, Lady Kerry requested: "Be so good to tell Sir James with my Sincere Compliments to him that Doctor Hawkesworth is very well and in good Spirits, he is a most Polite agreeable man, I am reading some of his Writings in the Adventurer which Answers the Descriptions Sir James gave me of them."[31]

Hawkesworth himself wrote to Caldwell, with evident satisfaction, of his new social contacts. On April 2, 1769, he wrote that from Lady Mary Howard he "gained new honour & importance by being the only person that she treated with Civility; she made me a Gracious Curtsey, and even paid me Complim^{ts}." A week later, on April 9, 1769, he thanked Caldwell for news that Lady Arabella Denny "intends to Write to Lord Shelburne on my behalf, the Interest she is pleased to take in my affairs is a much higher Reward than any I expected from my Work." In a postscript Hawkesworth added that he received an invitation from Lady Shelburne for her grand rout Tuesday the tenth. These were indeed satisfying times for a son of Grub Street who found himself moving among people of position and influence, though perhaps the transition was too great not to have produced some changes in a character often complimented for its benevolence and decency. Sir Joshua Reynolds, soon to paint Hawkesworth's portrait, found him, Edmond Malone relates, "an affected insincere man, and a great coxcomb in his dress." However just Reynolds' view of Hawkesworth, many sought his company. "I have received such a Billet from Lady Arabella Denny," he told Caldwell on May 1, 1769, "as I know of no person besides her Ladyship that cou'd write." Later, on December 21, 1770, in another letter to his friend showing his continued association with persons of high station, Hawkesworth observed: "I din'd with the Dowager Lady Shelburne on Sunday was Sev'n night at Twickenham; Lord Kingsborough was so good to give me a place in his carriage."[32]

In Hawkesworth's connection with Sir James Caldwell, then, one sees not only another aspect of his literary and editorial activity, but a friendship that ushered him into the world he would briefly inhabit as the celebrated author of Cook's *Voyages*. Before he undertook this great work, though, he turned his attention to the production of a new version of classic text that testifies again to his literary abilities and supports his claim to a place in English letters.

Although it is not clear when Hawkesworth decided to undertake a translation of *Les Aventures de Télémaque* by François de Salignac de La Mothe-Fénelon, his reasons for turning to this text are not hard to understand. Published in 1699, Fénelon's work became an acknowledged classic, seeing translation throughout Europe, including Turkey. Some five versions appeared in England before Hawkesworth produced an edition that long remained standard, one reprinted, at least in part, as late as 1962. One of the most famous seventeenth-century utopias, *Telemachus* is cast in the form of a travel book. Its hero's visits to Egypt, Tyre, Boetica, and Salentum are not designed to present mere typography and custom, though, but a representation of various ideal societies: in Egypt he finds a delightful order; in Tyre, a thriving trade and a virtuous population; in Boetica, a virtual arcadia, a community freed not only from vice but from passion itself; in Salentum, a complex state rationally divided into various classes, the whole rule by a philosopher king. Fénelon did not aim for escapism in the travels of his young prince but for specific commentary on the government of Louis XIV and a larger one on the modern world grown to viciousness. In form and content, then, *Telemachus* is related to Voltaire's *Candide* and, across the channel, Swift's *Gulliver's Travels* and Johnson's *Rasselas*. In its moral concerns as well as its exotic settings, moreover, it is closely akin to Hawkesworth's *Adventurer* fiction. In Telemachus and Mentor, his tutor, one sees parallels with Hamlet and Omar in *Almoran and Hamet*.[33]

In Fénelon's world, characterized by a classical austerity, a celebration of spartan denial and puritanical astringency, both coupled with an arcadianism and a devotion to the idea of the simple life generally, one sees a moral vision that must have appealed to Hawkesworth. It is evident that some thought him an ideal candidate to bring this classic afresh to the

English reading public. Joseph Cockfield, writing to the Reverend Weeden Butler on January 1, 1767, commented

> Mr. Hoole (when we spent some time at his house) mentioned in the course of conversation, that he had engaged himself with Dr. Hawkesworth to dine with Dr. Dodd. I am informed the Doctor intends to publish his edition of Telemaque by subscription, and that the book is to be printed in quarto. I should like to see his proposals if he has published them. The Doctor seems to be the only person suited for such an undertaking. In several of his papers in the Adventurer he seems to write like another Fenelon; he possesses the imagination of the Poet, his Essays have all the elegance and harmony of verse; he is often sublime, often serious, never light and trivial, except when he indulges in innocent gaiety, which is rather unfrequent.[34]

Hawkesworth's good friend, Sir James Caldwell, gave considerable support to this literary undertaking and was among those urging publication by subscription. "I am greatly obliged to you and Lady Caldwell," Hawkesworth wrote on January 11, 1767, "for your Advice about my Telemachus which is the same that I have received from other Friends & which therefore I believe I shall take." Caldwell undoubtedly felt that many would subscribe to a handsomely bound, illustrated translation of a celebrated classic, the product of a leading moralist and man of letters; more important, he and his wife were ready to give Hawkesworth assistance whenever necessary. Not only did they secure permission for him to dedicate the book to Lord Shelburne, Lady Caldwell's cousin and "one of his Majesty's Principal Secretaries of State," but actively solicited subscribers. "If you think it proper for me to apply concerning my Subscription to Mrs. Cramer Sir John Colthurst, or any other of the persons who have been Engaged by your friendly Interest," Hawkesworth wrote to Sir James on December 11, 1767, "let me know and I will instantly & gratefully do it, perhaps I have been remiss, but I thought where you had interfered I Ought to be wholly Neutral." Hawkesworth, deeply appreciative for this assistance, wrote to Lady Caldwell on March 4, 1768: "If I were less Sensible of the Zeal & Spirit of Sir James in my Subscription, I should perhaps say more about it, because then I might easily find words to Satisfy myself; as this is not the Case I say nothing."[35]

Printed by his friend and member of the Bromley circle William Strahan, Hawkesworth's translation was made available to his subscribers in late May 1768. His fluent dedication to Lord Shelburne is probably less interesting to a modern student of the book than its list of subscribers, which includes many friends as well as representatives from all important levels of society—the clergy, the nobility, members of Parliament and government, and such institutions as the Cambridge University Library. Even a brief sampling of this list suggests the book's appeal not only within the kingdom itself but to its far possessions as well: among the subscribers were the archbishop of Armag, primate of Ireland; Viscount Barrington, secretary of war; Edmund Burke; Charles Burney; the earls of Chesterfield and of Chatham; Benjamin Franklin, of Philadelphia; Francis Hopkinson, of Philadelphia; David Garrick; Mrs. Garrick; Philip Tisdal, attorney general of Ireland; Henry Thrale; and Joshua Reynolds. Perhaps the only slightly surprising omission is Johnson, but another man soon to play a significant role in Hawkesworth's life, the earl of Sandwich, does appear.[36]

Many famous writers tried their hand at translation from the French during the eighteenth century, among them Smollett, Goldsmith, Charlotte Lennox, and Johnson, who based his first prose work, *Father Lobo's Voyage to Abyssinia*, on the French text of Abbé Joachim Le Grand. Here and in the translations of a number of other French sources he attempted to put into practice his own theory of translation expressed in *Idler* nos. 68 and 69. In the latter he observes: "There is undoubtedly a mean to be observed. Dryden saw very early that closeness best preserved an author's sense, and that freedom best exhibited his spirit; he therefore will deserve highest praise who can give a representation at once faithful and pleasing, who can convey the same thoughts with the same graces, and who when he translates changes nothing but the language."[37] Hawkesworth, like Johnson, saw translation as something more than a mere mechanical exercise. In his preface to *Telemachus* he claimed that his principal view "was much more extensive, than to assist learners of the French language. I have attempted to render a work full of ingenious fiction, just reasoning, important precepts, and poetical imagery, as pleasing in English as it is in French, to those who read it as their native tongue" (p. xviii).

In *Telemachus*, then, Hawkesworth aimed to produce, not a gloss, but a work of art. While it would be difficult to substantiate his claim that previous translation of the French text were "totally destitute" (p. xvii) of poetic merit, it seems apparent that he attempted to seize qualities of his original not to be gained through mere mechanical manipulation of language. The following passages reveal how he worked with his French original; in comparing them one might conclude that Hawkesworth copes well with Fénelon's opulent description of Calypso's grotto and provides English readers with the essence, if not the exact language, of his source:

> On arriva à la porte de la grote de Calypso, où Télémaque fut surpris de voir avec une aparence de simplicité rustique tout ce qui peut charmer les yeux. Il est vrai qu'on n'y voyoit ni or, ni argent, ni marbre, ni colomnes, ni tableaux, ni statuës: mais cette grote étoit taillée dans le

roc, en voutes pleines de rocailles & de coquilles; elle étoit tapissée d'une jeune vigne qui étendoit également ses branches souples de tous côtés. Les doux Zéphirs conservoient en ce lieu, malgré les ardeurs du Soleil, une délicieuse fraîcheur. Des fontaines coulant avec un doux murmure sur des prés semés d'amaranthes & de violettes, formoient, en divers lieux, des bains aussi purs & aussi clairs que le crystal. Mille fleurs naissantes émailloient les tapis verds, dont la grote étoit environnée. Là on trouvoit un bois de ces arbres toufus qui portent des pommes d'or, & dont la fleur, qui se renouvelle dans toutes les faisons, répand le plus doux de tous les parfums: ce bois sembloit couronner ces belles prairies, & formoit une nuit que les rayons du Soleil ne pouvoient percer. Là on n'entendoit jamais que le chant des oiseaux, ou le bruit d'un ruisseau, qui, se précipitant du haut d'un rocher, tomboit à gros bouillons pleins d'écume, & s'enfuyoit au travers de la prairie. (Fénelon, p. 5)

When they arrived at the entrance of the grotto, TELEMACHUS was surprized to discover, under the appearance of rural simplicity, whatever could captivate the sight: there was, indeed, neither gold nor silver, nor marble; no decorated columns, no paintings or statues were to be seen; but the grotto consisted of several vaults cut in the rock; the roof of it was embellished with shells and pebbles; and the want of tapestry was supplied by the luxuriance of a young vine, which extended its branches equally on every side: here the heat of the sun was tempered by the freshness of the breeze; the rivulets, that, with soothing murmurs, wandered through meadows of intermingled violets and amaranth, formed innumerable baths that were pure and transparent as crystal; the verdant carpet which nature had spread round the grotto, was adorned with a thousand flowers; and, at a small distance, there was a wood of those trees that, in every season, unfold new blossoms, which diffuse ambrosial fragrance, and ripen into golden fruit: in this wood, which was impervious to the rays of the sun, and heightened the beauty of the adjacent meadows by an agreeable opposition of light and shade, nothing was to be heard but the melody of birds, or the fall of water, which, precipitated from the summit of a rock, was dashed into foam below, where forming a small rivulet it fled in haste over the meadow. (Hawkesworth, p. 4)

Hawkesworth received universal praise for his rendition of Fénelon's text. Few would have disagreed with the reviewer in the *Monthly Review* who noted simply: "There are several translations of this celebrated work, but the spirit and genius of the Author have never been so effectually represented." When reissued some years later, Hawkesworth's translation continued to draw praise. "Of the Translation of DR. HAWKESWORTH," a new editor wrote, "the critical world and the public have already given their opinion; and the merit of it is established beyond the reach of censure or of praise. Few translations, or even original productions in our language, can compare with it in brilliancy, elegance and harmony of style."[38]

The 1760s, then, was a particularly rich decade for Hawkesworth. In the list of subscribers to his *Telemachus* one sees the remarkable range of friends and associates who endorsed his literary genius. While *Telemachus* is closely linked to his previous writing, which embodied a commitment to virtue and virtue's enhancement through the power of art, it also clearly foreshadows the masterwork to come. Its year of publication, 1768, is of special significance. On August 26, 1768, another great voyager, James Cook, set out from Plymouth on the *Endeavour* to begin his heroic voyage around the globe, a journey that would, in fact, complete the map of the world for the first time. In a few years it would be Hawkesworth's mission to chart the voyage of this modern Telemachus, not through the classical worlds of Egypt, Tyre, Boetica, and Salentum, but to no less exotic places, as the *Endeavor*, in its search of Terra Australis Incognita, sailed through dazzling Patagonian nights to drop anchor at the Pacific's greatest jewel, the island of Tahiti.

VII HAWKESWORTH'S *VOYAGES:* CAPTAIN COOK AND THE GREAT VOYAGE CONTROVERSY OF 1773

> For a hundred and twenty years, so far as the first voyage was concerned, Hawkesworth was Cook.
>
> J. C. Beaglehole

On September 25, 1513, Vasco Nuñez de Balboa struggled across the Isthmus of Panama with his band of soldiers and became the first European to view the Pacific Ocean. He waded into the waters of the Gulf of San Miguel and claimed the "Great South Sea" and all its continents and islands in the name of his master the king of Spain. Thereafter Western man never rid himself of the lure of the Pacific and the lands vast and small whose shores its waters washed, the great Pacific, the globe's central geographical fact, an ocean measuring 10,000 miles from east to west, 10,000 miles from north to south.[1]

Through the centuries various European powers moved into Pacific waters—the Portuguese and the Spanish in the sixteenth century, the Dutch in the seventeenth, and the English and the French in the eighteenth. Pacific exploration, the result of the courage of legions of anonymous seamen, became personified in the exploits of such men as Ferdinand Magellan, whose circumnavigation of the world in 1522 remained a standard to test the courage of those who followed: Alvaro de Mendaña, Pedro Fernandez de Quiros, Luis Vaez de Torres, Abel Janszoon Tasman, William Dampier, Louis Antoine de Bougainville, and, most memorable in the English-speaking world, Captain James Cook.

In 1697 William Dampier fired the English imagination with his *New Voyage Round the World*, the carefully wrought journal of a buccaneer, privateer, merchant-sailor who had touched down at the earth's ends, including Australia itself. Eighteenth-century writers, such as Defoe in *Robinson Crusoe*, made travel and exploration the matter of great literature, and the Pacific itself figures prominently in *Gulliver's Travels*: Lilliput was northwest of Van Dieman's Land, and Gulliver sailed to what is now New South Wales; Brobdingnag was situated somewhere to the east of Japan, while Balnibarbi extended out towards California in northern Pacific reaches.

137

The War of the Spanish Succession and the South Sea Bubble of 1721 sustained public interest in the Pacific, as did George Anson's voyage around the world in 1741–44, and Britain watched French involvement in the area closely. Charles de Brosses in his *Histoire des Navigations aux Terres Australes* called for a French commitment to the Pacific in 1756, and his work was appropriated some years later by a Scotsman, John Callander, who demanded in his *Terra Australis Cognita* similar endeavors from the United Kingdom. For reasons somewhat unlike those that motivated Portuguese, Spanish, and Dutch exploration—the first two were stirred by the vision of converting Pacific infidels to Christianity (*conquista espiritual*), the third by stolid commercial interests—the French and the English at mid-century began intensive investigations of the Pacific. In the largest sense these voyages might be seen as a peaceful continuation of the conflict settled by the Treaty of Paris in 1763, though French and English Pacific exploration was as much motivated by scientific as military considerations; in Cook one sees a naval officer in command not so much of a warship, though firepower there was aplenty, as of a floating laboratory equipped to make extensive surveys of the natural world. Science in general benefited from such voyages, especially geography: it was Cook's voyages that defined the planet's oceans and surfaces and Cook more than any man who put to rest the *idée fixe* of countless generations of geographers of the great southern continent, the land mass at the globe's south supposedly balancing its known equivalent at the north—the last great land still awaiting its discoverer. "Symmetry demanded it," J. C. Beaglehole writes, "the balance of the earth demanded it—for in the absence of this tremendous mass of land what, asked Mercator, was there to prevent the world from toppling over to destruction amidst the stars?" *Terra Australis Incognita* "was a feeling, a tradition, a logical and now even a theological necessity, a compelling and inescapable mathematical certitude. Its discovery must come."[2] But no such land was discovered—not in Cook's celebrated voyage, or in those of John Byron (one of Anson's former officers), Philip Carteret, or Samuel Wallis, all of whom preceded Cook in Pacific expeditions. Whatever the motives that propelled them into the Pacific's vastnesses, motives that resist easy clarification, these men, in remarkable feats of navigation, helped establish British dominance in this part of the world, carrying their language and culture to the very ends of the earth.

In 1764 Commodore John Byron took command of an expedition to the South Seas whose principal objective was to establish an English base in the South Atlantic. This he achieved by taking formal possession of the Falkland Islands. Thereafter Byron proceeded into the Pacific, circled the globe, and anchored in the Downs on May 9, 1766. Though lacking some of the drama of subsequent voyages (Byron and his crew did, however, see the

Patagonian "giants" at the southern tip of South America), Byron's voyage stimulated the Admiralty's interest in future exploration. On August 22 of the same year Captain Samuel Wallis sailed in the *Dolphin*, accompanied by Philip Carteret in the *Swallow*, charged by the Admiralty not only with further Pacific exploration, but with discovery, if possible, of the southern continent. The *Swallow*, a wretched and ill-equipped ship, became separated from the *Dolphin* after having negotiated the treacherous Strait of Magellan. Wallis pushed on and achieved immortality as Tahiti's discoverer; Carteret, sensing abandonment and possible betrayal, sailed alone into the Pacific. He discovered Pitcairn Island, later of *Bounty* fame, named after the son of Major Pitcairn, who sighted it; rediscovered Santa Cruz and the Solomon Islands the Spanish had visited two centuries earlier; and returned home on May 20, 1769, after a voyage, which "though in fruitfulness it might be exceeded," J. C. Beaglehole writes, "for resolution, fortitude and skill had few rivals in that century."[3] Such was the momentum of Pacific exploration at the time that when Carteret completed his harrowing voyage, Cook had already been on the high seas for some ten months in the *Endeavour*.

Born in Yorkshire, the son of a day laborer of the village of Marton-in-Cleveland on October 27, 1728, James Cook rose to such eminence that during the American War of Independence all belligerents were under orders to treat him, if they should encounter him, as a commander of a neutral and allied power. Cook was, James A. Williamson writes, "the representative not only of England but of civilization, and civilization acknowledged it."[4] It was Cook's first Pacific voyage in the *Endeavour*, undertaken from 1768 to 1771, that firmly established him as the great commander and navigator of his age, forever after "the seamen's seaman" in Alan Villiers' phrase. Although under strict Admiralty control, the *Endeavour*'s mission was clearly scientific: in the later 1760s the European scientific community eagerly anticipated the transit of the planet Venus over the disc of the sun, an event predicted for June 3, 1769. The Royal Society insisted on England's participation in observing this important event and suggested that a South Pacific island was one of several favorable viewing points. Compared to previous expeditions to the Pacific, the *Endeavour* was handsomely fitted, partly through the lavish expenditures of Joseph Banks, the ship's principal scientist, a man of position and fortune, a member at twenty-six of the Royal Society. Joining him was Daniel Carl Solander, a pupil of Linnaeus. Such talent, both nautical and scientific, insured the *Endeavour*'s success.

While eighteenth-century astronomers could predict the exact date of the transit of Venus, contemporary geographers embraced more poetically inspired visions, and Cook was further charged with a search for the elusive southern continent. His directions, Beaglehole notes, were quite specific:

> As great an extent of the coast as possible was to be explored and its
> peculiarities noted; together with the nature of the soil and all its
> products, of which, where possible, specimens were to be brought
> back. The nature of the people, if people there should be, was also to be
> carefully examined, their friendship and alliance cultivated, and trade
> opened. Furthermore, with their consent, Cook was to take possession
> of convenient situations, or if the land was uninhabited, to annex it in
> due form.[5]

Some five months after setting out, on January 27, 1769, the *Endeavour*
passed Cape Horn and pressed west by north for Tahiti, following a course
well southward of previous explorations in hope of discovering the southern
continent. On April 13, 1769, Cook anchored in Wallis's anchorage in
Matavai Bay at Tahiti and on June 3 successfully observed the transit, the
temperature a tropical 119 degrees. "The naturalists were in heaven,"
Beaglehole writes, "while the high-spirited enthusiasm of Banks and the
universal curiosity of Cook elaborated a fuller and more accurate description of the country than any Pacific island had yet received. In the study of
native ceremony, Banks went so far as to strip off his clothes and be
blackened with charcoal and water; and Cook's journal is a model of
scientific detail and exact statement."[6] Relations between the explorers and
the natives were exceedingly good, though the Tahitians proved dexterous
thieves, stealing Solander's opera glass, Banks's snuffbox, Cook's stocking,
and, even worse, a sentry's musket and a quadrant. After exploring the
island Cook set sail on July 13, 1769, to investigate other islands in the
group, which he named the Society Islands; on August 9, 1769, he moved
southward in search of the southern continent, an exercise in futility,
obviously, but Cook was never one to disappoint: although he found no
continental mass, he visited and charted in remarkable detail New Zealand
and the east coast of Australia.

On October 6, 1769, Nicholas Young of the *Endeavour* first sighted the
northern island of New Zealand, receiving an extra gallon of rum for this
achievement. Cook encountered the Maoris, the native New Zealanders,
circumnavigated both the north and the south island, sailed the strait
between them, which bears his name today, and prepared charts that
remain a marvel for their accuracy.[7] In April 1770 the *Endeavour* approached Australia, and Cook sailed northwards to survey the yet un-
charted east coast, the dangers of which presented the *Endeavour*'s crew and
captain with the most serious crisis of the voyage. Late in the evening of
June 10, 1770, the *Endeavour*, having sailed inside the Great Barrier Reef,
struck the treacherous coral, and only the collective calm action of captain,

scientific personnel, and crew (the latter even abstaining from customary oaths) saved the ship from disaster. The ship was beached and underwent extensive repairs, during which time kangaroos were first sighted and shot, and it was not until July 4, 1770, that it could once again be floated. Further danger awaited Cook as he set out to find whether New Guinea and New Holland were joined. On August 15, 1770, a becalmed *Endeavour* drifted slowly toward destruction upon the reef. At a critical moment, however, a small breath of wind enabled the ship to move two hundred yards away before the next calm ensued. The ship missed the first opening through the reef, but safely navigated a second, a "Providential Channel."

Cook successfully sailed through the Torres Strait, demonstrating conclusively that New Holland and New Guinea were not connected and anchored at Batavia on October 10, 1770. After a difficult voyage around the Cape, which exacted a far greater toll than the previous part of the journey (twenty-two men died, including Green the astronomer and Monkhouse the midshipman), the *Endeavour* anchored in the Downs on July 13, 1771. Cook's achievement, Beaglehole comments, "was already after this one voyage the greatest which the history of discovery could record," and he writes in summary of this journey:

> [Cook] had not discovered the great southern continent, but he had more than any other man made doubtful the thesis of its existence. He had not discovered Tahiti, but he gave that island of Venus and of George III a complete and rounded existence. He had not discovered New Zealand, but he had brilliantly reduced it to the dimensions of fact. He had not discovered New Holland, but he had from a vague obscure crystallized New South Wales; and he had shown that this eastern coast at least was no archipelago, but continuous land. He was the second and not the first captain to sail between Australia and New Guinea; but the act had both the force and the effect of a new discovery. He had pursued these objects with a sure and astonishing tenacity, a capacity to make fruitful every league of a voyage, which compelled a positive and considerable result. The result had been attained with an accompaniment which amazed his expert contemporaries as much as did his additions to geography.[8]

The intense public interest in Cook's voyage around the world, as well as in the voyages of Byron, Wallis, and Carteret, was finally satisfied by the publication in early summer of 1773 of a handsome, three-volume, lavishly illustrated work whose very title is commensurate with the global nature of its contents: *An Account of the Voyages undertaken by order of his present Majesty for making Discoveries in the Southern Hemisphere, And successively performed by Commodore Byron, Captain Wallis, Captain Carteret, And Captain Cook, in the*

Dolphin, the Swallow, and the Endeavour: drawn up from the Journals which were kept by the several Commanders, And from the Papers of Joseph Banks, Esq. Its author was Dr. John Hawkesworth.[9] With this work he became forever linked with one of the nation's first citizens, and for generations Hawkesworth would transmit to the English-speaking world and, through translation, to many other nations the meaning of the great mid-century Pacific voyages.

The Admiralty wanted to issue an official, government-sanctioned account of Cook's celebrated voyage and of those of Byron, Wallis, and Carteret, who preceeded him into the Pacific. Such a version would replace the spurious and inaccurate texts that had already appeared, and would undoubtedly continue to appear, and would establish English claims in this part of the world. Most important, the authorized edition would illuminate a great national success, give positive proof of British dominance of the seas, and reveal in action the colonial spirit that took a people to the far points of the globe. George III was entitled to no less a commemoration of his captains' achievements on the seas than Queen Anne had enjoyed in Addison's celebration of Marlborough's victory on land at Blenheim in *The Campaign*. Hawkesworth, his patron, Lord Sandwich, the Admiralty's First Lord, and the bookselling establishment were all connected with the planning, writing, production, and distribution of one of the most famous publications of the age, one that soon came to be known simply as Hawkesworth's *Voyages*.

Hawkesworth secured the contract to write the *Voyages* through influence—principally that of his friends Charles Burney and David Garrick. Burney's role in securing the contract was instrumental, Garrick's supportive, though Garrick has generally been given more credit for his efforts. Hawkesworth might have met Charles Burney as early as 1745, when Burney was engaged as a musician in the household of Fulke Greville; and by the 1760s he was a frequent participant in the Burney circle, a member of the select company that included representatives of the arts and culture in general.

Dr. Burney was married for the second time in October 1767 to Mrs. Stephen Allen, the widow of a Lynn merchant, and the new Mrs. Burney, Charlotte Barrett writes, "who was herself highly intellectual, entered with intelligent delight into the literary circle which formed the solace and refreshment of her husband." A large and interesting group of people frequented their home, first in Queen Square and later in St. Martin's Street, among them, she records,

> Sir Robert and Lady Strange—the former so well known for his admirable engravings, and his lady for her strong sense and original

humour; Dr. Hawkesworth, the worthy and learned editor of Byron's and Cook's *First Voyages*; Garrick, and his amiable wife, the friend of Hannah More; Barry, the painter, whose works still adorn the Adelphi; Mr. Twining, the translator of *Aristotle*; Mason, the poet; Mr. Greville and his lady, the latter celebrated as the authoress of the beautiful "Ode to Indifference"; Dr. Armstrong; Arthur Young, the agriculturist, who had married a sister of Mrs. Burney's; John Hutton, the Moravian, the musical and clever La Trobes, and Nollekens, the sculptor. To these might be added many others of equal or superior celebrity, who formed part of Dr. Burney's society, as time and circumstance brought them within his reach.[10]

Frequent references to Hawkesworth in Fanny Burney's *Early Diary* during the late 1760s and early 1770s reflect his intimacy with the family. In early 1769 she wrote: "Our party last evening was large and *brilliant*. Mr. Greville, the celebrated Dr. Hawkesworth, Mr. Crisp and my cousin dined with us." She held Hawkesworth in high regard and commented that she had "never heard a man speak in a style which so much resembles writing. He has an amazing flow of choice words and expressions. . . . He is *remarkably* well bred and attentive, considering how great an author he is." But Fanny saw, as did others, that Hawkesworth had "a small tincture of affectation." Her fondness for the man grew, however. In August 1771 Fanny recorded, "The admiration I have of his works, has created great esteem for their author," though she observed at the same time that she found Hawkesworth "too precise to be really agreeable, that is, to be natural, like Mr. Crisp and my dear father." Yet in February 1773 she stated unequivocally: "I like the Doctor more and more every time I have the pleasure of seeing him; that stiffness and something resembling pedantry, which formerly struck me in him, upon further acquaintance and more intimacy either wear off or disappear. He was extremely natural and agreeable." Of Mary Hawkesworth, about whose person and manner there was universal agreement, Fanny wrote: "His wife is a very well-bred, obliging, and sweet-tempered woman."[11]

Not only does Fanny provide information about Hawkesworth's character and friendship with the family in her *Early Diary*, but she also gives specific details about the award of the contract to compile Cook's *Voyages*. Around September 1771 she observed:

My father has had a happy opportunity of extremely obliging Dr. Hawkesworth. During [Dr. Burney's] stay in Norfolk, he waited upon Lord Orford, who has always been particularly friendly to him. He there, among others, met with Lord Sandwich. His Lordship was speaking of the late voyage round the world and mentioned his having the papers of it in his possession; for he is First Lord of the Admiralty; and said that they were not arranged, but mere rough draughts, and said that he should be much obliged to any one who could recommend a proper person to *write the Voyage*.[12]

Dr. Burney thereupon recommended his friend Hawkesworth as one capable of undertaking such a task. The favor is confirmed in a marginal notation found in the *Morning Chronicle* for Saturday, June 19, 1773, in the Burney collection in the British Library, which also helps clarify Garrick's role in the matter. The note, probably in Dr. Burney's hand, reads: "It was D^r. Burney, who in recommending D^r. Hawkesworth to L^d. Sandwich at Houghton, referred his Lord^p. to Garrick for a confirmation of the character w^h. he had given of D^r. Hawkesworth as an ingenious & elegant writer, and an hon^{ble}. man."

Informed of the possibility of such an award, Hawkesworth immediately applied whatever pressure he could. On September 18, 1771, he wrote to Burney in great eagerness and some fear that such an opportunity might be missed. "There is nothing about which I would so willingly be employed," he comments, "as the work you mention. I would do my best to make it another Anson's Voyage. I am very unwilling to wait for Lord S.'s application without doing Something to anticipate or quicken it. Will you tell him by a Line that I most heartily concur in the proposal?" Hawkesworth cites Garrick as a referee ("I have written to Garrick requesting that he will do what he may") and suggests in addition references from Lord Lyttelton or Mrs. Montagu if Lord Sandwich "wishes to know further of me."[13] Hawkesworth was obviously well-connected: with the collective support of Burney and Garrick, both preeminent in their worlds; Elizabeth Montagu, the bluestocking and hostess of London literary parties; and Lord Lyttelton, a patron of letters and a friend of Fielding (who dedicated *Tom Jones* to him), he had little cause for worry. With their assistance, and with no apparent rival in view, the matter was quickly concluded.

The exact date of settlement is not known, but it must have been during September 1771. On the twenty-ninth of the month Daniel Wray stated in a letter to Lord Hardwicke: "The *Voyage* of the *Endeavour* has been settled: *Hawkesworth* is to be the writer, recommended by *Garrick*." Hawkesworth, writing to Burney on October 6, 1771, from Bromley, Kent, commented that "I have all the Journals of the Dolphin the Swallow & the Endeavour in my possession" and reported "that the Government will give me the Cutts & that the property of the work will be my own. Accept my best Thanks, dear Sir, for the Advantage which this work must necessarily procure me, which will be very considerable." In a postscript he indicated proof of the rise in his fortunes that the award had already generated. "I am going to spend a week at Lord Sandwich's at Hinchinbrook next week."[14]

A letter from Hawkesworth to Lord Sandwich written from Bromley, Kent, on November 19, 1771, shows that his labors on the *Voyages* were under way:

> I cannot help stealing a few Minutes from the Work which your Lordship is pleased to take an Interest so Flattering to myself, and so favourable to the Undertaking, to acknowledge the Receipt of the first Volume of Mr. Banks's Journal, and to assure your Lordship that as it is my highest Interest, it is also my earnest Desire to get my M.S. ready in time enough to have the Sanction of Mr Banks and Capt Cook to what I shall relate after them. I am happy in your Lordship's powerfull Influence with Mr Banks for the rest of his Journal. I flatter myself that I shall be able to prevent ill humour, and satisfy the utmost Delicacy of a Gentleman to whom I shall be so much obliged. I promise your Lordship that not an hour shall be bestowed upon any other Object, till the Account is finished, either of Business or Pleasure.[15]

By the fall of 1771 work on the *Voyages* was progressing well, and from then until its completion in 1773, Hawkesworth must have enjoyed deep contentment in being engaged in what promised to be his greatest work. Contrary to his last statement, however, there was also a good deal of other business and pleasure during this period. He maintained his powerful position as literary editor of the *Gentleman's Magazine*. When not in London, where he generally engaged himself at month's end in the various affairs of a well-connected man of letters, he spent his time in rural Bromley. Here for the first three weeks of each month he enjoyed comforts befitting a country gentleman and the company of a circle of friends and visitors drawn to a man of position and property. In April 1773 yet another honor would be secured—election as a director of the famed East India Company. The man of letters was thus translated into a man of business and fortune.

Founded in 1600, the East India Company reflected England's expanding interest in the world during Queen Elizabeth's reign, the result of Sir Francis Drake's great voyage of 1577–80 and of the desire to challenge the supremacy of the Portuguese East India trade. The company barely survived the Civil War but flourished after the Restoration, when demand in Europe for Eastern goods was steady and profitable: from east to west flowed indigo, calico, saltpeter, silks, sugar, tea and coffee (both highly popular in the reign of Queen Anne), drugs, porcelain, carpets, and lace. During the eighteenth century the company became deeply embroiled in politics, both domestic and foreign. Whigs generally resented Tory support of the company through loans during the reign of Charles II and James II, and company affairs were repeatedly in the public eye as it gradually found itself a leading power in the subcontinent of India. Although Robert Clive's military genius brought French defeat in India, the company's affairs were not so well managed. In 1772 it had to secure a government loan of a million pounds.[16]

Hawkesworth, then, sought to join a company with a long past and some immediate problems. His desire for such a position, something of an unlikely one for a man of letters, might not be immediately clear, though the prime motivation was undoubtedly financial. In seeking a directorship Hawkesworth entered a world of high finance: even to stand for such a post required an investment in company stock of £2,000. His election represented the culmination of several large financial transactions and the efforts of many friends. Hawkesworth had owned India stock as early as June 13, 1771, when he acquired £500 from Robert Browne, Esq., by virtue of a letter of attorney from Brigadier General Richard Smith of Queen Anne Street. On September 26, 1771, he transferred the same amount to William Devaynes of Spring Gardens. Not until the fall of 1772, on October 6, did Hawkesworth once again possess India stock, acquiring then £500 from Jonathan Green of the Haymarket; and he met the requisite £2,000 by purchasing on March 4, 1773, just a month before the election, £1,500 from Aaron Norden of Gold Square.[17]

The election itself took place on April 7, 1773, with balloting ending at six in the evening. The General Court, with Laurence Sulivan, Esq., deputy chairman, presiding, received the votes, which were to be counted and the results reported the next evening, a Thursday, at six. Hawkesworth barely achieved election, receiving only enough votes to finish twenty-third out of twenty-four directors chosen in spite of the influence of such men as Garrick. "You must know, my dear friend," Garrick wrote to the Abbé Morellet on April 9, 1773, "that the doctor is chosen an India director. We have all been at work for him, and his good character, with the good offices of his friends, have done the business. . . . His address now must be *To John Hawkesworth, Esq. at the India-House, Leaden Hall Street*, London."[18]

Hawkesworth was sworn in before Henry Crabb Boulton, Esq., and Frederick Pigou, Esq., on April 8, 1773, taking an oath prescribed by the charter of September 5, 1698; he secured appointment to three committees—House, Law Suits, and Preventing the Growth of Private Trade—the assignments made public in the *Lloyd's Evening Post and British Chronicle* for Monday, April 26, to Wednesday, April 28. Contrary to the general opinion that he rendered little service, the company's Court Book reveals Hawkesworth attended a number of meetings during 1773: although he missed meetings in June and July while he was out of London with Lord Sandwich, he attended thirty of the forty-two meetings held in

April, May, and August through October. His last recorded attendance was on Wednesday, November 3, 1773, only two weeks before his death. Hawkesworth himself wrote to a correspondent (identified only as "My dear Madam") in mid-1773 that he attended India House "almost every day from eleven to six," further evidence that he gave substantial service to the company during a hectic and controversial period of its history.[19]

Whatever satisfaction Hawkesworth gained from securing a directorship in a leading commercial enterprise of his time, a place of prominence that undoubtedly complemented his fame as compiler of Cook's *Voyages*, the year 1773 brought disaster. The rupture of his friendship with Garrick, a private and professional association that had flourished for years, would be only one, though perhaps the saddest, reverse Hawkesworth suffered.

Although Garrick's role in securing the *Voyages* contract for Hawkesworth was secondary to Burney's, he maintained an active interest in the work; among other activities, he became a liaison between Hawkesworth and the Abbé Morellet, who wished the *Voyages* translated into French. The French had their Bougainville as the English had their Cook, and both countries were fascinated with the South Sea reports filtering back to Europe. Garrick and the abbé corresponded during January 1773 about the matter of translating the *Voyages*; by April Morellet was deeply concerned about his failure to receive the necessary volumes, already having seen announcements of their publication. By late June, however, work was under way; and Jean Baptiste Antoine Suard, a friend of Garrick and Morellet who ultimately translated the work, wrote to Garrick on the twenty-fifth, "Nous traduisons à force le Voyage de Banks."[20]

Garrick's and Hawkesworth's friendship ruptured not over the mere matter of translation but over the more important one of money. William Strahan and Thomas Cadell gave Hawkesworth the enormous sum of £6,000 for the copyright to the *Voyages*, the largest payment of its kind during the whole of the century. It contrasts, for instance, with the £3,400 that William Robertson received for his *Charles V* a few years before, the £1,940 that Hume gained for the first two volumes of his *History*, and, significantly, with some £1,575 that Johnson received for the mighty *Dictionary* or the £100 for *Rasselas*. Few works testify better to the thorough commercialization eighteenth-century publishing had undergone than Hawkesworth's *Voyages*: it heralded all the best-sellers to come.[21]

For all its popularity, however—and the *Voyages* quickly appeared in a second edition—Strahan lamented his settlement with Hawkesworth. He was a shrewd businessman and attached himself to some of the most celebrated works of the century—*Roderick Random*, *Peregrine Pickle*, a volume of *Sir Charles Grandison*, part of *Tristram Shandy*, *The Man of Feeling*, and, in 1776, truly a miraculous year, *The Wealth of Nations* and *The Decline and Fall of the Roman Empire*. To him belonged as well Hawkesworth's

Voyages, but Dr. Johnson's printer cared far more for balanced ledgers than posterity's esteem. He complained to David Hume in a letter of April 9, 1774, of his overpayment for Hawkesworth's *Voyages*, "the event of which purchase," he writes, "if it does not cure Authors of their delirium, I am sure will have the proper effect upon booksellers."[22]

Strahan's was disappointment after the fact; the act of settlement itself infuriated Garrick, who thought his friend Thomas Becket should have been given the option to publish and felt betrayed when Hawkesworth settled with Strahan. Their correspondence during May 1773 reflects great strain, Garrick's bitterness, Hawkesworth's futile efforts at self-justification, and finally the dissolution of a friendship of decades' duration.

Hawkesworth's letter to Garrick on May 5, 1773, was apparently prompted by hearsay. "I am extreamly sorry to hear," he writes, "that I have incurred your Censure by the sale of my work, without submitting the conditions to Becket." He explains that after he had had applications from half the booksellers in London, none of whom offered more than five thousand pounds and no free copies, Strahan offered six thousand pounds and twenty-five free copies, worth more than an additional £75. Mindful, however, of Garrick's recommendation of Becket, Hawkesworth had suggested a fourth interest for Becket, which Strahan rejected. "Thus, you see," Hawkesworth continues, "my interest was *pitted* against Becket's: I supposed you would not wish that my Interest should be sacrificed to Becket's, and therefore I closed at once with Strahan's proposal." Becket, Hawkesworth explains, came later to India House and agreed that a fourth share at £1,500 was excessive. "Now, in the whole of this Affair," he concludes, "I think I have acted under the sense of friendship, and with the best return I could make to it, consistent with the regard which I supposed you to have in my Interest, which I never could imagine you meant to sacrifice to that of Becket in my own Affair." In a final effort to placate Garrick, Hawkesworth adds: "If you think otherwise, I am ready to make you any satisfaction in my power, no pecuniary Advantage being in my Estimation equivalent to acquitting the obligations of Friendship."[23]

Garrick would have none of Hawkesworth's protestations and on the next day, May 6, he recorded his displeasure. "He will not," he says of himself, "give ye Doctor the trouble, or himself again to enter into any further discussion of this very disagreeable business." Hawkesworth tried again on May 7 to amend things, pleading now that "notwithstanding the cold Expressions of your Note, I am once more desirous to subscribe myself, with cordiality and Friendship," but Garrick resisted all solicitations. Writing after May 7, 1773, he commented: "It may be the fault of my temper but I am so form'd, that when my Mind receives a Wound particularly from the hand of a friend, I cannot get it heal'd, so readily, as I could wish." The rupture of the friendship was final, and even the efforts of Mary Hawkesworth to repair it were unsuccessful. She wrote twice to Mrs. Garrick, on June 12 and 20, 1773, in the first letter explaining at some length the reasons her husband settled with Strahan and not with Becket, in the second describing the altercation merely as an unfortunate misunderstanding and acquitting "both parties of Intentional Wrong."[24]

Hawkesworth may not be blameless in the dispute, but his desire to settle at the greatest financial advantage is understandable. Garrick's apparent intransigence is more difficult to comprehend: at best, his role in securing Hawkesworth the *Voyages* contract was secondary to Burney's, and his championing of Becket is strange in light of the fact that in 1771 Becket partially stole Hawkesworth's thunder in the publication of the anonymous *Journal of a Voyage round the World.* Perhaps Garrick himself desired a financial return from the *Voyages* and saw such a hope dashed with Hawkesworth's settlement with Strahan. Whatever the truth of the matter, the £6,000 Hawkesworth received was tainted by the loss of a dear friend, and this was to be prelude to a larger pattern of catastrophe that would resolve itself in the months ahead in despair, sickness, and death. In contracting to write Cook's *Voyages*, Hawkesworth had unwittingly contracted for disaster.

While the sale of copyright lost Hawkesworth Garrick's friendship, his involvement in a protracted suit in Chancery damaged his reputation further. Hawkesworth was party to an attempt to frustrate the publication of a rival to the authorized *Voyages*, compiled by Stanfield Parkinson from the papers of his brother Sydney, Joseph Banks's botanical draughtsman, who failed to survive the *Endeavour* voyage. Stanfield and his sister received £500 from Joseph Banks for Sydney's effects and also to compensate his loss. While in temporary possession of his brother's papers, Stanfield transcribed them for publication, and his volume, prevented from publication by an injunction granted in January 1773, appeared after Hawkesworth's *Voyages* under the title *A Journal of A Voyage to the South Seas, in his Majesty's Ship, the Endeavour. Faithfully transcribed from the Papers of the late Sydney Parkinson* . . . .[25]

In retrospect the injunction frustrating the publication of Parkinson's rival text seems justified, compiled as it was by usurped documents, but appearances were against Hawkesworth and his supporters. They appeared to be a cabal of the rich and powerful suppressing material which was perhaps morally, if not legally, Parkinson's. The suit, like the rupture with Garrick, damaged Hawkesworth's reputation; although he undertook no public defense, he wrote at length about both issues to the correspondent identified only as "My dear Madam." "Mr. Garrick did not first recommend me to Lord Sandwich," he states, and adds, "I should have written the Book if there had been no such Man as Garrick in the World." Later he contends that he engaged Garrick to wait upon Sandwich in his absence, "which he did, and this is all the share he had in the transaction." Hawkesworth is faithful enough to the known facts, but he may underestimate the support, however secondary, Garrick provided. He also fails to recall that he had included Garrick among his potential supporters in the letter he wrote to Burney on September 18, 1773, quoted above.[26]

Concerning his role in the suit in Chancery to block the publication of Parkinson's *Journal* there is little reason to doubt his words. "As to Parkinson," he writes, "tho ye Suit is in my name, it is at Dr Fothergills expense, who by his affirmation [the Quaker's affidavit] alledges that the papers from which his Book is printed are Mr Bank's [*sic*] property that he saw them delivered to Mr Banks in consequence of the purchase & that Mr Banks afterwards lent them to Parkinson to read upon his [the Doc$^{tor's}$] answering for no improper use being made of them." Parkinson, Hawkesworth asserts, copied the papers and printed them. "This was surely justifiable cause for a Suit," Hawkesworth explains, "& as to my affidavit it is only that Banks executed a Bill of Sale to me of Parkinson's papers to make me plaintiff in the suit, & this fact, y^e *bill of sale* to which Mr Wallace's clerk, the Solicitor in ye Cause, is a subscribing witness proves to be true beyond the possibility of Cavil."[27]

Stanfield Parkinson's end was not to be a happy one; he was censured by his fellow Quakers, and finally drifted from frustration to madness itself. With Garrick and Parkinson, then, Hawkesworth found himself involved in delicate questions of property and propriety. While he appears after the fact to have been legally justified in all he did, he conducted himself less like the benign moralist of the *Adventurer* papers and more like a hardheaded businessman. A sensitive man, and one undoubtedly aware of these inconsistencies between his former preachments and present practices, he must have had occasion to reflect on the debilities that great wealth can bring a man of letters. Hawkesworth's disputes with Garrick and Parkinson merely hinted at worse things to come, for a furious controversy over the *Voyages* was soon to erupt. For a time, though, his labors completed, Hawkesworth found that people of position and eminence were as eager to receive the author of the *Voyages* as the public was the work itself.

In his *Literary and Miscellaneous Memoirs* Joseph Cradock shows that Hawkesworth enjoyed a busy social life before his *Voyages* were published in June 1773. During the spring of this year Cradock waited upon both Lord Clarendon and Lord Sandwich, finding at the latter's house an assemblage of "Admirals, Naval Officers, Naturalists, and Philosophers." Those who frequented Sandwich's table included Sir Richard Bickerton, Sir George Collyer, Mr. Owen Cambridge, Dr. Solander, Dr. Burney, Mr.

Bates, and Dr. Hawkesworth. "This was the frequent assemblage," Cradock writes and also notes that he "became intimate with Dr. Hawkesworth at Lord Sandwich's table at the Admiralty, where I constantly met him about the time of his publishing Cook's Voyages."[28]

It was not only with men of rank and influence that Hawkesworth kept company during this period, but also with old friends. James Beattie, in a *Diary* entry for May 19, 1773, wrote that he dined in the city (Breadstreet Hill) with Mr. Johnston, son-in-law to Mr. Strahan, along with Dr. and Mrs. Grant, the Hawkesworths, and Miss Kinnaird. "Dr. Hawkesworth appointed me to meet him tomorrow at the India-house in Leadenhall-street," Beattie continues, "as he wished to show me some part of the Book he is now publishing; particularly a dissertation on Providence."[29] Beattie missed the proposed meeting with Hawkesworth, however, in favor of one with Lord Mansfield; in so doing he denied himself a private reading of what was to become one of the most controversial sections in the *Voyages*.

By late spring Hawkesworth's work neared publication. An advertisement in the *Public Ledger* for Monday, May 3, 1773, announced that the *Voyages* would be published "during the course of this month," and a note states, "This work would have been published last Month, pursuant to a former Advertisement, if it had not been impossible to get the Engravings finished." Lord Sandwich, writing to Garrick from the Admiralty on April 6, 1773, confirmed that efforts were made to publish the book sometime in April and alluded to the problem that prevented publication: "Dr. Hawkesworth will be ready by the end of this month unless delayed by Mr. Rooker."[30] But Rooker, the engraver, apparently did delay, and it was not until Wednesday, June 9, 1773, that the quartos appeared. There is no indication Hawkesworth awaited any response but the applause of a pleased populace, no sign that within days his reputation would begin eroding as public clamor grew over the book's perceived shortcomings. If ever a writer could be said to be at career's peak, it was John Hawkesworth during June 1773—his masterwork was published, his name linked with national heroes, his fortune secured through Strahan's bountiful payment. He left London to accompany his patron, Lord Sandwich, on board the yacht *Augusta* to inspect the dockyards at Portsmouth, in company with the rich and powerful, and finally to meet the king himself.

Details of the king's visit to Portsmouth, Sandwich's peregrination, and, on occasion, the activities of Hawkesworth himself, appeared in the papers during June 1773. The *Morning Chronicle* for Monday, June 28, 1773 reported: "Doctor Hawkesworth was observed, on Tuesday last [June 22] to get out of a coach, in company with Sir George Warren, in the High Street of Portsmouth." But the column reflects the scorn Hawkesworth received from all quarters. "Quere," it continues, "Did this fortunate stringer together of written events go to Portsmouth at the government's expense, to take an account of every occurrence at the sea review; and will he be as well paid for a history of fire and smoke, as he has been for a compilation which turns out to be all smoke and no fire?" The *London Evening-Post* for July 1–3 fixed Hawkesworth's whereabouts in an "Extract of a letter from Gosport" dated June 29, 1773, which stated, "Lord Sandwich and the yachts are out pleasuring round the Isle of Wight, from which they are to go to Plymouth to view the dock, &c. and then return home."

One can imagine Hawkesworth's pleasure in keeping company with men of rank. Joseph Cradock provides a brief portrait of his association with Sandwich and his party.

> When Lord Sandwich was about to embark at Portsmouth, with Sir Joseph Banks, Dr. Solander, and a very large party of friends, the Doctor was invited to accompany them, and was not a little gratified by the compliment that was paid him; but when his Lordship mentioned something of a *cork-wig*, the Doctor was all astonishment. "A cork-wig! my Lord; I have never heard of such a thing." "Oh, yes," says Lord Sandwich, "always on these little water excursions we put on our cork-wigs, and I have ordered one to be prepared for you." The Doctor paused, looked very grave, and at last recollected an engagement that would absolutely prevent him from having the honour of attending his Lordship. However, finding that no excuse would be accepted, he at last submitted to the punishment. The Doctor, however, finding the laugh to run against him, was resolved to retaliate. When on board, and at leisure, he tried to turn the tables upon them, if possible. The Esquimaux Indians had lately been in England, and he determined to write a ludicrous voyage in character of one of them. This proved to be very witty, and was most highly relished and complimented by Lord Sandwich and all the party.

The sketch that Hawkesworth composed in good-natured retaliation for the bantering he endured has not survived, but Cradock recollected something that Lord Sandwich quoted "as highly characteristic." An Eskimo failed to respond to a whole gallery of English beauties but did so to another of nature's marvels—the sun painted "in full splendour, and of great magnitude, on a sign-post."[31]

The episode Cradock preserves probably reflects Hawkesworth in a characteristic light during these days. While part of the Sandwich party, he was not one of them, and perhaps a bit uneasy in their presence. Still, he held his own, as one might expect from a man whose friends included Garrick, Franklin, and Johnson. For all that the First Lord of the Admiralty highlighted Hawkesworth's social insecurity, he did not do so out of maliciousness, and Hawkesworth skillfully parried Sandwich's teasing.

Sandwich, in fact, probably introduced Hawkesworth to the king, whose presence generated great excitement in Portsmouth in late June.

The *Public Advertiser* for June 25, 1773, reported his visit in detail:

> As soon as the King came to Portsmouth, the Town was put under Military Discipline; the Walls were shut, and Persons on Horseback, in Carriages, or on Foot, were denied a Passage through Lamport Gates to the Common. . . . Many of the Nobility and Persons of the first Fashion are here, among others Lord North, Lord Sandwich, Lord Dartmouth, and Dukes of Devonshire, Leinster, Chandos, and Richmond. . . . The Water is now crowded with Vessels of every Size and Dimension; the Sight is beyond Expression beautiful; the King is now going on Board the Barfleur. At Night the whole Town will be illuminated.

The Osborn sketch at Yale alone provides the information that Hawkesworth met his sovereign. "He was introduced to the King at Portsmouth" is the extent of the comment,[32] but the meeting certainly took place. According to a letter written from Portsmouth on June 23 and published in the *Public Advertiser* from June 25, the king went on board "the Augusta Yacht, and sailed into the Harbour, accompanied by the William and Mary Fubbs, with an incredible Number of Pleasure Boats and Spectators." The *St. James's Chronicle* for June 29 reported that the king was also on board the Augusta on June 25. On either of these occasions Hawkesworth could have been introduced to him. Such an introduction would have been appropriate, bringing together the man whose government supported the great explorations of Byron, Wallis, Carteret, and Cook and the man who recorded them. No account of their conversation exists, but Hawkesworth's felicitous dedication to the king in his *Voyages* captures the spirit, perhaps, if not the substance, of the comments he might have made to George III:

> After the great improvements that have been made in Navigation since the discovery of America, it may well be thought strange that a very considerable part of the globe on which we live should still have remained unknown; that it should still have been the subject of speculation, whether a great portion of the Southern Hemisphere is land or water; and, even where land had been discovered, that neither its extent nor figure should have been ascertained. . . . Your Majesty has, not with a view to the acquisition of treasure, or the extent of dominion, but the improvement of commerce and the increase and diffusion of knowledge, undertaken what has so long been neglected; and under Your Majesty's auspices, in little more than seven years, discoveries have been made far greater than those of all the navigators in the world

collectively, from the expedition of Columbus to the present time.

To have been appointed to record them, and permitted to inscribe the narrative to Your Majesty, is an honour, the sense of which will always be retained [by me] with the warmest gratitude. . . ." (Hawkesworth's *Voyages*, 1:n.p.)

Leaving the king, Lord Sandwich, and the distinguished company on the *Augusta*, Hawkesworth returned to London to pursue his varied affairs, attending on Wednesday, July 21, a directors' meeting at the East India Company. He probably did not know at the time that he had returned to disaster, that during the next several months he and his *Voyages* would be at the center of an intense controversy. He would suffer criticism by people of note, condemnation by nautical experts, and censure by the sea captains themselves. Worse, perhaps, he would be hounded and defamed almost daily in the papers by legions of anonymous correspondents who searched his volumes for assorted violations, particularly of taste, morality, and religion. The latter attacks are preserved in the newspaper files of the Burney collection in the British Library. History is not without its unconscious ironies.

Horace Walpole complained unceasingly about the *Voyages* during the summer of 1773, unable, even, to reserve criticism until the volumes were published. Writing to the Reverend William Mason from Strawberry Hill on May 15, 1773, he commented: "So much for what we *have* been reading; at present our ears listen and our eyes are expecting East Indian affairs, and Mr Banks's voyage, for which Dr Hawksworth has received *d'advance* one thousand pounds from the voyager, and six thousand from the booksellers, Strahan and Co., who will take due care that we shall read nothing else till they meet with such another pennyworth." More grumbling followed when the volumes appeared and Walpole began his weary trek through the large pages. To Mason he commented again on June 28: "We have nothing new but what is as old as Paul's—the *Voyages* to the South Sea. The Admiralty have dragged the whole ocean, and caught nothing but the fry of ungrown islands, which had slipped through the meshes of the Spaniard's net." He continued to fume, noting that the voyagers "fetched blood of a great whale called Terra Australis incognita, but saw nothing but its tail. However Lord Sandwich has given great ocean's King a taste for salt water, and we are to conquer the Atlantic, or let the sea into Richmond garden, I forget which." In July Walpole's agonies were at an end. On the fifth he informed Mason, "I have almost waded through Dr. Hawkesworth's three volumes of the voyages to the South Sea. The entertaining matter would not fill half a volume; and at best is but an account of the fishermen on the coasts of forty islands." Such was his exasperation with the text that he apparently extracted a promise from Madame Du Deffand never to read the book. "Je vous promets de ne point lire les trois volumes de voyages" she wrote to Walpole on July 14, 1773.[33]

Perhaps Walpole wished to spare Madame Du Deffand not so much the dullness of the text but those salacious passages and possible theological heresies that riveted public attention, especially that of the ladies and the clergy. Mrs. Elizabeth Montagu, writing to her sister on June 20, 1773, alluded to these problems, though with a good deal more sense than many of her contemporaries:

> I daresay you have been well entertaind by Bankes's Voyage etc, tho poor Hawkesworth is so abused in every paper. I do not approve what he has said concerning Providence in his Introduction, but I cannot enter into the prudery of the Ladies, who are afraid to own they have read the Voyages, and less still into the moral delicacy of those who suppose the effronterie of the Demoiselles of Ottaheité will corrupt our Misses; if the girls had invented a surer way to keep intrigues secret, it might have been dangerous, but their publick amours will not be imitated.[34]

Such objectivity was rare, however, and the views of Mrs. Montagu's friend, Mrs. Elizabeth Carter, typify the attitudes of many. At first her comments to Mrs. Montagu were mild; on June 19, 1773, she noted that she was sorry to find that Hawkesworth had "departed in any instance from the tendency of his former writings." On July 20, however, she stated: "I am very sorry to find that this last performance is so unworthy of him. I have not seen it, and certainly never shall have the least curiosity to read it from the accounts that you, and some of my other friends, have given me of it." By August 14, still not having read the book, she joined the general condemnation: "The very wrong tendency of the preface, . . . and the scandalous indecency of some parts of the book, have raised my indignation, and entirely prevented my feeling any curiosity about it." She continued in her righteous vein: "It gives one pleasure to find that this nation has still virtue enough left to be shocked and disgusted by an attack upon religion, and an outrage against decency, such as Dr. Hawkesworth's last performance, which I find is most universally disliked."[35]

Thus, for one reader—and undoubtedly for many more—the *Voyages* were tried and condemned by hearsay alone. Tahitian maidens, Hawkesworth found to his sorrow, were no match for English bluestockings: morality, at least as the bluestockings perceived it, prevailed. Not surprisingly, they received strong support from the clergy itself, especially in the person of John Wesley, who took strong exception to the apparent indecencies of the text. He recorded in his journal for December 17, 1773:

"Meeting with a celebrated book, a volume of Captain Cook's *Voyages*, I sat down to read it with huge expectation." Wesley, however, scanned Hawkesworth's pages with equivalent measures of disbelief and moral disapproval, especially the latter. "Men and women coupling together in the face of the sun, and in the sight of scores of people!" he wrote in shock. While Wesley tended to mirror contemporary bluestocking outrage in his journal, other writers, such as William Cowper and Johnson, supported Walpole's skepticism about the value of South Sea exploration. Of Walpole, in fact, J. C. Beaglehole writes with some justice: "If ever a man was predestined to misunderstand, and undervalue, such a book as this [the *Voyages*], it was Horace Walpole; not all the efforts of polite literature could, one feels, have made a sufficient bridge between Tahiti or Queen Charlotte's Sound and Strawberry Hill. The smell of tar and coconut oil would always have been disagreeable." Writing to the Reverend John Newton, Cowper concluded rather sourly: "The principal fruits of these circuits, that have been made around the globe, seem likely to be the amusement of those that stayed at home."[36]

Boswell's *Life of Johnson* is flavored on a number of occasions with talk of the recent ventures to the South Seas. Johnson was no champion of the primitive life, resisting all Boswell's persuasions on the subject. One assumes that the young Scotsman, ever with an eye for the ladies, read Hawkesworth's account of Tahiti with more than academic interest.

On Friday, May 7, 1773, about a month before the *Voyages* appeared, Johnson, Boswell, Goldsmith, and others dined with Edward and Charles Dilly, booksellers in the Poultry. Of this gathering Boswell writes in part:

> Hawkesworth's compilation of the voyages to the South Sea being mentioned;—JOHNSON. 'Sir, if you talk of it as a subject of commerce, it will be gainful; if as a book that is to increase human knowledge, I believe there will not be much of that. Hawkesworth can tell only what the voyagers have told him; and they have found very little, only one new animal, I think.' BOSWELL. 'But many insects, Sir.' JOHNSON. 'Why, Sir, as to insects, Ray reckons of British insects twenty thousand species. They might have staid at home and discovered enough in that way.'

The subject was almost an ideal one to test Johnson, especially as it brought him, almost the quintessence of urban man, in confrontation with the supposed values of primitive life. Johnson clearly preferred civilization's artifices.

> BOSWELL. 'I am well assured that the people of Otaheite who have the bread tree, the fruit of which serves them for bread, laughed heartily

when they were informed of the tedious process necessary with us to have bread;—plowing, sowing, harrowing, reaping, threshing, grinding, baking.' JOHNSON. 'Why, Sir, all ignorant savages will laugh when they are told of the advantages of civilized life. Were you to tell men who live without houses, how we pile brick upon brick, and rafter upon rafter, and that after a house is raised to a certain height, a man tumbles off a scaffold, and breaks his neck, he would laugh heartily at our folly in building; but it does not follow that men are better without houses. No, Sir, (holding up a slice of a good loaf,) this is better than the bread tree.'

"I refute it *thus*." So with breadfruit, as with Bishop Berkeley, the pragmatic Johnson emerges, equally disdainful of metaphysics and South Sea manners.[37]

While severe critiques of Hawkesworth's *Voyages* appeared in the private correspondence and journals of people of note, and his volumes were the subject of astringent conversation in the Johnson circle, Hawkesworth also endured public abuse, particularly in Alexander Dalrymple's impassioned pamphlet entitled *A Letter from Mr. Dalrymple to Dr. Hawkesworth, Occasioned by Some Groundless and Illiberal Imputations in his Account of the Late Voyages to the South*, dated Soho-Square, June 22, 1773. Dalrymple's heavily italicized attack is so furious—no aspect of the book escapes his wrath—that it might appear to be the work of a crank. But Dalrymple, hydrographer to the East India Company and later first hydrographer to the Admiralty, was no crank. He, instead of Cook, might have led the *Endeavour* expedition if the Admiralty had not insisted on a naval officer, and it galled him to see the captains' journals converted into a profitable best seller by a mere man of letters. Undoubtedly many of Dalrymple's arguments have merit—complaints, for example, about obvious discrepancies between the charts and the narrative in the *Voyages*. Unfortunately, he expends space and energy in attacking Hawkesworth for the supposed theological errors of his General Introduction—for his "Providential heresy" already cited by Mrs. Carter and Mrs. Montagu—and he doggedly defends his belief in the existence of a southern continent, a myth put to rest by the *Endeavour* voyage itself.

The man in a position, then, to make a serious assessment of the worth of the *Voyages* misdirected his energies and left himself exposed to a counterattack by Hawkesworth in his Preface (unpaginated) to a second edition of the work dated August 2, 1773. This was Hawkesworth's only published reply to his critics, and at this time, refreshed, probably, by his recent travels with Lord Sandwich, he was calm and even jocular about this assault. Dalrymple's fixation on the southern continent, Hawkesworth finds, reminds him of an old woman who visited his grandmother whose mind had been turned by having been almost all her life at law. "I cannot but impute the illiberal turn of Mr. Dalrymple's Letter to a similar cause," Hawkesworth comments. "He is as sore upon the subject of the southern continent as the old woman was upon that of the law." Sarcastically he concludes: "I am very sorry for the discontented state of this good Gentleman's mind, and most sincerely wish that a southern continent may be found, as I am confident nothing else can make him happy and good-humoured."

Hawkesworth's words produced no good humor in Dalrymple and drove him into real silliness in a subsequent attack in *Mr. Dalrymple's Observations on Dr. Hawkesworth's Preface to the Second Edition*, dated September 18, 1773. At one point he writes, "The only time I ever was in his company Dr. Hawkesworth, intending to pay Mr. Banks a compliment, failed miserably in his attempt." This is not the sort of material that breeds confidence in Dalrymple's assessment of the *Voyages*, but objections he raises are not to be discounted, especially one that casts doubt on the textual authenticity of Hawkesworth's edition. "The Gentlemen whose *acquiescence* he plumes himself upon," Dalrymple writes in reference to the captains themselves, "may be induced to let this Book pass without any notice from various motives, but every man who has had any conversation with them, must be satisfied their silence cannot be construed into an *acquiescence* of the *justness* of all the *sentiments* the Doctor has published." And Dalrymple questions "if the *manuscript* they *saw* is *exactly* the same with what *he* has *published?*"[38]

Dalrymple was not alone in raising this question. It was of special concern to a young German bookseller named Spener, who wished to publish a translation of the *Voyages* by John Frederick Schiller. On November 14, 1773, Schiller wrote to Joseph Banks that an eminent mineralogist, a Mr. Ferber, returned to Berlin from England to assert

> That not only the respective Commanders, Mess[rs]. Byron, Wallis, Carteret &c. had publicly protested against D[r]. H's account of their voyages, as containing misrepresented facts, but also that especially Mess[rs]. Banks and Solander, had publicly declared that they had never delivered any papers of their's into that Editor's hands, and that the Public was to wait for their own Narrative, which was to be published within 3 or 4 Years.

Speaking apparently for Spener, who as the seller of the translation needed assurance of its authenticity, Schiller continued:

> Since it is notorious that D[r]. H's work has been published for national purposes under the sanction of the Admiralty and of [the] Government

as being accurately authenticated by the repeated evidence and approbation of all the chief persons concerned in it; and since amidst all the
paroxisms of envy and malevolence, not one of all the numerous crew
by whom that work has been slandered and plundered by turns, has to
my Knowledge hitherto dared to question the authenticity of any one
single fact contained in it; I am sensible, that any additional written
private evidence, however respectable, would probably be considered
here as superfluous and indecent.[39]

The authenticity of the text of the *Voyages* was, in spite of Schiller's
attempt to downplay the issue, much in question, and not merely by
translators but by two of the captains, Carteret and Cook himself. Not only
did Carteret leave two lists citing his specific objections to Hawkesworth's
text, but he felt that his editor had so corrupted his materials that he
prepared a new version, finally published in 1965. His condemnation of
Hawkesworth is blunt:

When a Man's Voyage is printed not only in his Lifetime but also to his
Face & in the place where he is resident, it must certainly be imagined
that there is nothing either omitted or added by the publisher that is
contrary to the will or desire of the writer, and that the whole is strictly
true & well warranted by the original manuscript given into his Hands;
But . . . this is unfortunately not the Case with respect to an account of
a voyage I made round the globe in his majesty's Ship the Swallow
which has been lately given to the publick by the late D^r. H.[40]

Cook's complaints about Hawkesworth's *Voyages* were somewhat restrained, but it is clear he felt unfairly reported. During his visit to St.
Helena in May 1775, Cook wrote in his journal in reference to the *Voyages*,
"I never had the perusal of the Manuscript nor did I ever hear the whole of it
read in the mode it was written, notwithstanding what Dr Hawkesworth
has said to the Contrary in the Interduction." Boswell reports Cook's
further dissatisfaction with the official text. On April 2, 1776, he had dined
with the famed captain and a large company at Sir John Pringle's, observing
Cook to be "a grave steady man, and his wife, a decent plump English-
woman." Cook, Boswell observes, "said Hawkesworth made in his book a
general conclusion from a particular fact, and would take as a fact what they
had only heard. He said it was not true that Mr. Banks and he had revised all
the book; and in what was revised Hawkesworth would make no alteration
(I think he said this too)." Cook also claimed that "a disregard of chastity in
unmarried women was by no means general at Otaheite, and he said
Hawkesworth's story of an *initiation* he had no reason to believe." Hawkesworth, Boswell said to Cook, "has used your narrative as a London tavern
keeper does wine. He has *brewed* it."[41]

Although Hawkesworth suffered attacks by people of note—Johnson and Walpole—and censure from bluestockings as well as naval experts, including two of the captains themselves, his worst trial came from a host of defamers in the press. Connoisseurs of the literature of abuse would be richly rewarded by a perusal of the London papers during the summer of 1773, when anonymous correspondents savaged Hawkesworth in what might be termed collectively "The Great Voyage Controversy of 1773." Critics, in fact, did not wait until the *Voyages* were published. As early as May 15, 1773, "Candour" castigated Hawkesworth in the *Morning Chronicle* for excessive financial gain. "Common fame," he complains to Hawkesworth, "says you have disposed of *your compilation* for the enormous sum of six thousand pounds. Pray, Sir, with what face could you make such a demand upon your Printer, or what infatuation seized him to comply with your extortionate demands?" Few aspects of Hawkesworth's involvement with the *Voyages* escaped public notice; while many complained of his unreasonable financial reward, at least one made public reference to his part in the lawsuit against Stanfield Parkinson. "A Friend to the Injured" berated Hawkesworth in the *Public Advertiser* for June 5, 1773, the heat of his opening comment sustained throughout his attack. "The specious Gloss with which you attempt to varnish over the grossest Duplicity extorts from me this Address," he asserts. "Going to Lincoln's-inn-hall on Friday last, prepossessed very highly in your Favour, it was with equal Surprize and Indignation I learned from the Pleadings in Court that the Injunction you had obtained to stop the Publication of Sydney Parkinson's Journal of the Voyage of the ship Endeavour was granted on a most groundless Application."

It was on June 14, however, that one of Hawkesworth's severest critics, one signing himself "A Christian," opened up an attack in the pages of the *Public Advertiser*, which would last, words apparently without end, until August 28.[42] His subject would be Hawkesworth's controversial comments on Providence in his General Introduction. In retrospect, whatever following he had at the time, "A Christian" emerges as one of those dedicated believers who cause one to loathe, not the faith, but the faithful. Rarely during the Age of Johnson was religious orthodoxy so badly served, and for weeks Hawkesworth endured this man's religious frenzies. "A Christian" writes constantly on the stretch, his prose tense with the spirit of the Inquisition. In contending with Hawkesworth's offending Providential passage he contests not with error so much as with sin itself, and Dr. Hawkesworth becomes its chief purveyor. Here is a sample of his righteous wrath in the June 15 issue:

Your Adventurers, your Almoran and Hamet, and other Works prove you to be a Man of Religion and Virtue; and consequently this Sentiment [Hawkesworth's Providential heresy] (which I am willing to hope you have heedlessly published) may do more Mischief than could have been occasioned by the most immoral Productions of the most abandoned Writers—for where the Authors are known to be irreligious and vicious, their Writings are read with Caution,—Poison is expected to be found in every Leaf, and it's Venom by being apprehended—finds no Admittance within the Heart.

Attacks multiplied during the summer and Hawkesworth could not have examined a paper without risk of seeing himself defamed. "Bossu" in the *St. James's Chronicle* for June 17 lamented "that a Work which would have nobly employed the sublime Genius of a Montesquieu should have been committed to the trim, limited Talents of a Moral Essayist." A correspondent signing himself "A.B." in the *Public Advertiser* for June 21 joined the many who attacked Hawkesworth for his views on Providence. "People in high Rank, as well as others, have blamed you for it," he remarks and submits as proof of Hawkesworth's error, verses from the Book of Common Prayer. "A Patagonian" in the *Morning Chronicle* for June 19 excoriated Hawkesworth for a variety of offenses and added a heated postscript: "Having dispatched your *dedication*," he states, "I shall, in a future letter, consider your general *introduction* and then your *particular* one to the voyage of the ship Endeavour, from the contents of both which, it appears that your religious principles are as inconsistent as your moral practice, and that neither of them are a whit more defensible than your pretensions to science and literature."

While a variety of anonymous defamers came and went in the pages of the papers during the summer, "A Christian" remained, the faith's staunch defender when weaker guardians pursued other interests. He attacked Hawkesworth again on July 3 in the *Public Advertiser* for promulgating a doctrine "diametrically opposed to the Religion of Christ," charged that he had also taken pains *"to debauch the Morals of our Youth at home,"* and, in a crescendo of moral fervor, exclaimed that

> our Women may find in *Dr. Hawkesworth's Book* stronger Excitements to vicious Indulgences than the most intriguing French Novel could present to their Imaginations—and while our Mariners no longer look up to the Almighty for Deliverance from Shipwreck—or feel Gratitude rise in their Breasts on being saved from impending Evils—our Libertines may throw aside the *Woman of Pleasure*, and gratify their impure Minds with the Perusal of infinitely more lascivious Recitals than are to be found in that scandalous Performance!

And on it goes, words and abuse without end—not alone from "A

Christian," but from numerous other correspondents, among them "A Thinking Woman," who echoed Elizabeth Carter in writing in the *St. James's Chronicle* for July 17, 1773, that she had once found a Johnson and a Hawkesworth "sufficient against a whole Army of modern Freethinkers, and half-fledged Deists." But Hawkesworth, she observes, has fallen from purity to profanity. "Ask your heart, Dr. H——th," she cries, "what possible good can such wanton and loose Representations do in an Age already too much corrupted?" Questions continue to cascade from her pen: "And shall *you* give these Accounts? Shall *you*, the supposed Friend of Virtue, be the insidious Underminer of it; and do all in your Power, under the hypocritical Sanction of a favourite Name, to pollute more Minds, of Youth especially, than the most profest of Libertines?"

On the same date came yet another attack from "A Christian," again in the columns of the *Public Advertiser*, again hot with italics and vituperation. He asserted that "it would be highly criminal to remain silent when a *Dr. Hawkesworth* makes an *open* Profession of a Sentiment, *the favourite Theme of Bolingbroke and Hume!*" and, he continued, "we must dread the pernicious Influence of the Contagion which *you* have wantonly scattered abroad among the People." He lamented that the author of the pious *Adventurer* had so degenerated: "*Who* can possibly turn over the delightful Pages of the Adventurer, and not feelingly regret the Defection of a Man who had *once* painted Religion in Colours so lively, beautiful, and attractive, that even the most dissolute were surprised into an Admiration of the Ways of Virtue,— and Instruction, under the Semblance of Pleasure, pointed out the Road to Happiness!" This was not "A Christian's" last response to Hawkesworth, but it will be his final one here. He alone would have been a sufficient load for Hawkesworth to bear, but sadly there were many others eager in the name of virtue and morality to whip him into repentance or, perhaps, insensibility. One can conclude with the condemnation of "A Believer in the Particular as well as the General Providence of God," writing in the *Public Advertiser* for July 2, 1773, who presented a distillation of the anger generated by the *Voyages*. He writes: "You are *lawful Game*, and ought to be *hunted* by every Friend of Virtue. You have verified the Maxim, that, those who are destitute of the fundamental Principles of Religion and Morality, will grasp at Gold with Avidity, though it cannot be seized without Injustice."

This, then, is a sample of the abuse Hawkesworth suffered in the papers during the summer of 1773.[43] Such was his trial by public opinion, though these few citations scarcely convey the weight and extent of the assault. In spite of these heavy attacks, he might have taken some comfort from the few correspondents who wrote in his behalf. These were, apparently, friends as well as those who continued to respect him and his work, though both found it the better part of discretion to sign their contributions with initials or pseudonyms. As early as June 22 "J.H." in the *Public Advertiser* came to the defense of the *Voyages* and its author. He sees the *Voyages* as presenting the record of an impressive national achievement, a demonstration of the vigor and accomplishment of a great people, which, if it did not guarantee future commercial benefits, revealed a benign penetration of European influence into island civilizations. Of Hawkesworth he writes, in a second letter on the twenty-fifth, "I need say little to you about Dr. Hawkesworth's Part of the Performance, as *you* expect nothing mediocre from his Pen; he has exceeded even *my* Expectation."

"L.O." in the same paper for July 6 provided a strong personal defense of Hawkesworth, a writer who has, he suggests, "given Dignity to Truth, and added Elegance to Virtue." In his company L.O. has found "the Researches of Sense, the Brilliancy of Wit, and the Blandishments of Good-humour, without finding my Mind polluted by Vice, or distracted by Sophistry." L.O.'s words of support were a prelude to an equally strong defense in the *Public Advertiser* for July 7 by "Atticus alter," who confessed that he was "utterly at a Loss to discover a rational Motive for the Torrent of Abuse which has been so illiberally poured out upon that excellent Writer." He defends the text: "The Countries discovered are described with the greatest Care and Precision; the Manners of the People are delineated with the strictest Justice, and accurate Charts are given of every maritime Particular that can be useful to our Navigators in future Expeditions—yet our Critics are not satisfied." He defends as well the book's price, pointing out to the outraged that large quarto works even without cuts sell at a guinea a volume. Finally, he defends Hawkesworth's profit: "The Employment was as honourable as it was advantageous, and the meanest Son of Grub-street is mortified because it was not bestowed on himself."

Perhaps the most eloquent vindication of Hawkesworth was that submitted (once again) by "L.O.," who wrote in the *Public Advertiser* for July 13 with virtual Johnsonian tone:

> If a Life passed in repeated and successful Endeavours to apply uncommon Talents to the Instruction and Entertainment of others, with small private Advantage, and with unspotted Integrity, may become in its latter Days the Sport of Newspaper Paragraphs and scurrilous Letters without Names; if the fair Fame of successive Years can be thus impeached, can be thus extinguished by Evidence such as has been exhibited against Dr. Hawkesworth, let Virtue hide her Face, let Merit remain in Obscurity, their Presence can only afford us Trouble, and their Fate bring us Reproach.

Whatever comfort Hawkesworth might have gained from such support, he could not ignore the fact that the papers mirrored, perhaps as no other source, the great public dissatisfaction with his *Voyages*. He was to live out his last months in a poisoned atmosphere, his reputation damaged beyond repair at least in his lifetime. The controversy in the papers would end not because of the defenses of his supporters but more out of exhaustion of all parties concerned. "A Detestor of Dullness, though no Friend to wretched Journalists" revealed in a letter to the *Public Advertiser* for August 5, 1773, that even the most dedicated consumer of the literature of abuse could become cloyed by the attacks and counterattacks generated by the *Voyages*. "I wish you would dismiss Hawkesworth and his long- winded Commentator, who signs himself A CHRISTIAN," he urges. "The Critic fits, it is true, the Author; but I see no Reason why your Paper, Time out of Mind the Vehicle of Wit and Humour, should be converted into an Opiate to your Readers, merely to please a dull Methodist, who writes neither with the Elegance of a Scholar nor the Manners of a good Christian." And "Fog" in the same paper for September 1 rejoiced at the departure of "Christian." "Good Night to you, Mr. Long-wind! And a pretty putrid blast you have been. You smell rank of an Irish Bog. Had the *Endeavour* felt such in her flagging Sails, she, in spite of *your* Providence, had gone to the Bottom." To Hawkesworth he writes, "Farewell also, you Bromley graduate! Had you been guilty of no Sin against Religion, but your having given Being to this abominable *Christian*, you ought to be d——n'd."

Hawkesworth's volumes, then, were subjected to endless criticism both in public and private, and his text cited for a variety of offenses, from the excesses of his dedication to the king to the excesses of the book's price (three guineas). Whatever the range of supposed faults, three commanded greatest attention: Hawkesworth's unorthodox views on Providence, the moral tone of the edition, and the reliability and authenticity of the text. Of the three the last question is probably of greatest interest to modern students of Hawkesworth and Cook, though the other two provide useful angles of vision on the mind and temper of the age in the crucial areas of belief and conduct.

Few aspects of the *Voyages* generated as much controversy as Hawkesworth's "Providential heresy"—his refusal to admit the possibility that divine intervention saved Cook and his crew in times of impending disaster. It was this view, discussed at some length in his General Introduction to the *Voyages*, that caused objections from Mrs. Montagu and Elizabeth Carter in private correspondence as well as the fulminations of "A Christian" in the columns of the *Public Advertiser*. Who would have expected from the sober moralist of the *Adventurer* and *Almoran and Hamet* the unorthodoxies that begin, quite suddenly in the General Introduction, with Hawkesworth's request for the "right of private judgment" in "not having attributed any of the critical escapes from danger that I have recorded, to the particular interposition of Providence" (Hawkesworth's *Voyages*, 1:xix). Certainly "A Christian" and other believers fell upon such words and read with increasing vexation worse ones to come. Having followed, at least vicariously, Cook and the other brave captains over the globe's great oceans, Hawkesworth apparently had little trepidation about entering dangerous theological waters.

Hawkesworth's view is no more than that God manifests His presence in the world continually—that good and evil are distinctions man makes and are not inherent in the system of things. "If the fall of a sparrow, as well as its preservation, is imputed to providence," he writes, "why not the fall as well as the preservation of a man? and why should we attribute to Providence only what appears to be good in its immediate effect, when we suppose that the whole concatenation of events, whether the preservation or destruction of particular parts, tends ultimately to the good of the whole?" Such thinking, Hawkesworth contends, "derogates from the honour of the great Universal Cause, who, acting through all duration, and subsisting in all space, fills immensity with his presence, and eternity with his power" (1:xx).

Arguments like these were probably damaging enough in the abstract, but when applied to a specific episode, Cook's miraculous escape from certain destruction off the coast of New Holland, too much was too much. Here are Hawkesworth's offending lines:

> It is true that when the Endeavour was upon the rock off the coast of New Holland, the wind ceased, and that otherwise she must have been beaten to pieces; but either the subsiding of the wind was a mere natural event or not; if it was a natural event, providence is out of the question, at least we can with no more propriety say that providentially the wind ceased, than that providentially the sun rose in the morning. If it was not a mere natural event, but produced by an extraordinary interposition, correcting a defect in the constitution of nature, tending to mischief, it will lie upon those who maintain the position, to shew, why an extraordinary interposition did not take place to prevent the ship's striking, than to prevent her being beaten to pieces after she had struck. (1:xxi)

In substance Hawkesworth's words mirror the deistic convictions of such solidly representative figures of the period as Pope and Franklin, the former his favorite poet, the latter one of his closest friends. In fact, though, he offended the sensibilities of many in the age, and it is through their response that one realizes that generalizations about the thinking of a period on matters so profound are risky.

On September 20, 1773, Elizabeth Carter wrote to Mrs. Montagu: "Your account of your dear nephew's accident quite made me shudder. What a providential escape, that the sweet boy did not lose his eye. The philosophical Dr. Hawkesworth, if what I have heard of his system is fairly represented, would gravely argue, that if Providence had any thing to do with it, the penknife had never come near the eye." Several years after the initial furor, Hawkesworth's providential heresy continued to rankle. The Reverend Dr. Porteus, writing to Dr. James Beattie on January 11, 1776, commented: "I congratulate you, and Mrs. Beattie, most cordially, on the many dangers you have escaped, since we saw you, both in your own persons, and that of your little boy. Your escape from the precipice, where your chaise was overturned, was really next to miraculous." The event, he argues, "affords a strong argument in favour of a particular providence, and might very well be opposed to all the profound reasoning of Dr. Hawkesworth against it."[44]

More immediately, Hawkesworth's providential assertions surfaced in Boswell and Johnson's tour of the Hebrides when the two endured a fearsome storm off the Isle of Skye. On Saturday, October 16, 1773, readers of the *St. James's Chronicle* received a humorous reference to the event that occurred on the third of the month. A correspondent wrote that Hawkesworth, hearing "that his old acquaintance Dr. Johnson was confined by tempestuous weather to the Island of Sky, and how unsafe it was to venture to Sea in a small Boat, cried, I know my Friend's Danger very well, and if he ventures from Shore, nothing but a *particular Providence* can save him." But to Boswell the subject was humorless. Having endured the storm's fury, not to mention the fear of fire on board, "and the perpetual talking, or rather shouting, which was carried on in Erse," he observed that piety afforded him comfort:

> Yet I was disturbed by the objections that have been made against a particular providence, and by the arguments of those who maintain that it is in vain to hope that the petitions of the individual, or even of congregations, can have any influence with the Deity; objections which have been often made, and which Dr. Hawkesworth has lately revived in his Preface to the Voyages to the South Seas; but Dr. Ogden's excellent doctrine on the efficacy of intercession prevailed.

Johnson, who Boswell reports, "was quite in a state of annihilation," rode out the storm unconcerned, it appears, with providential intercessions.[45]

There were times when silence was to be preferred to expostulation, and on one occasion Boswell found that Johnson resisted commentary on questions that, in Boswell's words, "excruciated philosophers and divines, beyond any other"—questions involving God's prescience, free will, the efficacy of prayer, and divine intervention. Boswell observed that they "cramped the vigorous powers of his understanding. He was confined by a chain which early imagination and long habit made him think massy and strong, but which, had he ventured to try, he could at once have snapt asunder." Hawkesworth might better have emulated such Johnsonian self-restraint before he sailed blithely into murky theological depths. It was not to the *Voyages'* good editor, or even to such men as Pope and Franklin, that many of the time turned for clarification of dark issues but to those with less complex notions. Many surely would have agreed with Cook himself, who, Hawkesworth's arguments notwithstanding, saw that the means of his escape from the reef was that "I have named *Providential Channell.*"[46]

Although vigorous moral objections to the *Voyages* have already been noted in the comments of Mrs. Carter and John Wesley, as well as those who despaired publicly, though anonymously, in the press, it is clear that the age was somewhat divided over matters of sexual propriety and felt itself pulled at times as much back to its licentious Restoration past as toward its Victorian future: Congreve and Wycherley tugged at as many minds as did Mrs. Grundy and Thomas Bowdler. If "A Christian," when he was not harping on themes theological, could find in the *Voyages* "stronger Excitements to vicious Indulgences than the most intriguing French Novel," the same papers that carried his moral diatribes could advertise, as did the *Morning Chronicle* for July 2, 1773, the twelfth number of the *Covent-Garden Magazine; or, Amorous Repository*, "calculated solely for the Entertainment of the Polite World," featuring among its contents, "The operation of Tattowing, the girls in King George's Island, and a description of the Timorodee Dance" as well as an "Anecdote of the celebrated Mr. B——ks." If legitimate interest and genuine curiosity led shortly to the printing of a second edition of the *Voyages*, and led many other readers to purchase shilling parts entitled *Genuine Voyages to the South Seas, published in sixty Weekly Numbers*, there was an audience, too, for more salacious materials—the poetic bawdry, for example, of "*An Epistle from Mr. Banks, Voyager, Monster-hunter, and Amoroso, to Oberea, Queen of Otaheite.*" Here one sees blended a righteous recounting of a moralist's fall from grace and matter more libidinous:

> The fatal bribe he took; but, ah! his soul
> Rose high, and sought the great empyreal goal:
> That goal, I trust, is gain'd; the mortal frame
> Sunk down, and left the *shadow of a name*:
> Yet, bles'd that name to time's remotest end,
> For he was virtue's *once*, and Britain's friend.
> The God who sunk him low, has rais'd him high
> And giv'n him genuine empire in the sky:

> Those heav'ns his studious readers long have seen
> Receiv'd their leader, ere I hail my Queen.
> All hail! sweet *Oberea*, queen of charms,
> Whom oft I've clasp'd within my wanton arms!
> Desire was mutual, but the fault was mine;
> For you, fond souls, who dwell beneath the line,
> In mutual dalliance hold perpetual play,
> The golden age repeating ev'ry day.[47]

While collateral materials such as these provide some insight into the moral tone of the *Voyages*, the text itself remains the best source. It requires no searching nor even particularly curious mind to grasp what offended the sensitivities of many readers during the summer months of 1773. One can understand, for instance, the shock many must have experienced in reading in Hawkesworth the following frank account of the encounter between lovely Tahitian maidens and true-born Englishmen, the latter seeking understandable relief from their cramped months on board ship.

> The women are all handsome, and some of them extremely beautiful. Chastity does not seem to be considered as a virtue among them, for they not only readily and openly trafficked with our people for personal favours, but were brought down by their fathers and brothers for that purpose: they were, however, conscious of the value of beauty, and the size of the nail that was demanded for the enjoyment of the lady, was always in proportion to her charms. The men who came down to the side of the river, at the same time that they presented the girl, shewed a stick of the size of the nail that was to be her price, and if our people agreed, she was sent over to them, for the men were not permitted to cross the river. This commerce was carried on a considerable time before the officers discovered it, for while some straggled a little way to receive the lady, the others kept a look-out. When I was acquainted with it, I no longer wondered that the ship was in danger of being pulled to pieces for the nails and iron that held her together. (Hawkesworth's *Voyages*, 1:481)[48]

Scandalous, indeed, it must have been to read of such commerce, to see the common English nail proving a harder currency than sterling and one of His Majesty's ships threatened with destruction by the licentious urges of those bent on pursuing the pleasures of the flesh. But this was not Hawkesworth's invention; it was simply his version—a more attenuated one, to be sure—of Wallis's journal entry that reads:

> The women in General are very handsome, some really great Beauties. Yet their Virtue was not proof against a Nail. for they would prostitute

themselves for a Nail. the lower sort for a small one and the Nail must be larger in proportion [to] the Ladys Beauty. even the Fathers and brothers brought them to the people and shew'd sticks preportion'd to the Nail they were to give, and would then send them a Cross the River. it was some time before the Officers found this out for the Men never pass'd and our people used to stragle but a little way whilst the other kept a look out, and it was this that occasion'd the Stealing all the Nails they could come at. (Wallis's journal, fol. 42)

Hawkesworth clearly preserves here the substance if not the style of the original.

Indeed, there are occasions when he appears to modify the blunter commentaries of the captains, perhaps to spare the sensitivities of some of his readers. On Sunday, June 21, 1767, for example, Wallis recorded that "the women particularly came down and stript themselves naked and made all the alluring Gestures they could to intice them [the crew] on shoar—" (fol. 35). Hawkesworth recasts the entry, having officers *report* to Wallis that the women came down to the beach "and stripping themselves naked, endeavoured to allure them by many wanton gestures, the meaning of which could not possibly be mistaken. At this time, however, our people resisted the temptation" (1:439). The modifications here are slight, but Hawkesworth does remove Wallis from direct participation in the episode, and the comment he adds may not reflect the meaning of Wallis's ambiguous dash.

An even clearer instance is Hawkesworth's tempering, through euphemism and circumlocution, of an erotically charged passage in Banks's account of the morals of the women of Rio de Janeiro. "This town," Banks writes, "as well as all others in South America belonging either to Spanyards or Portuguese has long been infamous for the unchastity of its women" (*Banks's "Endeavour" Journal*, 1:199), a comment Hawkesworth rewrites, "It is, I believe, universally allowed, that the women, both of the Spanish and Portuguese settlements in South America, make less difficulty of granting personal favours, than those of any other civilized country in the world." (Hawkesworth's *Voyages*, 2:30). Hawkesworth also modulates Banks's recounting of Dr. Solander's experience in receiving nosegays from the ladies of the town (he and two others received whole hatfuls as they traversed the city streets), which quite clearly had sexual overtones. Hawkesworth, however, insists that "great allowance must certainly be made for local customs; that which in one country would be an indecent familiarity, is a mere act of general courtesy in another" (2:31).

Hawkesworth also appears to exercise caution in handling the erotically colored episodes involving Joseph Banks on Tahiti on Friday, May 12, 1769, the meaning of which is not clear. It may have been a version of a ceremony called "taurua," in which cloth is presented, or, J. C. Beaglehole explains, "it may have symbolized the generous feelings entertained by the female population of the district towards the young and attractive Banks."[49] At any rate, what the English read in Hawkesworth was less explicit than the private record of Cook or Banks. Hawkesworth writes that pieces of cloth were put down between Banks and his visitors, and a girl "stepped upon them, and taking up her garments all round her to the waist, turned about, with great composure and deliberation, and with an air of perfect innocence and simplicity, three times" (Hawkesworth's *Voyages*, 2:125). Cook is more direct: "One of the Young Women," he writes, "then step'd upon the Cloth and with as much Innocency as one could possibly conceve, expose'd herself intirely naked from the waist downwards, in this manner she turn'd her Self once or twice round" (*Cook's "Endeavour" Journal*, p. 93). Banks, a party to the event, presents the most graphic record: "The foremost of the women, who seemd to be the principal, then stepd upon them [the cloths] and quickly unveiling all her charms gave me a most convenient opportunity of admiring them by turning herself gradually round: 3 peices more were laid and she repeated her part of the ceremony. . . . She then once more displayd her naked beauties and immediately marchd up to me" (*Banks's "Endeavour" Journal*, 1:275).

Whatever energies Hawkesworth expended to spare the more delicate of his readers, these were insufficient to prevent castigation and almost willful misinterpretation. Wallis, for example, reported that on Monday, July 13, 1767, the Tahitian queen, Oborea, or Purea, as she was called, visited the ship; he describes the subsequent departure of the queen and members of the crew, some of whom were ailing. The queen ordered four young girls to perform a medicinal massage on the sick, including Wallis himself, who comments that "it had done me much service and the others declared the same" (Wallis's journal, fol. 39). Later, to prevent Wallis's feet from getting wet, the queen, Wallis writes, "took me by the Arm and lifted me over every Haugh with as much ease as I could (when in health) a child" (fol. 39). Hawkesworth records the substance of Wallis's commentary carefully, altering only the language. But about this passage Horace Walpole fumed to Lady Ossory on June 21, 1773: "Doctor Hawksworth is still more provoking—an old black gentlewoman of forty carries Capt. Wallis cross a river, when he was too weak to walk, and the man represents them as a new edition of Dido and AEneas." He condemns the massage as well: "Indeed Dido the new does not even borrow the obscurity of a cave when she treats the travellers with the rites of Love, as practised in Otaheite."[50] Thus, at least one reader of Hawkesworth's *Voyages* was eager, it seems, to misconstrue what possibly could be misconstrued. *Honi soit qui mal y pense*, one hopes Lady Ossory might have reminded him.

But Hawkesworth was no censor, and if he appears to tone down certain episodes, others, undoubtedly to his sorrow after the fact, bask in the full Tahitian sun. On Sunday, May 14, 1769, Cook described an act of Tahitian intercourse performed in public, which Hawkesworth records with considerable fidelity to his original save an initial clumsy attempt at humor. Consider the response of a Mrs. Carter, remembering Hawkesworth as a moralist, author of elegant *Adventurer* papers, and purveyor of the solid wisdom of *Almoran and Hamet*:

> Such were our Matins; our Indians thought fit to perform Vespers of a very different kind. A young man, near six feet high, performed the rites of Venus with a little girl about eleven or twelve years of age, before several of our people, and a great number of natives, without the least sense of its being indecent or improper, but, as appeared, in perfect conformity to the custom of the place. Among the spectators were several women of superior rank, particularly Oberea, who may properly be said to have assisted at the ceremony; for they gave instructions to the girl how to perform her part, which, young as she was, she did not seem much to stand in need of. (Hawkesworth's *Voyages*, 2:128)

One can almost imagine fierce viragos and other guardians of public decency in damp and fog-bound Britain recoiling at this image of Tahitian humanity revealed in the sun's bright light and transmitted unblushingly to English readers. Even worse, instead of getting on with his text, Hawkesworth digresses with a philosophical rumination on the event that purveys a dangerous moral relativism:

> This incident is not mentioned as an object of idle curiosity, but as it deserves consideration in determining a question which has been long debated in philosophy; Whether the shame attending certain actions, which are allowed on all sides to be in themselves innocent, is implanted in Nature, or superinduced by custom? If it has its origin in custom, it will, perhaps, be found difficult to trace that custom, however general, to its source; if in instinct, it will be equally difficult to discover from what cause it is subdued or at least over-ruled among these people, in whose manners not the least trace of it is to be found. (P. 128)

No wonder, then, many found Hawkesworth morally offensive as others found him religiously suspect. Living as we do in a sexually frank age, we might find his record of Tahitian activities mild in contrast to the possibilities of behavior suggested in the personal columns of the popular press; but in the late eighteenth century many shunned the supposed indecencies of his work, and those more inventive—Walpole, for instance —inferred them where none existed. Yet a collation of Hawkesworth's version with his originals suggests that far from being a purveyor of the salacious, the moralist and man of letters wrote with concern for his age's sensibilities, with some awareness that Tahiti and Britain were separated not only by the globe's oceans but by contrasting attitudes towards human conduct. The controversy that erupted over the supposed sexual violations of the *Voyages* is much like that issuing from Hawkesworth's purported heretical religious views: both are more an index to the age's values than to those of the *Voyages'* author.

Regarding Hawkesworth himself a more important question remains to be answered, one that involves not only the serious charge raised by the captains that he violated his materials, but the larger one of just what Hawkesworth did with his originals, what strategies he employed in the making of one of the remarkable books of the century.

Whatever hurt Hawkesworth the moralist felt in hearing his work attacked for putative moral and religious abuse, Hawkesworth the naval historian might have suffered even greater pain from challenges to the authenticity of the text itself. Moral and religious questions are, after all, difficult to resolve and test the best minds of any age. In matters religious, moreover, his principal attacker, "A Christian," sounded much like a crank, and Hawkesworth had only to review the works of Pope and to remember his conversations with Franklin to find support for his mild deism. But doubts about the reliability of his text were more serious: to have betrayed his originals constituted for a man of letters, as violation of orders for a man of service, a dereliction of duty, the gravest of offenses. Evidence suggests that for Hawkesworth and others involved in the project, textual authenticity was a principal concern.

Hawkesworth had written to Lord Sandwich from Bromley on November 19, 1771 (as noted above), that he was already hard at work on the text, earnest, he says, "to get my M.S. ready [in] time enough to have the Sanction of Mr Banks and Capt Cook to what I shall relate after them." He alludes here to Cook's anticipated departure, referred to again in his preface to the second edition of the *Voyages*: "The two volumes which contain an account of the voyage of the Endeavour were written in little more than four months after the papers were put into my hands, because it was expected that Captain Cook would in that time sail on another expedition"(n.p.). Clearly Cook was to review Hawkesworth's text, and Hawkesworth writes in his General Introduction:

> That no doubt might remain of the fidelity with which I Have related the events recorded in my materials, the manuscript account of each

voyage was read to the respective Commanders at the Admiralty, by the appointment of Lord Sandwich, who was himself present during much the greatest part of the time. The account of the voyage of the Endeavour was also read to Mr. Banks and Dr. Solander, in whose hands, as well as in those of Captain Cook, the manuscript was left for a considerable time after the reading. Commodore Byron also, Captain Wallis and Captain Carteret, had the manuscripts of their respective voyages to peruse, after they had been read at the Admiralty in their presence, and such emendations as they suggested were made. (Hawkesworth's *Voyages*, 1:vi)

But these words conflict with Cook's denial and Carteret's disclaimer. How, then, can one explain the discrepancy? Is Hawkesworth lying, or are the captains? No one, it seems, was fully party to the truth of the matter or deliberate in purveying untruths about it. J. C. Beaglehole suggests, for example, that Hawkesworth's statement above does not place him with certainty at such reviews of his text, a view supported in an anonymous letter (by "a Seaman") in the *Public Advertiser* for July 17, 1773, who wrote that "Dr. H. submitted his Papers to the Examination and Correction (not of Scribblers, Witlings and Women) of a select Number of the most able and intelligent Seamen of long Experience, great Service and high Rank in their Profession." These men, he argues, "saw it, considered it, and greatly approved of the Stile, Manner, and Contents." This account suggests that middlemen, not necessarily the commanders themselves, reviewed the finished text and vouched for its authenticity. At worst, then, Hawkesworth might be guilty of asserting as fact in his General Introduction what he had learned at second hand from Lord Sandwich. Joseph Cradock records, moreover, that Hawkesworth himself was present at one review of his work at the Admiralty.

> When a meeting of friends was held at the Admiralty to consult about the South Sea voyages that were to be published by Dr. Hawkesworth, and the Preface was to be read by the Doctor; I presumed so far as to make one objection at the commencement. It was there asserted, that no crowned head, before his then present Majesty, had ever patronized any similar publication, and I exemplified the elaborate work of the Abbé d'Auteroche, which had been magnificently printed at the expence of the Empress of all the Russias.[51]

In spite of the captains' comments and those of such critics as Dalrymple, Hawkesworth appears innocent of any deliberate misstatement about attempts to authenticate his text. One might observe, too, that protests about the fidelity of the *Voyages* to their originals surfaced *after* the great controversy developed. The edition became (a nautical cliché forces itself here) a sinking ship, and few wished to ride it bravely to the bottom. The captains involved, moreover, must have been preoccupied with other matters than the conversion of their papers into a printed text, and Banks, the best educated of those who submitted material to Hawkesworth, appeared least concerned about its final disposition. He, in fact, granted Hawkesworth the right to blend his commentary with Cook's and in Cook's own voice, an act of self-abnegation accorded a special introduction by Hawkesworth, who was delighted that Cook's stolid prose could be illuminated with the more expansive and articulate observations of the young scientist. Banks's donation of materials might have been prompted by the highest motives or, equally, from a lack of recognition that they were of any special worth. Surely he hardly anticipated the uncomfortable notoriety that they would bring him and the captains.

Of such speculation there is probably no end, and of Hawkesworth one can conclude that while he might have misconstrued the means by which his text was authenticated, there were attempts to do so. The question evaporates into smoke, however, when his work is collated with its original sources. Even a cursory reading suggests that Hawkesworth's *Voyages* is no edition of the journals of Byron, Carteret, Wallis, Cook, and Banks, but a version based upon them, that Hawkesworth was no mere compiler of one of the most famous works of the age, but its author.

Hawkesworth's *Voyages* was condemned by many at the time for its supposed moral and theological abuses; it has been censured by modern editors for obvious failures to reproduce the originals upon which it is based; it has yet to be assessed for what it really is—the work of a professional man of letters contending with a great mass of materials, wrenching from them a coherent work at once historical and literary. As naval historian Hawkesworth recorded the great achievements of the brave circumnavigators of the 1760s and 1770s; as a man of letters, aided by metaphor, allusion, and the capacity to push the disparities of history into pattern, he helped shape one of the deepest of national myths, that of the Empire itself and the role the brave British captains and their crews played in creating it.

Hawkesworth composed the *Voyages* according to principles he enunciated over twenty years before in his fourth *Adventurer*, an important critical document discussing a theory of genres. Hawkesworth's views are amplified by Johnson in *Idler* no. 97, and the arguments of the two periodical essays are manifest in the General Introduction to the *Voyages*. In *Adventurer* no. 4 Hawkesworth suggests that the function of literature is to instruct by entertainment and stresses the affective principle that permeates his dramatic criticism in the *Gentleman's Magazine*. While the epic poem succeeds in engaging the passions, Hawkesworth argues, other species of writing—history, biography, even the novel—suffer by contrast. So, too, with voyages and travels, which share the defect of history: "No passion is strongly excited except wonder; or if we feel any emotion at the danger of the traveller, it is transient and languid, because his character is not rendered sufficiently important; he is rarely discovered to have any excellencies but daring curiosity; he is ever the object of admiration, and seldom of esteem." Johnson echoes Hawkesworth in *Idler* no. 97 when he writes of travel books that "nothing is found but such general accounts as leave no distinct idea behind them, or such minute enumerations as few can read with either profit or delight." Johnson complains that the writer of such works "conducts his reader thro' wet and dry, over rough and smooth, without incidents, without reflection." The author of travel books must remember, Johnson suggests, that "he that pleases must offer new images to his reader, and enable him to form a tacit comparison of his own state with that of others."[52]

The problems of the genre were very much in Hawkesworth's mind when he began composing the *Voyages*. "When I first undertook the work," Hawkesworth writes, "it was debated, whether it should be written in the first or third person: it was readily acknowledged on all hands, that a narrative in the first person would, by bringing the Adventurer and the Reader nearer together, without the intervention of a stranger, more strongly excite an interest and consequently afford more entertainment" (Hawkesworth's *Voyages*, 1:iv). In each voyage, then, Hawkesworth became an "I," the voice of the captain speaking directly to the reader of his exploits, a strategy dictated by literary rather than historical concerns. It is as a man of letters that Hawkesworth writes:

> An account that ten thousand men perished in a battle, that twice the number were swallowed up by an earthquake, or that a whole nation was swept away by a pestilence, is read in the naked brevity of an index, without the least emotion, by those who feel themselves strongly interested even for Pamela, the imaginary heroine of a novel that is remarkable for the enumeration of particulars in themselves so trifling, that we almost wonder how they could occur to the author's mind. (P. vii).

The captains were, of course, real heroes and the particulars of their travels far from trifling, but both would be subjected to the subtle shading of character and episode when the novelist got the better of the naval historian.

Hawkesworth, then, was not to be dominated by his materials, and a creative spirit pervades his introduction, one sanctioned by his and Johnson's theorizing on travel writing. Almost as if in reference to *Idler* no. 97 he comments in his introduction:

> But it was objected that if it was written in the name of the several Commanders, I could exhibit only a naked narrative, without any opinion or sentiment of my own, however fair the occasion, and without noting the similitude or dissimilitude between the opinions, customs, or manners of the people now first discovered, and those of nations that have been long known, or remarking on any other incident or particular that might occur. (1:iv–v)

With the apparent approval of all concerned parties Hawkesworth enlivened his originals with his own "sentiments" and "observations." Many of these are short; some are allusions, classical or derivatively classic (his translation of Fénelon's *Telemachus* was much in mind when he composed the *Voyages*); some are more discursive, such as his dissertations on death, the nature of fire, and the Romish religion. Such intrusions, coupled with Hawkesworth's characterization of the captains themselves, reflect the inappropriateness of the word "edition" to describe the *Voyages*, and these alterations do not reveal the fundamental alteration observed throughout the text. Quite simply, Hawkesworth consistently rewrites his originals, elevating the workmanlike prose of the commanders, and even Banks's more articulate assessments, into textured literary periods and paragraphs. Most readers today would prefer the honest simplicities of the captains to the more ornate utterances of a polished man of letters, but to fault Hawkesworth in this instance is to judge him by the stylistic conventions of our time, just as he was judged in his own time by eighteenth-century definitions of taste and morality. Hawkesworth would have been blamed, in fact, had he not exerted the same stylistic energies in Cook's behalf as he had for Swift in his esteemed biography of the Dean. It is unlikely that he could have refrained, for with Hawkesworth as with his good friend Johnson, there was no disguising innate powers to use language with force, clarity, and that analogizing power that separates the expository from the literary.

Hawkesworth's literary strategies are best seen, not in the abstract, but in a collation of the *Voyages* with their originals. Contrast, for example, Byron's report of an encounter with a wild beast near Tierra del Fuego with Hawkesworth's rendition.

> Two of the Men going to the Well on the S° side this morning, saw a
> large Tyger there & having no fire Arms with them they threw Stones
> at him, but he did not move till more of the Men came up when he
> walked leisurely away. (*Byron's Journal*, p. 39)

Hawkesworth, seeing possibilities in elaboration and allusion, reconstructs
the scene.

> The two men who first came up to the well found there a large tyger
> lying upon the ground; having gazed at each other some time, the men
> who had no fire-arms, seeing the beast treat them with as much
> contemptuous neglect as the lion did the knight of La Mancha, began to
> throw stones at him: of this insult however he did not deign to take the
> least notice, but continued stretched upon the ground in great tranquil-
> lity till the rest of the party came up, and then he very leisurely rose and
> walked away. (Hawkesworth's *Voyages*, 1:21–22)

No mere editor is at work here, no historian interested primarily in an
objective presentation of material. The substance of Byron's statement is
preserved, but the essence is Hawkesworth's. He is not content with fact
alone but rather, in the words of *Idler* no. 97, allows the reader "to form a
tacit comparison of his own state with that of another." His method here is
referential, specifically literary, though on other occasions it is sociological.
Commenting, for example, on the inhabitants of distant Madeira, who
stubbornly resisted changes in winemaking, Hawkesworth compares them
to the parish poor of England, afflicted with a similar kind of *vis inertiae*, "for
whom the law must not only make a provision, but compel them to accept
it, or else they will be still found begging in the streets" (2:6). Here a
comparative mood pervades the *Voyages*. Let others, especially the French,
celebrate the exotic; Hawkesworth chooses to remain more neoclassically
inclined. Through the captains he had surveyed the globe and its inhabitants from China to Peru, concluding in spite of the romantic particularities
of place and people that it was still possible to stress the unity rather than
the disparity of this vast scene. Better, then, the generalization (the poor of
England resemble those of Madeira) or the literary reference (Don Quixote
can follow us literally to the ends of the earth) that subsumes apparent
differences; better to consider the tulip rather than its streaks.

The *Voyages*, though, is so rich and complex a work, and Hawkesworth's motives in composing it so varied, that it resists any single reading.
If in the above passage one sees the remote tamed by the familiar, almost the
opposite is true in the following citation, also from Byron's voyage, where
Hawkesworth converts history, if not into literature, at least into matter
that would satisfy a reader's appetite for romantic adventure. The episode
takes place at Port Famine, Tierra del Fuego:

Three of our People that have a little Tent ashore at the bottom of this Bay where they are washing close to a little Rivulet, & just at the skirts of the wood, were terribly alarmed last night by the roaring of some large wild Beasts who approached very near their Tent & did not leave them till near day break. All they had for it was making a large fire, which kept them off. (*Byron's Journal*, p. 53)

I had set up a small tent at the skirts of a wood, soon after the ship came to an anchor, where three men were employed in washing: they slept on shore; but soon after sunset were awakened out of their first sleep by the roaring of some wild beasts, which the darkness of the night, and the solitariness of their situation in this pathless desart, rendered horrid beyond imagination: the tone was hollow and deep, so that the beasts, of whatever kind, were certainly large, and the poor fellows perceived that they drew nearer and nearer, as the sound every minute became more loud. From this time sleep was renounced for the night, a large fire was immediately kindled, and a constant blaze kept up: this prevented the beasts from invading the tent; but they continued to prowl round it at a little distance, with incessant howlings, till the day broke, and then, to the great comfort of the affrighted sailors, they disappeared. (Hawkesworth's *Voyages*, 1:39–40)

Again, Hawkesworth is less editor and more creative artist; Byron's commentary is not simply a source to be transmitted, but an occasion for an imaginative attenuation, a virtual recreation in which the mere facts of an encounter are shaped into a scene and a state of mind. Byron's "People" become Hawkesworth's "affrighted sailors," confronted at earth's end with destruction by the beasts of the night. Byron's editor might legitimately charge that his holograph journal "bears the same relationship to the Hawkesworth version as a realistic preliminary pencil sketch does to the finished impressionistic portrait; and, in this case, the portrait bears a closer resemblance to the artist, Hawkesworth, than it does to the sitter, Byron.[53] His complaint, though, is misdirected. Byron's voyage simply establishes what the others confirm—that Hawkesworth was no editor but a man of letters as he worked with his originals, one conscious of the travel genre within which he wrote. In his elaboration of his source above he specifically contends with Johnson's objection to such works in which "nothing is found but general accounts as leave no distinct idea behind them."

While Hawkesworth engages in sustained rewriting of the journals, making more elegant the captains' functional prose, reflecting, musing, commenting on his texts when so moved, he indulges in more subtle alterations that may be of greater interest: in all the voyages he tends to idealize both the captains and their missions, which brought them into confrontation with alien civilizations and peoples. It was not so much the myth of the noble savage and the idea of primitive life that Hawkesworth loosed upon the world—the French would see to that—but rather, as a shrewd student of the *Voyages* remarks, "the prototype of that hero of Victorian boys' sea fiction, the magnanimous British commander . . . for all that Cook was embarrassed by his editor's intrusions and inaccuracies, the edition of his first voyage was the first contribution to his ennoblement as a national figure."[54]

Such ennoblement is seen not only in Hawkesworth's treatment of Cook, but first in his rendition of Byron. When, for example, in mid-February 1765 Bougainville's ship followed the *Dolphin* into the Strait of Magellan, Byron wrote with an honest bluntness appropriate to an Englishman, at least in the privacy of thought and journal: "I was in great hopes she would have run ashore upon one of the Banks between Point Possession & the first Narrow, for the Navigation is extremely difficult to those who are not well acquainted. But the misfortune was, the Storeship kept so far a Stern that she served as a Pilot to the Stranger" (*Byron's Journal*, p. 65). Hawkesworth omits this comment and through its omission preserves good form, so necessary to an English officer in foreign parts.

If, with the French, proper conduct should be observed, at least in theory, so too the white man's dealings with simple islanders should be above censure. Hawkesworth, through delicate rephrasing of Byron's journal entries involving contact with natives of King George's Isles in early June 1765, places him in a light Byron scarcely deserves by his own account:

> Our People would have gladly saluted them with a few Balls, but as they had no Orders from me they desisted. However if it had been possible for us to have come to an Anchor, It would have been a most convenient place for us, for if we could not have made these Savages our friends, we should presently have drove them off, & as the Island was so small, I could easily have guarded every part of it, so that I should have been under no apprehension of being molested from the Savages of the Great Island. (*Byron's Journal*, p. 96)

There is nothing particularly shocking in Byron's commentary; he is a naval officer thinking primarily of military matters—the safety of ship and men, the latter more eager than their captain to commit violence. But Hawkesworth felt some modulation necessary: "But nothing," Hawkesworth writes as Byron, "could justify the taking away their lives for a mere imaginary or intentional injury, without procuring the least advantage to ourselves" (Hawkesworth's *Voyages*, 1:95).

Shortly afterwards, however, several natives were killed in a confrontation with Western firepower, and on Tuesday, June 11, 1765, Byron, seeing a potentially threatening gathering of natives, fired "a Shot over their heads & they all disappeared in a moment" (p. 100). But Hawkesworth elaborates upon the captain's blunt comment and in so doing creates a heightened sense of humanity that Byron probably would not have claimed: "As I thought they might be troublesome, and was unwilling that they should suffer by another unequal contest with our people, I fired a shot over their heads which produced the effect I intended, for they all disappeared in a moment" (1:100–101). What emerges, then, are two Byrons, one of his journal, one of Hawkesworth's making. The two are not distinct, of course, and the captain of the *Voyages* is very much a reflection of the man of the journal, but the tendency to elevation is there. The historical Byron was principally interested in the safety of his ship, and he saw his encounters with alien humanity as a matter of dealing with "savages," not occasions for moral reflection. His attitude toward them is presented by Hawkesworth with more delicacy than his journal suggests. Byron writes, for example, of a native's "thousand Asses tricks" (p. 112) on shipboard, rephrased by Hawkesworth as mere "antic" tricks (1:112); and Hawkesworth also omits Byron's comment that "I believe there was never a Set of more dexterous Thieves in the World" (p. 112).

Hawkesworth employs similar techniques in his rendition of Wallis's and Carteret's voyages. In presenting Wallis's account of Tahiti Hawkesworth, as noted above, makes some concessions to the sexual sensitivities of his readers; in his writing of Carteret's story he may have, the captain's modern editor suggests, compromised the facts of history itself. Certainly, no other commander was more outspoken than Carteret in condemning Hawkesworth's version of his voyage; as we have already seen, he not only answered Hawkesworth with two long lists of specific objections to the official text, but also prepared his own account, only recently published.[55] Comparing Carteret's account with passages in the *Voyages* concerning the very source of Carteret's anguish—his apparent abandonment by Wallis at the western opening of the Strait of Magellan on April 11, 1767—it is obvious that the tone of the captain and that of his supposed editor are very different.

The Carteret of Hawkesworth's version speaks in a more controlled voice than the captain of the journal composed subsequent to the publication of the *Voyages*, who clearly felt that a mere man of letters could not grasp the significance of his troubled voyage. In reference to the doomed *Swallow*, for instance, Hawkesworth writes as Carteret: "I was now convinced that I had been sent upon a service to which my vessel and her equipment were by no means equal, but I determined at all events to perform it in the best manner I was able" (Hawkesworth's *Voyages*, 1:528–29). But Carteret himself suggests:

The Reader I am certain will better comprehend, than I can write, the astonishment I was in, on perusing these Orders, & to find I was sent on a Service, to which the ill quallity of my Ship, and the manner she was equiped in, made her in every respect inadequate. And from the Nature of these orders, I was convinced, that they could not be strictly complyed with; Nor with any credit to my self, or material Service to my Country, but on the contrary, foresaw many difficulties, & dangers, possibly not to be overcome. These were dispiriting considerations indeed; but as there was no choise left, I detirmined at all events, be the risque what it might, to execute them in the best manner. (*Carteret's Voyage*, 1:111–12)

Few could argue that Hawkesworth successfully conveys Carteret's frustration in being assigned so ill-equipped a ship as the *Swallow*; neither, in fact, does he describe fairly the captain's state of mind at the time of separation in the Strait of Magellan. Where Hawkesworth's commander observes stoically, "From this time, I gave up all hope of seeing the Dolphin again till we should arrive in England" (1:531), Carteret himself noted bitterly, "But . . . I was now fully convinced, from many circumstances which had happened from the time we left England, till the present, that Capt. Wallis never intended to be troubled with the Swallow, after he had been safely piloted through the Streights" (1:120).

The worst, then, that one could say about Hawkesworth here is that he did, perhaps even at the Admiralty's insistence, modulate the captain's protest; the best, that in his rendition of Carteret, as with the other chief officers, he attempted to portray the controlled, stiff-lipped British commander doing duty uncomplainingly. The above, surely, are among the most unconscionable alterations that Hawkesworth made in Carteret's text. It might be observed, too, that Carteret's objections to Hawkesworth's version, formidable as they are at first reading, prove of somewhat less consequence on closer examination and in several cases are quibbles about style rather than substance. However one attempts to resolve the question, it illustrates once again the limitation of the word "edition" to describe the work. In no voyage more than Cook's is this fact made manifest.

Although it appears last in the *Voyages*, Cook's incredible journey received Hawkesworth's first and most enthusiastic treatment; it is here one sees most clearly the imprint of his person through intrusion and commentary, through philosophical ruminations, and, most of all, in his sustained rewriting of his sources. To his delight Hawkesworth had access not only to Cook's papers, but also to those of Joseph Banks, the naturalist on board the *Endeavour*, one with a philosophical turn of mind and powers of articulation in significant contrast to the stolid Cook, whose commentary at times is as abbreviated as his commands. The papers of the two are

perfectly complementary, as Hawkesworth observes in his special introduction, which is largely an appreciation of Banks's contribution to the
Voyages. "The papers of Captain Cook," he writes, "contained a very
particular account of all the nautical incidents of the voyage, and a very
minute description of the figure and extent of the countries he had visited,
with all the bearing of the headlands and bays that diversify the coasts."
Such material, Hawkesworth notes, "abundantly shewed him to be an
excellent officer, and skilful navigator" (2:xiii–xiv). But in Banks's papers
Hawkesworth found "a great variety of incidents which had not come
under the notice of Captain Cook, with descriptions of countries and
people, their productions, manners, customs, religion, policy, and language" (p. xiv). In a salute to Banks, Hawkesworth writes with the felicity
of phrase that came naturally to him: "It is indeed fortunate for mankind,
when wealth and science, and a strong inclination to exert the powers of
both for purposes of public benefit, unite in the same person; and I cannot
but congratulate my country upon the prospect of further pleasure and
advantage from the same Gentleman, to whom we are indebted for so
considerable a part of this narrative" (pp. xiv–xv).

The "I" of Cook's voyage, ostensibly the great captain himself, is at
once a blend of Cook, Banks, and Hawkesworth, and a few examples
should illustrate how the latter emerges as author rather than editor of
Cook's *Voyages.* Both Cook and Banks, for example, comment on the Tierra
del Fuegians, a miserable specimen of humanity living a grim Hobbesian
existence in remote southern regions. Cook writes that these nomads "are
extreeamly fond of any Red thing and seemed to set more Value on Beeds
than any thing we could give them" (*Cook's "Endeavour" Journal*, p. 45);
Banks comments that they were "to all appearance contented with what
they had nor wishing for any thing we could give them except beads; of
these they were very fond preferring ornamental things to those which
might be of real use and giving more in exchange for a string of Beids than
they would for a knife or a hatchet" (*Banks's "Endeavour" Journal*, 1:224); and
Hawkesworth states:

> They seemed to have no wish for any thing more than they possessed,
> nor did any thing we offered them appear acceptable but beads, as an
> ornamental superfluity of life. . . . But it is certain, that they suffered
> nothing from the want of the innumerable articles which we consider,
> not as the luxuries and conveniencies only, but the necessaries of life: as
> their desires are few, they probably enjoy them all; and how much they
> may be gainers by an exemption from the care, labour and solicitude,
> which arise from a perpetual and unsuccessful effort to gratify that
> infinite variety of desires which the refinements of artificial life have
> produced among us, is not very easy to determine: possibly this may

counterbalance all the real disadvantages of their situation in comparison with ours, and make the scales by which good and evil are distributed to man, hang even between us. (Hawkesworth's *Voyages*, 2:59)

Cook's and Banks's facts concerning the Tierra del Fuegians are converted
into Hawkesworth's reflection; it is no editor at work but a creative writer
who ably fulfills the Johnsonian requirements that practitioners of the
travel genre avoid conducting readers "thro' wet and dry, over rough and
smooth, without incidents, without reflection," and satisfy the reader's
need to "form a tacit comparison of his own state with that of another."

More often, however, Hawkesworth's alterations are stylistic rather
than substantive: he consistently elevates Cook's spare style and even
burnishes Banks's more eloquent periods. The visit of the Tahitian queen
Oberea to the *Endeavour* on Friday, April 28, 1769, for example, receives
various treatments. Cook writes, "This Woman is about 40 years of Age
and like most of the other Women very Masculine" (*Cook's "Endeavour"
Journal*, p. 85); Banks, more eloquently, suggests that she "appeard to be
about 40, tall and very lusty, her skin white and her eyes full of meaning,
she might have been hansome when young but now few or no traces of it
were left" (*Banks's "Endeavour" Journal*, 1:266); and Hawkesworth, with
further elaboration, presents his reader with the assessment, "She seemed
to be about forty years of age, and was not only tall, but of large make; her
skin was white, and there was an uncommon intelligence and sensibility in
her eyes: she appeared to have been handsome when she was young, but at
this time little more than memorials of her beauty were left" (Hawkesworth's *Voyages*, 2:105). One progresses, then, from adequate journalism in
Cook to the delicacy of a novel of manners in Hawkesworth. (Sydney
Parkinson might serve twentieth-century tastes best in his description of
the queen as "a fat, bouncing, good-looking dame."[56])

Perhaps more important than his stylistic alterations and philosophical
intrusions is Hawkesworth's tendency to idealize Cook as he had the other
commanders. Their conduct was generally exemplary, Cook's especially,
but on one occasion, for example, a Tahitian native, having stolen a musket
on Saturday, April 15, 1769, suffered the fatal consequences of Western
firepower, an event reported in some detail by Cook and Banks as well as by
Hawkesworth. Portions of Hawkesworth's version with no basis in the
originals are italicized.

We had not been gone long from the Tent before the natives again
began to gather about it and one of them more daring then the rest
push'd one of the Centinals down, snatched the Musquet out of his
hand and made a push at him and then made off and with him all the

rest, emmidiatly upon this the officer order'd the party to fire and the Man who took the Musquet was shott dead before he had got far from the Tent but the Musquet was carried quite off. . . . Old Owhaa as I have said before was the only one of the Natives that stay'd by us and by his means we prevail'd on about 20 of them to come to the Tent and their sit down with us and endeavour'd by every means in our power to convence them that the man was kill'd for taking away the Musquet and that we still would be friends with them. At sunset they left us seemingly satisfied and we struck our Tent and went on Board. (*Cook's "Endeavour" Journal*, pp. 79–80)

On our return we found that an Indian had snatchd a sentrys musquet from him unawares and run off; the midshipman (may be) imprudently orderd the marines to fire, they did fire into the thickest of the flying croud some hundreds in number several shot, and pursueing the man who stole the musquet killd him dead but whether any others were killd or hurt no one could tell. No Indian was now to be seen about the tent but our old man, who with us took all pains to reconcile them again; before night by his means we got together a few of them and explaining to them that the man who sufferd was guilty of a crime deserving of death (for so we were forcd to make it) we retired to the ship not well pleasd with the days expedition, guilty no doubt in some measure of the death of a man who the most severe laws of equity would not have condemnd to so severe a punishment. (*Banks's "Endeavour" Journal*, 1:257)

Upon this [the musket's theft] the petty officer, a midshipman, who commanded the party, *perhaps from a sudden fear of farther violence, perhaps from the natural petulance of power newly acquired, and perhaps from a brutality in his nature*, ordered the marines to fire: the men, *with as little consideration or humanity as the officer*, immediately discharged their pieces. . . .
    . . . We endeavoured to justify our people as well as we could, and to convince the Indians that if they did no wrong to us, we should do no wrong to them: they went away without any appearance of distrust or resentment; and having struck our tent, we returned to the ship, but by no means satisfied with the transactions of the day. (Hawkesworth's *Voyages*, 2:91–92)

Generations read Hawkesworth's words as Cook's, yet collation suggests the distance between the *Endeavour*'s captain and his putative editor is great. The latter was obviously drawn to the more reflective Banks, whose moral doubts probably generated the flowing Johnsonian triplet suggesting Cook's supposed state of mind. In fact, Cook was virtually emotionless about the event—the native stole a musket, he was shot (the firing into the crowd is omitted), and the matter was "justified" to the natives. One can almost see the pragmatic captain walking briskly to the ship, satisfied with the resolution of the events.[57]

Hawkesworth's *Voyages*, one of the significant works of the eighteenth century, is finally receiving the kind of study it deserves. A complex text with attractions for students in various disciplines, it resists any single reading. It is clear, though, that it is much less and a great deal more than an edition, the term most frequently used to describe it and an obvious misnomer. Sandwich in his discussions with Burney referred to the captains' papers as "mere rough draughts" and sought "a proper person to *write the Voyage.*" The title page of the work carries the word "account," not "edition," and in his dedication to the king, Hawkesworth speaks of his role as that of a "recorder" of the journals and his work as a "narrative," not an edition. Hawkesworth shaped the mass of materials turned over to him according to principles enunciated years before in his fourth *Adventurer*, principles amplified in his General Introduction. He approached his originals not simply as an editor but as a man of letters, and the *Voyages* consistently reflect this fact. In his vision of the captains' missions Hawkesworth helped fuel a myth that was to motivate the nation for more than a century—the myth that an island kingdom through sea power and administrative genius could impose a Pax Britannica on a major portion of the world, as Cook and Wallis had quickly dominated the tiny island of Tahiti. Obviously no single work, even one so rich as Hawkesworth's *Voyages*, created such a myth; its sources are various. Hawkesworth, though, joins an arc that later included Kipling and East of Suez, one that diminished finally, as empire faded, in Forster and Orwell. He is a recorder of a part of that remarkable demonstration of energy of a people who would stop at nothing less than the export of their language and their culture to the ends of the earth.

Hawkesworth did not live to defend his *Voyages*, and it is difficult to conjecture how he might best have answered his numerous critics. While it provides no comfort for one who expired as an object of scorn and derision, it does justice to his memory to observe that modern students of his masterwork have become increasingly appreciative of the magnitude of the task he faced in composing his controversial text. Hawkesworth, it should be remembered, attempted in a matter of months to bring order and structure to a mass of materials that have subsequently occupied the attention of three editors for some years, one of whom spent a lifetime mastering the complexities of the subject. Perhaps it would be most economical here simply to note that Hawkesworth's eighteenth-century critics might best have been referred to his own assessment of another great work of encyclopedic complexity. Of Johnson's *Dictionary* he wrote in the *Gentleman's Magazine* for April 1755:

> It is evident that such a work will in many particulars admit improvement from a mind utterly unequal to the whole performance; but let not any of those, who by long poring over minute parts, have discovered what was necessarily overlooked by an eye that could comprehend the whole, assume an air of superiority, or hope to escape the indignation of genius and learning, which, in the language of *Milton*, can *burn after them* for ever, if in the malignity of their folly they depreciate, for trivial imperfections, a work, in which perfection was not possible to man. (25:150)

With so rich a work as the *Voyages*, commentary has no termination. No student of Cook and Hawkesworth, however, better deserves final commentary than the former's great editor and biographer. Of Hawkesworth's famed *oeuvre* J. C. Beaglehole writes:

> Demerits desregarded, his work entered into the canon; the second English edition of 1773 was followed by a New York edition, and by French and German translations, in 1774; by a third English edition in 1785 and an Italian one in 1794. In the following century it reached other languages. Reprinted again and again in one form or another it became a sort of classic unacknowledged by historians of literature, the indispensible introduction to 'Cook's Voyages,' whether laid out in full, or pillaged and abridged; a classic not of English prose but of English adventure; and for a hundred and twenty years, so far as the first voyage was concerned, Hawkesworth was Cook.[58]

In surely one of the more arcane uses to which it has been put, Hawkesworth's *Voyages* guided Fletcher Christian and the *Bounty* mutineers to tiny Pitcairn Island.[59] For Hawkesworth the text brought no such liberation, and for the final days of his life there would be little but suffering, disappointment, and sorrow.

VIII THE FINAL DAYS

> The poetry I would have printed in order of time, which
> he seems to have intended by noting the dates, which
> dates I should like to preserve, they show the progress of
> [his] Mind, and of a very powerful Mind.
>
> Samuel Johnson to John Ryland, April 12, 1777, on
> the making of an edition of Hawkesworth's works.

Hawkesworth lived only six months after the publication of his
Voyages, and accounts of his death reflect his severely damaged reputation.
A New and General Biographical Dictionary recorded that some claimed he
died "of high living; others, of chagrin from the ill reception of his 'Narrative.'" Edmond Malone darkened the circumstances of his passing, alluding to possible suicide. Attacks upon Hawkesworth on account of the
Voyages, he writes, "affected him so much that, from low spirits he was
seized with a nervous fever, which on account of the high living he had
indulged in had the more power on him; and he is supposed to have put an
end to his life by intentionally taking an immoderate dose of opium."
Nineteenth-century commentators on Hawkesworth's life repeated, and
promiscuously intensified, such charges. James Boaden, the editor of
Garrick's correspondence, suggested that "Hawkesworth literally died of
prosperity," and Charles Robert Leslie and Tom Taylor asserted in their *Life
and Times of Sir Joshua Reynolds* that he "was so elated with his good fortune
that he is said to have died of it." As late as 1882, Leslie Stephen, in his
Samuel Johnson, echoed Malone in writing that Hawkesworth "was so bitterly attacked by a 'Christian' in the papers, that he destroyed himself by a
dose of opium."[1]

While neither "high living" nor an overdose of opium is the probable
cause of Hawkesworth's death, both accusations reveal popular impressions of the fallen moralist at the time. The charge of high living undoubtedly stemmed from Hawkesworth's connection during the last years
of his life with persons of great influence though questionable moral probity, such as his patron, the earl of Sandwich. Yet Hawkesworth's continued close association with the Burney family and their strong support of

187

an old friend indicate that he had suffered no fundamental alteration in character. While there is no way of disproving the charge that he committed suicide by an overdose of opium, this too seems unlikely and could have been inspired by those who wished to blacken his reputation further by suggesting that he compounded the moral and theological errors of his masterwork with a last violation of one of the deeper prohibitions of the Christian faith. The rumor of death from opium came, moreover, to Malone second, even third, hand ("From the Bishop of Salisbury. The opinion from Dr. Fordyce," a parenthetical comment reads in "Maloniana"), and the assertion is made by no other student of Hawkesworth's life. While a sick, depressed writer might have deliberately consumed such a fatal dose, this would have been the same man who described in a review in the *Gentleman's Magazine* for February 1763 the unhappy fate of those who "discovered, too late, that life is not destroyed by this drug without a dreadful struggle, nor death brought on but with great agony." This powerful substance, Hawkesworth notes, "produces a heat and weight at the stomach, extravagant spirits, convulsive laughter, short and quick breathing, nauseas, vertigoes, vomiting, hickups, outrageous madness, contraction of the jaw, convulsions, profuse sweats, universal relaxation, and death."[2]

Whatever the specific cause of his death, Hawkesworth suffered from a frail constitution unable to endure both the strain of the composition of the *Voyages* and the public outcry that greeted his text after its publication. After its completion there were clear signs of debility: Garrick, in a letter to the Abbé Morellet dated April 9, 1773, referred to Hawkesworth's "late fatigue"; Mary Hawkesworth wrote to Mrs. Garrick on June 20, 1773, of a mind "whose powers have for a long time been exerted almost to agony, but manifestly so as to have nearly destroy'd yᵉ Fragile Fabrick [of] the Body"; and Fanny Burney described Hawkesworth at his last appearance at the Burneys, during mid-October 1773, as "thin, livid, harassed!" While Hawkesworth listened approvingly at this final visit to the Burneys as the doctor read from a manuscript of his *History of Music*, his thoughts, and much of the evening's discussion, apparently turned to the disaster of the *Voyages*. Hawkesworth lamented his fate to Burney, commenting sadly on the catastrophe that had obliterated a lifetime's honest labor and had fatally blemished the purest of reputations. He did, however, tell Burney that he would give a "general answer to the invidious, calumniating and most unjust aspersions which had been so cruelly and wantonly cast on him," and Burney did his best to support his suffering friend. "There was hardly a man in the kingdon who had ever had a pen in his hand," he commented to Hawkesworth, "who did not think that he could have done it [the *Voyages*] with more propriety." Hawkesworth's enemies, Burney continued, "were all occasioned by his success, for if he had failed, every voice would have said, 'poor man, 'tis an ingenious, well written book, he deserved more encouragement.' " It is unlikely, though, that Burney's words gave much comfort, and Fanny herself observed solemnly that the author had "reason to detest the fortune which only preceded detraction and defamation." When Hawkesworth left the Burneys this evening, he had only a month to live.[3]

One wonders whether during these last terrible months, if Hawkesworth ever recalled his own superlative summary of the life of Jonathan Swift, those words that so grimly forecast his present state and a future response to his life and labors. While Swift was "viewed at a distance with envy," Hawkesworth had written, "he became a burden to himself; he was forsaken by his friends, and his memory has been loaded with unmerited reproach: his life, therefore, does not afford less instruction than his writings, since to the wise it may teach humility, and to the simple content."[4] Whatever desperation Hawkesworth must have felt during this troubled period, it gave way, at least temporarily, to a tranquility of spirit promoted by the deep religious commitment that one sees in a poem he dictated to his wife a month before his death. His thoughts are scarcely those of the fallen moralist various critics hounded and are an eloquent, though unpublished, reply to the "Christian" who accused him of heresy during the preceding summer.

> In Sleep's serene oblivion laid,
>   I safely past the silent night;
> At once, I see the breaking shade,
>   And drink again the morning light
>
> New born—I bless the waking hour.
>   Once more, with awe, rejoice to *be;*
> My conscious soul resumes her power,
>   And springs, my gracious God, to Thee.
>
> Oh guide me through the various maze
>   My doubtful feet are doom'd to tread;
> And spread thy shield's protecting blaze
>   When dangers press around my head.
>
> A *deeper Shade* will soon impend
>   A *deeper Sleep* my eyes oppress;
> Yet still thy Strength shall me defend,
>   Thy goodness still shall deign to bless.

That *deeper Shade* shall fade away
   That *deeper Sleep* shall leave my eyes;
Thy *light* shall give eternal day!
Thy *love*, the rapture of the skies![5]

These somber, yet joyous, verses suggest not only that Hawkesworth knew that his appointed hour was near, but also, and more significantly, that he had placed the hurt of the *Voyages*, the worst blow he had received during his life, in the larger spiritual perspective that precludes ultimate concern with the things of this world. Although few days remained, he attempted to pursue the business of life as usual. On October 16, 1773, for example, he communicated with an old friend, Charlotte Lennox. There is mention in this letter of her proposed new edition of *The Female Quixote*, which she hoped to enhance with illustrations by Giovanni Battista Cipriani, engraved by Francesco Bartolozzi, both of whom were involved with the *Voyages*. Not surprisingly, she had solicited the advice of one who had only recently engaged their services. Hawkesworth states as well that he had missed seeing Sir Joshua Reynolds, and he promises Mrs. Lennox, who had asked his advice on future literary projects, that he "will not dismiss the Subject from my Thoughts, and will do myself the pleasure to receive your further Commands the next time I am in London." Hawkesworth's letter shows him in a characteristic light as friend and advisor to one of the leading literary talents of his time, a role he had assumed for nearly a generation. Many others besides Mrs. Lennox would soon have cause to miss his good counsel. Although this is apparently Hawkesworth's last surviving letter, his final known public appearance took place on November 3, 1773, when he attended a meeting at the East India Company. Illness struck soon thereafter.[6]

Fanny Burney recorded (as Madame D'Arblay) that "a slow fever had robbed the invalid of sleep and appetite; and had so fastened upon his shattered nerves, that, after lingering a week or two, he fell a prey to incurable atrophy; and sunk to his last earthly rest exactly a month after the visit to Dr. Burney." Hawkesworth died on Wednesday evening, November 17, 1773, at the home of his friend Dr. William Grant in Lime Street, as the *Gentleman's Magazine*, among others, reported. There seems little question that whatever the immediate physical cause of death, the awful environment of turmoil he had inhabited the preceding months fatally compromised his will to live. Madame D'Arblay herself observed trenchantly: "Who shall venture to say where begins, and where ends, the complicate[d] reciprocity of influence which involves the corporeal with the intellectual part of our being?" Hawkesworth, she continues,

foresaw not the danger, to a constitution already, and perhaps natively, fragile, of yielding to the agitating effects of resentful vexation. He brooded, therefore, unresistingly, over the injustice of which he was the victim; instead of struggling to master it by the only means through which it is conquerable, namely, a calm and determined silence, that would have committed his justification to personal character;—a still, but intrepid champion, against which falsehood never ultimately prevails.[7]

The papers, which had damned him during the summer, carried admiring eulogies, the fullest appearing in Johnson's favorite, the *London Chronicle*, for November 16–18:

> He was a Gentleman of a clear and solid understanding, and good natural parts, which enabled him, more than any advantage he derived from a liberal education, to make no inconsiderable figure in the learned world. His social disposition, the chearfulness of his temper, his vivacity, his good nature, his general knowledge, the virtuous and benevolent tendency of his conversation, added to his great facility of expressing himself with ease, elegance and perspicuity upon a variety of subjects, rendered him a very agreeable, instructive, and entertaining companion to a numerous and respectable acquaintance of both sexes, by whom his loss will be severely felt and deeply lamented.

The *Lloyd's Evening Post, and British Chronicle* for November 17–19 also noted his passing, commenting, "In every literary accomplishment, and every social virtue, the Public will not soon lament a Writer of superior genius, or his numerous friends a man more justly dear and amiable." The *Public Advertiser*, which carried the diatribes of "A Christian" throughout the summer, evidently sensed the inconsistency of eulogy in its pages and published only the sparest of notices for Friday, November 19: "Wednesday Night died of a lingering Fever, John Hawkesworth, LL.D. of Bromley in Kent."

Hawkesworth was buried in the parish church of Bromley, Kent, on November 22, 1773, the Reverend Thomas Bagshaw presiding.[8] A marble monument was erected in his memory, subsequently destroyed along with a major portion of the church during World War II. Again Hawkesworth's luck was poor, for the headstone of Johnson's wife, Tetty, survived the same raid and may be seen today in the church. In death, if not in life, defenders came to Hawkesworth's aid, shocked perhaps at the passing of a friend too much ignored in his time of need. An angry correspondent in a letter directed to Mr. H. Baldwin, No. 108 Fleet Street, which appeared in the *St. James's Chronicle* for November 16–18, 1773, wrote:

> Your serious Attention is desired to the following lines.
> While Life and Vigour last, a Man is the sole Judge of an Affront

offered to his Person or Character. Amidst the various Attacks levelled at DR HAWKESWORTH in the past Year from the public Prints, he felt no Emotion but Contempt: He is now past all human Emotion.

But there remain, SIR, some who loved and honoured him, who respect his Memory too much to suffer any INSULT to be offered it with IMPUNITY.

Other testimonies appeared in contexts public and private, among them "An Epitaph on John Hawkesworth, L.L.D.," which was published in the *Gentleman's Magazine* for December 1773. It reflects the feeling and respect of a correspondent signing himself "F.F.," probably Hawkesworth's close friend Francis Fawkes, the clergyman and classicist to whose *Poetical Calendar* Johnson contributed a character of Collins. He wrote:

> HAWKESWORTH, adieu! thou most ingenuous mind,
> Firm friend to truth, in wisdom's school refin'd!
> Great was thy praise in learning to excel,
> But greater far the praise of living well:
> Great was thy pow'r the vitious to controul,
> But boundless thy benevolence of soul:
> Belov'd by all—to virtue's precepts true,
> Thou lively, cheerful, social friend, adieu! (*GM* 43:614)

Mrs. Piozzi observed in her *Anecdotes* that "Hawkesworth, the pious, the virtuous, and the wise, for want of that fortitude which casts a shield before the merits of his friend, fell a lamented sacrifice to wanton malice and cruelty, I know not how provoked; but all in turn feel the lash of censure in a country where, as every baby is allowed to carry a whip, no person can escape by chance." In *Thraliana* she testified that Hawkesworth "doubtless was one of the few, both as a Man and a Writer." While such generous sentiments as these must have given Mary Hawkesworth some comfort, her husband's death, and the circumstances that generated it, affected her deeply. The *Voyages*, she wrote to Sir James Caldwell on July 20, 1776, delivered "the *Coup de grace* to all my hopes of happiness on earth."[9]

Although Fanny Burney provided one of the kindest commentaries on Hawkesworth's passing ("The world has lost one of its best ornaments,—a man of letters who was worthy and honest") Johnson gave the most flattering testimony to Hawkesworth's memory by undertaking in 1776, with Mary Hawkesworth and John Ryland, an edition of the writer's collected works. According to a letter Mary Hawkesworth wrote to Sir James Caldwell, a family friend, Johnson had Hawkesworth's papers in hand before June 14, 1776 (the date of her letter), and she cites Johnson's procrastination as the barrier to publication. By July 20 of the year she reported to Caldwell that she expected material from Johnson daily, but he apparently was not to be rushed. He wrote to John Ryland on September 21, 1776, concerning the undertaking and again on November 14, 1776, sending Ryland a portion of the papers with the comment, "I purpose to send the rest very soon, and I believe you and I must then have two or three interviews to adjust the order in which they shall stand." The edition was still in process the following spring, and Johnson's letter to John Ryland on April 12, 1777, shows the extent of his involvement:

> Sir
> I have sent you the papers. Of this parcel I have ejected no poetry. Of the letters there are some which I should be sorry to omit, some that it is not proper to insert, and very many which as we want room or want matter we may use or neglect. When we come to these we will have another selection. But to these I think our present plan of publication will never bring us. His poems with his play will I think make two volumes. The Adventurers will make at least one, and for the fourth, as I think you intend four which will make the subscription a Guinea, if you subscribe, we have so much more than we want that the difficulty will [be] to reject.[10]

Johnson clearly took charge of the edition, suggesting contents as well as marketing strategies. No more competent editor could be found in the kingdom, no one better able to exercise astute literary judgments. "I am for letting none stand that are only relatively good as they were written in youth," he comments to Ryland. "The Buyer has no better bargain when he pays for mean performances, by being told that the authour wrote them young." But the problem was that of abundance. "I have yet not mentioned Swift's Life, nor the Novel," he continues, alluding to Hawkesworth's biography of the Dean and his *Almoran and Hamet*, an imitation of *Rasselas*. Johnson reserves highest praise for Hawkesworth's poetry, which, he suggests, "I would have printed in order of time, which he seems to have intended by noting the dates, which dates I should like to preserve, they show the progress of [his] Mind, and of a very powerful Mind."[11]

Mary Hawkesworth apparently received papers from Johnson by August 27, 1777, but for unexplained reasons no collected edition of Hawkesworth's works appeared.[12] Once again he suffered from ill luck, and the consequences of this failure can hardly be underestimated. Had such an edition appeared, under Johnson's aegis, Hawkesworth's place in the literary history of the period might have been significantly altered. Some years earlier, in his concluding *Adventurer*, Hawkesworth had written in almost stoic anticipation of his fate as a writer:

I have subscribed this paper with my name. But the hour is hastening, in which, whatever praise or censure I have acquired by these compositions, if they are remembered at all, will be remembered with equal indifference, and the tenour of them will only afford me comfort. Time, who is impatient to date my last paper, will shortly moulder the hand that is now writing it in the dust, and still the breast that now throbs at the reflection: but let not this be read as something that relates only to another; for a few years only can divide the eye that is now reading from the hand that has written. This awful truth, however obvious, and however reiterated, is yet frequently forgotten; for, surely, if we did not lose our remembrance, or at least our sensibility, that view would always predominate in our lives which alone can afford us comfort when we die.[13]

Hawkesworth's assessment of his future prospects was overly gloomy, and students of the literary-journalistic-theatrical worlds of the late eighteenth century have become increasingly aware of the extent and quality of his work. It would be difficult to cite a figure of the time who better embodied the profession of letters. A staunch adherent to Johnson's dictum that "no man but a blockhead ever wrote, except for money,"[14] Hawkesworth nevertheless left a body of writing as worthy for its literary merit as for its popular appeal. He, too, was a shaper of British culture, however much he manifests in his career the commercialization of letters in the latter half of the eighteenth century.

While specific works in his canon—his *Adventurer*, his biography and edition of Swift, his *Almoran and Hamet*, the plays he revised and wrote for Garrick—offer varied resources for students of the cultural and literary history of the period, not to mention enduring samples of a pure English prose for the general reader, in no place are the dimensions of his career more evident than in the *Gentleman's Magazine*. Perhaps no aspect of his contribution to the age is less appreciated and more deserving of further study. A principal force in the magazine during much of the age, he assessed, as literary editor, a great mass of fiction, nonfiction, drama, and poetry. In the process he passed judgment on most of the important writers of the day—Charlotte Lennox, William Hogarth, Henry Fielding, Arthur Murphy, Oliver Goldsmith, Laurence Sterne, Tobias Smollett, James Boswell, George Colman, Charles Burney, to name only a few. Most important, he gave extensive coverage to the works of his friend, Samuel Johnson, significantly boosting his contemporary reputation.

The man of letters was equally a man of his world, and to follow Hawkesworth is to encounter, in a special light, many celebrated figures of the time. A friend and associate of Benjamin Franklin, Samuel Richardson, the Dodsleys, William Strahan, Sir James Caldwell, Christopher Smart,

Edward Cave, Lord Sandwich, the Burneys, to cite several, he stands framed by two of the most eminent figures of the century, Samuel Johnson and Captain Cook, defined by the former, defining the latter. His relationship with Johnson was of greatest consequence, and his career mirrors his mentor's: each abandoned poetry for the more congenial medium of prose; each secured reputation through periodical essays; each contributed to the rise of the *Gentleman's Magazine*; each wrote eastern tales and translated from the French; each became the editor of a great literary figure; each labored to complete a work of encyclopedic dimensions—Johnson the *Dictionary*, Hawkesworth the *Voyages*. To suggest such parallels in their writing is not to insinuate a real comparison of literary talent, but to indicate that the term "minor," which Hawkesworth deserves when compared to Johnson, need not be so much a term of opprobrium as an index to the relative distance between the good and the great. Hawkesworth is linked to Johnson, then, and secured in English literary history through a lifelong connection with him.

Hawkesworth is equally secured by his relationship with Captain James Cook and the *Voyages*. The magnum opus that destroyed his reputation and probably cost him his life ironically guarantees him a place in English cultural history. Whatever the demerits of the *Voyages*—and it has endured unfair assessment by both eighteenth-century and later critics—it remains a prime introduction to Cook and the meaning of the South Seas, a sourcebook of fact and myth blended together presenting one of the great sagas of navigation and discovery.

To be associated, then, with two such figures is not an unhappy lot for such a writer as Hawkesworth. It ensures that as long as interest remains in Johnson and Cook—and this should persist as long as John Bull's spirit walks the earth—his substantial accomplishments will be noted.

To have described, even at this length, the dimensions of Hawkesworth's life and work is not to have exhausted him as a subject for future investigation that should further enhance his reputation and clarify his contributions to the later eighteenth century. Still, if one seeks now to identify a single quality of person or craft by which he deserves to be remembered, it might not be a single work, however important the *Voyages*, however central the moral concerns of the *Adventurer*, however imposing the great review canon in the *Gentleman's Magazine*, but his literary style. It is in his prose style that Hawkesworth is most Johnsonian, most deserves comparison with his great mentor.

Of Johnson's prose, that enduring manifestation of his greatness and genius whatever subject matter he cared to address, Boswell writes with characteristic felicity: "His sentences have a dignified march; and, it is certain, that his example has given an elevation to the language of his country, for many of our best writers have approached very near to him; and, from the influence which he has had upon our composition, scarcely any thing is written now that is not better expressed than was usual before he appeared to lead the national taste." Few writers of the period stood better witness in their prose works to the example of Johnson's prose style than Hawkesworth. In Boswell's own words, his "imitations of Johnson are sometimes so happy, that it is extremely difficult to distinguish them, with certainty, from the compositions of his great archetype."[15] As in Johnson's prose, so in Hawkesworth's, one finds a consistent commitment to the proper use of the language that sustains and elevates our lives, a commitment reflecting the conviction that style is not so much a nicety as a necessity that preserves order and sanity. Like Johnson, he resisted the incessant corrosions and the flippancy of matter to which language is subjected, and it is for this dedication and his lifelong effort to add sense and clarity to the language and literature of the nation that he might best be remembered.

A study of Hawkesworth's life suggests, finally, that the eighteenth century gained illumination not merely from such great writers as Johnson but from a number of lesser figures worthy to be numbered among his school. Among them one must count Dr. John Hawkesworth of Grub Street obscurity and Admiralty fame—an eighteenth-century man of letters.

Notes / Index

Abbreviations and Short Titles

Adventurer	*The Adventurer*, ed. John Hawkesworth, 4 vols. (London, 1793).
Biographia Dramatica	*Biographia Dramatica*, comp. David Erskine Baker, Isaac Reed, and Stephen Jones, 3 vols. (London, 1812).
BL	British Library, London
Burney, *Early Diary*	*The Early Diary of Frances Burney, 1768–1778*, ed. Annie Raine Ellis, 2 vols. (London, 1889).
Chalmers, *British Essayists*	Alexander Chalmers, "Historical and Biographical Preface to *The Adventurer*," in *The British Essayists*, vol. 23 (London, 1802).
Garrick Letters	*The Letters of David Garrick*, ed. David M. Little and George M. Kahrl, 3 vols. (Cambridge: Harvard Univ. Press, 1963).
GM	The *Gentleman's Magazine*
Hawkins, *Life of Johnson*	Sir John Hawkins, *The Life of Samuel Johnson, LL.D.*, 2d ed. (London, 1787).
Hyde Collection	Hyde Collection at Four Oaks Farm, near Somerville, New Jersey.
Johnson's England	*Johnson's England*, ed. A. S. Turberville, 2 vols. (1933; rpt. Oxford: Clarendon Press, 1967).
Johnson Letters	*The Letters of Samuel Johnson*, ed. R. W. Chapman, 3 vols. (Oxford: Clarendon Press, 1952).
JRULMS.	The John Rylands University Library of Manchester. Letters prefixed B 3/10/ are copies found in Caldwell's letter books. Others are originals.
Life	*Boswell's Life of Johnson*, ed. G. B. Hill, rev. and enl. by L. F. Powell, 6 vols. (Oxford: Clarendon Press, 1934–50; 2d ed. of vols. 5–6, 1964).

Nichols, *Illustrations*   John Nichols, *Illustrations of the Literary History of the Eighteenth Century*, 8 vols. (London, 1817–58).

Osborn Sketch   Untitled, anonymously authored sketch found in the papers of William Hayley (1745–1820). Now in the James Marshall and Marie-Louise Osborn Collection, Beinecke Library, Yale University.

PRO   Public Record Office, London

Shaw, *Memoirs—*   William Shaw, *Memoirs of the Life and Writings of the Late*
    Piozzi, Anecdotes   *Dr. Samuel Johnson*; Hester Lynch Piozzi, *Anecdotes of the Late Samuel Johnson, LL.D.*, ed. Arthur Sherbo (London: Oxford Univ. Press, 1974).

Thraliana   *Thraliana: The Diary of Mrs Hester Lynch Thrale (Later Mrs. Piozzi), 1776–1809*, ed. Katherine C. Balderston, 2 vols. (Oxford: Clarendon Press, 1942; 2d ed., 1951).

Universal Magazine   "Memoirs of the Life of Dr. John Hawkesworth," *Uni-*
    "Memoirs"   *versal Magazine*, 111 (1802): 233–39.

Yale *Idler &*   *The Idler and the Adventurer*, ed. Walter J. Bate, John M.
    Adventurer   Bullitt, and L. F. Powell, vol. 2 of The Yale Edition of *The Works of Samuel Johnson* (New Haven: Yale Univ. Press, 1963).

YSJ   James L. Clifford, *Young Samuel Johnson* (1955; rpt. London: Mercury Books, 1962).

Notes

Chapter I: Early Years and Removal to Bromley

1 *Early Diary*, 1:262–63.

2 Ibid., pp. 263–64.

3 There are a number of biographical commentaries on Hawkesworth. The earliest appears in *Biographia Dramatica*, 1, pt. 1:316–17. This entry was probably compiled by Isaac Reed about 1782. Others include *A New and General Biographical Dictionary* (London, 1784), 6:477–78; the *Universal Magazine*'s "Memoirs" of Hawkesworth's life (1802); Alexander Chalmers's "Historical and Biographical Preface to *The Adventurer*," in *The British Essayists*, vol. 23 (London, 1802); Leigh Hunt, *Classic Tales* (London, 1807), 4:219–36; Alexander Chalmers, "Hawkesworth," in *The General Biographical Dictionary* (London, 1814), 17:235–42 (which repeats much of his 1802 commentary above); R. Freeman, *Kentish Poets* (Canterbury, 1821), 2:176–234; Edward E. Morris, "Doctor John Hawkesworth, Friend of Dr. Johnson and Historian of Captain Cook's First Voyage," *Gentleman's Magazine* 289 (1900):218–38. There are several unpublished studies of Hawkesworth, the most valuable the Osborn Sketch in the James Marshall and Marie-Louise Osborn Collection, Beinecke Library, Yale University. Apparently based on first-hand knowledge of one who knew Hawkesworth well, it is essential in illuminating many aspects of his life. Also useful are H. E. Webster, "John Hawkesworth: A Biography and a Critical Study of his Work in the Periodicals" (M.A. thesis, Univ. of London, 1949); R. E. Gallagher, "John Hawkesworth: A Study towards a Literary Biography" (Ph.D. diss., Northwestern Univ., 1957). I survey Hawkesworth's literary career briefly in "John Hawkesworth: Friend of Samuel Johnson and Editor of Captain Cook's *Voyages* and of the *Gentleman's Magazine*," *Eighteenth-Century Studies* 3 (1970):339–50.

4 Information about the Hawkesworth family is found in Records of St. Pancras parish (i.e., of St. Pancras Old Church, Pancras Road, and of St. Pancras, Euston Road, St. Pancras), deposited in the London County Record Office, London. The marriage of Hawkesworth's parents, Hawkesworth's baptism, and Thomas Hawkesworth's baptism are recorded in P90/ PAN1/ 1,3. I could not locate Honor's baptismal record, though her marriage license (see n. 16 below) enables one to determine the year of her birth. Guildhall MS. 6667/8 records the baptism of a Peter Hawkesworth in the parish of St. Andrew Holborn on August 29, 1718. His parents bear the same names as John's, and he may have been another brother who failed to survive. No evidence survives concerning the assertion in *Biographia Dramatica* that Hawkesworth was of "the sect of Presbyterians, and a member of the celebrated Tom Bradbury's meeting, from which

he was expelled for some irregularities" (1, pt. 1:316). A search at Dr. Williams's Library in London produced no information about this charge, and there are no references to Hawkesworth in Walter Wilson, *The History and Antiquities of Dissenting Churches* (London, 1808).

5   Osborn Sketch, fol. 1.

6   Ibid., fol. 1.

7   Hawkins, *Life of Johnson*, p. 252.

8   Freeman, *Kentish Poets*, 2:178.

9   PRO, I.R. 1. 15, fol. 164.

10   Freeman, *Kentish Poets*, 2:177. Osborn Sketch, fol. 1. The bitter winter is described in *YSJ*, pp. 222–23.

11   John Nichols, *Literary Anecdotes of the Eighteenth Century* (London, 1815), 9:500–501.

12   *Adventurer*, 1:80. This edition is based on the second, revised edition published in 1754. Subsequent references to this work will appear in the text.

13   Nichols, *Literary Anecdotes*, 9:501–2.

14   I quote from a letter (not in Hawkesworth's hand) dated 1738, found in the Osborn Collection, Yale University.

15   "Sketch of the Character of the late Dr. Hawkesworth," *Annual Register* 18 (1775):53–54. Hereafter cited as *Annual Register* "Sketch."

16   Letter in the Hyde Collection. The John Ryland–Honor Hawkesworth license (Guildhall Matrimonial Allegations, 1742, fol. 256) lists Honor as twenty-three years of age as of June 11, 1742, the date of the license. The marriage took place on June 19 (PRO, L.C. 5/211, p. 53).

17   1742 letter, Hyde Collection. Hawkesworth probably refers to Pope's "humbling" by Colley Cibber, who had attacked Pope in a pamphlet published in 1742. See Peter Quennel, *Alexander Pope: The Education of a Genius, 1688–1728* (New York: Stein and Day, 1968), p. 238.

18   *Life*, 1:47.

19   Osborn Sketch, fol. 2.

20   Freeman, *Kentish Poets*, 2:179. Their marriage license is found in the Lambeth Palace Library, MS. V/Cant iv cont. 1744, i. John Hawkesworth of "the Parish of Saint Andrew Holborn in the County of Middlesex Aged Twenty Three Years a Batchelor" alleges "that he intends to Marry with Mary Brown of the Parish of Saint Clements Danes in the Same County Aged Twenty two years and a Spinster." The ceremony is noted in London County Record Office, P90/PAN 1/2,4. Joseph Cradock, *Literary and Miscellaneous Memoirs* (London, 1828), 4:185.

21   Hawkins, *Life of Johnson*, pp. 310–11. There are some sixteen folio manuscript pages of notes by Norman and others in the Bromley Central Library, which provide considerable evidence about the Hawkesworths in Bromley. Freeman, *Kentish Poets*, 2:183 *n*. The burial of Mary Hawkesworth's mother, Sarah Brown, is recorded in the church register and the register of John Dunn (a local undertaker), both in the church of St. Peter and St. Paul, Bromley.

22   The MS. letter, in Mary Hawkesworth's hand, is found in the Hyde Collection.

23   Details about the house are found in *Archaeologia Cantiana: Being Transactions of the Kent Archaeological Society* (London, 1880), 13:151–53. E. L. S. Horsburgh,

Bromley, Kent, from the Earliest Times to the Present Century (London: Hodder and Stoughton, 1929), p. 31. MS. notes in Bromley Central Library. Deeds to the property were kindly searched for me by former library archivist J. C. M. Shaw. The name of Hawkesworth is found in the mortgage of 1751 (Bromley Central Library, B200) and then in B11, 12, 13, 15, and 202. Assessment books are preserved in the library, but a gap in the records from April 1737 to March 1757 prevents our knowing the exact date of the beginning of the Hawkesworth tenancy in the Thornhill Mansion. Mary Hawkesworth's burial is recorded in the church register for September 28, 1796. Her property holdings are noted in the Bromley Central Library, MS. notes.

24 Freeman, *Kentish Poets* 2:180. Edward Walford, *Greater London: A Narrative of Its History, Its People, and Its Places* (London, 1882), 2:84. MS. notes in the Bromley Central Library provide details about the excavation. *Johnson Letters*, 3:260.

25 Freeman, *Kentish Poets*, 2:185, 192.

26 Details about the Bell Hotel are taken from an undated newspaper clipping in the Bromley Central Library, Bromley Local Collection, Illustrations Box no. 1.A— Bromley Palace. *Life*, 2:451.

27 Freeman, *Kentish Poets*, 1:342; 2:185.

28 Vestry minutes are preserved in the Bromley Parish Church. Hawkesworth's letters to Caldwell are JRULMSS. B3/10/137 and B3/10/ 138.

29 Hawkesworth left no will, only an administration. Mary Hawkesworth's will is in Somerset House, Ref. PCC Harris, fol. 505, 1796. Dunn's register of baptisms (see n. 21 above) reveals the employment of a footman at the Hawkesworth home, a John Wood, who became a father three times between 1769 and 1771.

30 Hawkesworth's sittings for Reynolds are noted in Charles Robert Leslie and Tom Taylor, *Life and Times of Sir Joshua Reynolds* (London, 1865), 1:348, 375, 465; 2:55. The sittings took place during September 1769, January 1770, October 1772, and July 1773. Burney, *Early Diary*, 1:263. For Goldsmith's comment, see Shaw's *Memoirs—Piozzi's Anecdotes*, p. 55.

Chapter II: Johnson, the *Adventurer*, and Dr. Hawkesworth

1 Shaw, *Memoirs—Piozzi, Anecdotes*, pp. 7, 10.

2 Ibid., p. 70. There is a variant of this comment in *Thraliana* that reads: "After my coming to London you will be at a Loss again; though Jack Hawkesworth and Baretti both, with whom I lived quite familiarly, can tell you pretty nearly all my Adventures from the Year 1753" (1:173). The time that the Thrales took Johnson up is hard to date exactly but occurred around 1765. See *Life*, 1:520–22.

3 *Universal Magazine* "Memoirs," p. 234. Osborn Sketch, fol. 2.

4 The best summary of Johnson's early years is James L. Clifford's *Young Samuel Johnson* (London: Mercury Books, 1962). Hereafter cited as *YSJ*. I survey some of his early journalism in "No 'Dialect of France': Samuel Johnson's Translations from the French," *University of Toronto Quarterly* 36 (1967): 129–40.

5 *Annual Register* "Sketch," p. 53.

6 *Life*, 2:75. W. S. Lewis, *Three Tours through London in the Years 1748–1776–1797* (1941; rpt. Westport, Conn.: Greenwood Press, 1971), p. 13.

7 Derbyshire County Record Office, Fitzherbert Papers, D239, Matlock. "Anecdotes & Occurrences in the Life of Sarah Perrin, Afterwards Fitzherbert," pp. 14–15. I wish to thank James L. Clifford for alerting me to this material. Information provided by Miss J. C. Sinar, county archivist, suggests that the two episodes took place in the late 1740s and early 1750s.

8 *YSJ*, p. 227.

9 *YSJ*, pp. 228–31.

10 *YSJ*, pp. 180–81, 235.

11 Hawkins, *Life of Johnson*, pp. 222–23, 233.

12 *Life*, 1:190. *Universal Magazine* "Memoirs," p. 234.

13 For a convenient summary of this complex affair see James L. Clifford, "Johnson and Lauder," *Philological Quarterly* 54 (1975):342–56. The best student of the subject is Michael Marcuse. See his "The *Gentleman's Magazine* and the Lauder/Milton Controversy," *Bulletin of Research in the Humanities* 81 (1978):179–209.

14 Donald Greene argues for Johnson's authorship of the *Gentleman's* explanation and apology entitled "Some Account of the Present State of the Controversy Concerning Milton's Imitation of the Moderns" (*GM* 20 [Dec. 1750]:535–36) in "Some Notes on Johnson and the *Gentleman's Magazine*," *PMLA* 74 (1959):83–84. Johnson's last words on the matter are in Arthur Murphy's account of his life in G. B. Hill, ed., *Johnsonian Miscellanies* (1897; rpt. New York: Barnes & Noble, 1966), 1:398.

15 Hawkins, *Life of Johnson*, pp. 286–87. For the dating of this episode see James L. Clifford, *Dictionary Johnson* (New York: McGraw-Hill, 1979), pp. 42–43.

16 Osborn Sketch, fol. 2.

17 Britain converted to the Gregorian calendar in September 1752. Thereafter Johnson fixed the date of Tetty's death as March 28. The best summary of Mrs. Johnson's death is by James L. Clifford in *Dictionary Johnson*, chap. 6. I draw here on *Life*, 1:238; Hill, *Johnsonian Miscellanies*, 2:359. See my "Dr. Johnson and Dr. Hawkesworth: A Literary Friendship," *The New Rambler* 111 (Autumn 1971): 2–21.

18 *Life*, 1:241. Hawkins, *Life of Johnson*, pp. 314–15.

19 *Life*, 1:99, 234. Clifford, *Dictionary Johnson*, p. 17.

20 For Johnson's letter to Charlotte Lennox see Duncan Isles, "The Lennox Collection," *Harvard Library Bulletin* 18 (1970):343. Albert E. J. Hollaender, keeper of manuscripts at the Guildhall Library, London, wrote to me on October 1, 1970, in reference to burial outside a home parish: "A clause in a testator's will or a decision by the responsible relict(s) coupled with the consent of the incumbent of the out-parish to receive the body for interment was usually sufficient and over the centuries many residents of the metropolis are known to have been buried outside of London, sometimes even at great distance from both the Cities of London and Westminster and deep in the country." Hawkesworth, in fact, may have secured permission himself from his friend, the Reverend Bagshaw, to inter Tetty in Bromley.

21 Burial information is found in the church registers of St. Peter and St. Paul, Bromley. Besides James L. Clifford, I am much indebted to Harry MacLeod Currie and David D. Brown for their help in clarifying some of the problems

connected with Tetty's burial at Bromley. At the time of my investigation of this subject they were Bromley residents and members of the church in which she is buried. The Reverend Canon A. R. Winnett commented to the Johnson Society of London on November 21, 1970, that Johnson's delay in ordering a headstone for Tetty would not have been unusual at the time. The letter ordering the headstone is in *Johnson Letters*, 3:181.

22 Osborn Sketch, fol. 2. *Universal Magazine* "Memoirs," p. 234. Hawkins, *Life of Johnson*, p. 293. Arthur Sherbo identifies M'Ghie as a participant, who apparently failed at translating one of the paper's mottoes, in one of the best specialized studies of the work, *Samuel Johnson, Editor of Shakespeare, with an Essay on the "Adventurer,"* Illinois Studies in Language and Literature, 42 (Urbana: Univ. of Illinois Press, 1956), pp. 148–49.

23 *Life*, 1:215.

24 *Adventurer*, 4:240–42. Subsequent references to this edition are in the text.

25 Hawkins, *Life of Johnson*, p. 293. Chalmers, *British Essayists*, 23:x; 30:xxviii. The best studies of this periodical include Sherbo's *Johnson, Editor of Shakespeare*, L. F. Powell's introduction to the Yale *Idler & Adventurer*, and Clifford's *Dictionary Johnson*, chap. 7. The definitive, though unpublished, study of the *Adventurer* is by Philip Mahone Griffith, "A Study of the *Adventurer* (1752–1754)" (Ph.D. diss., Univ. of North Carolina, 1961). The complicated problem of authorship in the *Adventurer* is best untangled by David Fairer in "Authorship Problems in *The Adventurer*," *Review of English Studies*, n.s. 25 (1974):137–51. The rival claims of Bathurst and Thornton are argued by Philip Mahone Griffith, "The Authorship of the Papers Signed 'A' in Hawkesworth's *Adventurer*: A Stronger Case for Dr. Richard Bathurst," *Tulane Studies in English* 12 (1962):63–70, and Victor J. Lams, "The 'A' Papers in the *Adventurer*: Bonnell Thornton, not Dr. Bathurst, Their Author," *Studies in Philology* 64 (1967):83–96.

26 BL, Add. MS. 42,560, fol. 24, Joseph Warton to Thomas Warton, Nov. 17, 1752. Fairer, "Authorship Problems," p. 140. Joseph Warton to James Boswell, March 30, 1790, in *The Correspondence and Other Papers of James Boswell Relating to the Making of the "Life of Johnson,"* ed. Marshall Waingrow (New York: McGraw-Hill [1969]), p. 311.

27 *The Rambler*, ed. W. J. Bate and Albrecht B. Strauss, vol. 5 of the Yale Edition of *The Works of Samuel Johnson* (New Haven and London: Yale Univ. Press, 1969), p. 318. Hereafter cited as Yale *Rambler*. Hawkesworth's ailment is mentioned in John Payne's letter to Dr. Warton of February 2, 1754, which is reprinted in Dr. Powell's introduction to the Yale *Idler & Adventurer* and originally appeared in *Willis's Current Notes* for February 1857, p. 14. Fairer, "Authorship Problems," pp. 137–39, calls attention to an autograph manuscript of Payne's letter in the Hyde Collection that differs in several respects from the printed version. *Johnson Letters*, 1:48.

28 Richardson's letter is found in the Victoria and Albert Museum, Forster Collection 457 (48.E.5). I quote from the Yale *Idler & Adventurer*, p. 332.

29 The same size and format as the *Rambler*, the *Adventurer* also appeared on the same days of the week (Tuesday and Saturday), prefaced with a Latin or a Greek motto. With no classical training, Hawkesworth had to rely entirely on his

friends for this feature of the paper, which is best illuminated by Arthur Sherbo (see n. 22 above). Griffith, "A Study of the *Adventurer*," provides a detailed account of the revisions made by the paper's various authors between the first and second editions.

30 Yale *Rambler*, 3:24.

31 See Gerald B. Kauvar, "Coleridge, Hawkesworth, and the Willing Suspension of Disbelief," *Papers on English Language and Literature* 5 (1969):91–94. Since one deals here with something of a critical commonplace, it may not be possible, as Kauvar argues, to locate its origin in a single source.

32 The standard study of oriental fiction, on which I draw here, is Martha Pike Conant, *The Oriental Tale in England in the Eighteenth Century* (New York: Columbia Univ. Press, 1908). This should be supplemented by Robert D. Mayo, *The English Novel in the Magazines, 1740–1815* (Evanston, Ill.: Northwestern Univ. Press, 1962), which provides extensive commentary on Hawkesworth's oriental pieces and his fiction in general.

33 Nathan Drake, *Essays, Biographical, Critical, and Historical, Illustrative of the "Rambler," "Adventurer," and "Idler"* (London, 1810), 2:10.

34 *Letters from the Late Most Reverend Dr. Thomas Herring, Lord Archbishop of Canterbury, to William Duncombe, Esq., deceased, From the Year 1728–1757* (London, 1777), p. 354.

35 Drake, *Essays*, 2:16–17, gives details of Gay's mishap, first described, apparently, in Johnson's *Life of Gay*.

36 Swift to Pope in a letter dated September 29, 1725, in *The Correspondence of Jonathan Swift*, ed. Harold Williams (Oxford: Clarendon Press, 1963), 3:103. Hereafter cited as Williams, *Swift Correspondence*.

37 Arthur Murphy, *Gray's-Inn Journal* (London, 1756), 2:5. Griffith in "A Study of the *Adventurer*" (pp. 20–21) provides information about the paper's circulation and Payne's profits. He examines its contemporary success in " 'A Truly Elegant Work': The Contemporary Reputation of Hawkesworth's *Adventurer*," in *The Dress of Words: Essays on Restoration and Eighteenth-Century Literature in Honor of Richmond P. Bond*, ed. Robert B. White, Jr., University of Kansas Library Series, 42 (Lawrence: Univ. of Kansas Printing Service, 1978), pp. 199–208.

38 Griffith, "A Study of the *Adventurer*," pp. 252–62, traces the paper's subsequent reputation. Drake, *Essays*, 2:18.

39 *A Series of Letters Between Mrs. Elizabeth Carter and Miss Catherine Talbot from the Year 1741 to 1770*, ed. Rev. Montagu Pennington (London, 1809), 2:109. Courtenay's comment is in *Life*, 1:223.

40 *Life*, 1:252. Chapman's comment is found in his review of Allen T. Hazen's *Samuel Johnson's Prefaces and Dedications* in *Review of English Studies* 14 (1938):361.

41 James Sutherland, "Some Aspects of Eighteenth-Century Prose," in *Essays on the Eighteenth Century, Presented to David Nichol Smith*, ed. James Sutherland and F. P. Wilson (Oxford: Clarendon Press, 1945), p. 103. This volume is hereafter cited as D. Nichol Smith *Festschrift*.

42 Chalmers, *British Essayists*, 23:xxvii. Drake, *Essays*, 2:7.

43 *Life*, 1:252–53.

44 Peter Gay, "The Spectator as Actor: Addison in Perspective," *Encounter* 29 (Dec.

1967):31. C. S. Lewis, "Addison," in D. Nichol Smith *Festschrift*, p. 7.
45 Hawkins, *Life of Johnson*, p. 311.
46 Lambeth Palace Library, Faculty Office Muniment Book, FII/1756/31; FI, fol. 111v.
47 Hawkins, *Life of Johnson*, pp. 311–12.
48 *Life*, 1:489. Hill, *Johnsonian Miscellanies*, 2:297–98.
49 Hawkins, *Life of Johnson*, 360.

Chapter III: Biographer and Editor of Swift

1 Swift to Pope, September 29, 1725, in Williams, *Swift Correspondence*, 3:102.
2 Hawkesworth was only one of several involved in editing Swift during the century. Others included William Boyer, Deane Swift, and John Nichols. The best examination of this complex subject is by Pierre Danchin, "The Text of *Gulliver's Travels*," *Texas Studies in Literature and Language* 2 (1960): 233–50.
3 *Life*, 1:7. For lives of Swift see Sir Harold Williams, "Swift's Early Biographers," in *Pope and His Contemporaries*, ed. James L. Clifford and Louis Landa (Oxford: Clarendon Press, 1949), pp. 114–28. Wayne Warncke, "Samuel Johnson on Swift: The *Life of Swift* and Johnson's Predecessors in Swiftian Biography," *Journal of British Studies* 7 (May 1968):56–64. Paul J. Korshin, "Johnson and Swift: A Study in the Genesis of Literary Opinion," *Philological Quarterly* 48 (1969): 464–78. Jordan Richman, "Subjectivity in the Art of Eighteenth-Century Biography: Johnson's Portrait of Swift," *Enlightenment Essays* 2 (1971):91–102. I would like to thank former University of Connecticut graduate students in English André Dupré and Donna Brown for sharing their work on Hawkesworth, Johnson, and Swift with me.
4 *The Works of Dr. Jonathan Swift*, ed. John Hawkesworth (London, 1766), 1:2. Hereafter cited as Hawkesworth, *Swift*. I quote from the large octavo edition in twelve volumes. Subsequent references appear in the text.
5 Absolute proof of Swift's marriage to Stella has never been produced.
6 Thomas Sheridan, *The Life of the Rev. Dr. Jonathan Swift* (London, 1784), n. pag. (Introduction). Warncke, "Johnson on Swift," p. 58.
7 Samuel Johnson, "Swift," in *Lives of the English Poets*, ed. G. B. Hill (1905; rpt. New York: Octagon Books, 1967), 3:1. Subsequent references appear in the text.
8 *Johnson Letters*, 2:390. Item 267 (17) in the *Sale Catalogue* is described by Donald Greene as "Faulkner's edition, 1735, or Hawkesworth's, 1755, or a combination of them, or a miscellaneous collection of individual works" in *Samuel Johnson's Library: An Annotated Guide*, English Literary Studies, Monograph Series, no. 1 (Victoria, B.C.: Univ. of Victoria, 1975), p. 108.
9 Deane Swift commented to John Nichols that "Hawkesworth's edition of Swift's Works is the vilest that was ever published" (Nichols, *Illustrations*, 5:376). Danchin, "Text of *Gulliver's Travels*," p. 237, says, "There does not seem to be much doubt that he was a carelss editor." Danchin's study shows, though, the difficult editorial problems that Hawkesworth faced.
10 Sir Harold Williams elaborated on his choice of the Irish edition in *The Text of "Gulliver's Travels"* (Cambridge: Cambridge Univ. Press, 1952). The value of this

text is disputed by Arthur E. Case in "The Text of *Gulliver's Travels*," in *Four Essays on "Gulliver's Travels"* (Princeton: Princeton Univ. Press, 1945), and by W. B. Todd's review of Williams' 1952 study in *Library*, 5th ser. 8 (1953):280–82. Danchin, a supporter of the Irish edition, is severe in his assessment of Hawkesworth's editorial role. He concludes: "His unfairness in not recognizing the merits of the man he copied has probably but one explanation: he wanted to show his own edition as superior to its Dublin rival. And his preface, after all, seems to have no other than a commercial aim" ("Text of *Gulliver's Travels*," p. 244). Faulkner himself, though, apparently held no grudge. Some years later, on July 14, 1763, he wrote from Dublin to Sir John Caldwell: "How are D^r. Hawkesworth and M^r. Johnson? I hope they are both well, and that you will be pleased to make my best Wishes and Respects to them, and should be glad to know, *if the former got my present of Swift's Works to him*" (JRULMS. B 3/16/88).

11 *Life*, 2:319.

12 Kathleen Williams, ed., *Swift: The Critical Heritage* (New York: Barnes & Noble, 1970), p. 19. She reprints a number of Hawkesworth's notes in her survey of critical views on Swift.

13 Norman O. Brown, *Life Against Death: The Psychoanalytic Meaning of History* (Middletown, Conn.: Wesleyan Univ. Press, 1959), p. 180. *The Works of William Makepeace Thackeray with Biographical Introduction by His Daughter, Anne Ritchie*, vol. 7, *"The History of Henry Esmond, Esq.," and the Lectures* (New York, 1899), p. 446. George Orwell, "Politics vs. Literature: An Examination of *Gulliver's Travels*," in *The Collected Essays, Journalism, and Letters of George Orwell* (Harmondsworth: Penguin Books, 1970), 4:261. Aldous Huxley, *Do What You Will* (London: Chatto & Windus, 1929), p. 99. John Middleton Murray, *Jonathan Swift* (London: Jonathan Cape, 1954), pp. 432–48.

14 Hawkesworth's extensive involvement with the *Journal to Stella* has been carefully explored by Sir Harold Williams in "Deane Swift, Hawkesworth, and *The Journal to Stella*" in D. Nichol Smith *Festschrift*, pp. 33–48, and in Williams' *Jonathan Swift: Journal to Stella*, 2 vols. (Oxford: Clarendon Press, 1948).

15 Williams, *Journal to Stella*, 2:503, 537–38. John Nichols writes of Hawkesworth's omissions in *GM* 47 (Nov. 1777):531: "But, if the letters are to be at all published, I can by no means think it right that any part of them should be *suppressed*, as they certainly exhibit the most faithful picture of the times that is any where to be met with: and in this particular I am very happy to be countenanced by our author's worthy kinsman Mr. Deane Swift, who appears to have faithfully published that part of the Journal which came into his hands."

16 For all his shortcomings as Swift's editor, Hawkesworth still remains a figure of some importance in any study of Swift. He is, for example, the source of some forty-one letters in Sir Harold Williams' edition of Swift's correspondence, and A. C. Guthkelch and D. Nichol Smith depend upon him occasionally in their edition of *A Tale of a Tub*.

Chapter IV: Hawkesworth, Garrick, and the Theater

1 "Smith," in *Lives of the English Poets*, ed. G. B. Hill (New York: Octagon Books, 1967), 2:21.

2 *Garrick Letters*, 1:235. Sometimes the dates of Garrick's letters can only be approximated. In the first sentence here Garrick refers to Voltaire's *Amélie; ou, Le Duc de Foix* (Paris, 1752).

3 *The London Stage, 1660–1800* (Carbondale: Southern Illinois Univ. Press, 1960–68), *Part IV: 1747–1776*, ed. George Winchester Stone, Jr., 3 vols. (1962), 2:722ff.

4 *Garrick Letters*, 1:248, 250.

5 Ibid., p. 249. Hawkesworth's connection with Greville and Burney is also noted in Roger Lonsdale, *Dr. Charles Burney: A Literary Biography* (Oxford: Clarendon Press, 1965), p. 21.

6 Hawkesworth's assistance is noted in *Life*, 4:535. I quote from Hawkesworth's holograph letter in the Hyde Collection, which is reprinted in part in *Letters of Samuel Johnson*, ed. G. B. Hill (Oxford, 1892), 1:60–61. Besides offering comfort to Greville, Hawkesworth's words confirm Boswell's assertion that Johnson did not read books through. *Life*, 2:226.

7 *Garrick Letters*, 1:249, 255.

8 For this summary I draw on W. J. Lawrence, "The Drama and the Theatre," in *Johnson's England*, 2:160–89, and George Winchester Stone, Jr., *The London Stage, 1747–1776: A Critical Introduction* (Carbondale: Southern Illinois Univ. Press, 1968), vol. 4.

9 *Amphitryon* (London, 1756), n. pag. Hawkesworth's adaptation, which may be found in the Huntington Library, Larpent Collection, LA 126, is based on the 1732 edition of Dryden's play (London: printed for J. Tonson). Subsequent citations to both versions appear in the text, differentiated by "Dryden" or "Hawkesworth." Other Hawkesworth plays in manuscript at the Huntington include *Oroonoko*, 1759 (LA 162), *Edgar and Emmeline: A Fairy Tale*, 1761 (LA 185), and two brief oratorios—*Zimri*, 1760 (LA 169) and *The Fall of Egypt*, 1774 (LA 369). The first oratorio was performed at Covent Garden in 1760, the second at Drury Lane in 1774, a year after Hawkesworth's death. John Stanley composed the music for both works, which reveal themes dear to Hawkesworth, especially the necessity and rewards of virtue. See Stone, *The London Stage, Part 4: 1747–1776*, 2:778 and 3:1796.

10 For the play's run see Stone, *The London Stage, Part 4: 1747–1776*, 2:570–72ff., and *The London Stage, Part 5: 1776–1800*, ed. Charles Beecher Hogan, 3 vols. (1968), 1:77ff.; 2:635, 706. Warburton's comment is in *The Private Correspondence of David Garrick*, ed. James Boaden (London, 1831–32), 1:78. Hereafter cited as Boaden, *Garrick Correspondence*. Thornton's assessment is in *Biographia Dramatica*, 2:27.

11 *Garrick Letters*, 1:246, 248.

12 Stone, *The London Stage, Part 4: 1747–1776*, 2:586. The Shakespeare reference is in *Biographia Dramatica*, 1, pt. 1:360. Hume's praise is found in his dedication to Home in *Four Dissertations* (London, 1757), pp. v–vi. Little and Kahrl first attributed *A Letter to Mr. David Hume*, . . . to Hawkesworth in *Garrick Letters*, 1:260. Dates of publication for this and *Douglas Analyzed* are from the *Public Advertiser*.

13 Hawkesworth, *A Letter to Mr. David Hume*, pp. 3–5.

14 Ibid., pp. 6, 8–10.

15 Ibid., pp. 18–19. Garrick's final response to Hawkesworth is in *Garrick Letters*, 1:260.

16 *Garrick Letters*, 1:xxxviii–xxxix.

17 Ibid., pp. 305–6.

18 Ibid., pp. 268, 271–72. Cautherly's career is detailed on p. 305.

19 *The Rout* was performed on December 20 and 21, 1758. See Stone, *The London Stage, Part 4: 1747–1776*, 2:701–2. *Garrick Letters*, 1:299. Hawkesworth not only defended his friend in the columns of the *Gentleman's Magazine*, but reviewed plays there of which Garrick was complete or partial author. These include *The Guardian* (*GM* 29 [Feb. 1759]:84–86), *The Clandestine Marriage* (*GM* 36 [March 1766]:124–28), *Neck or Nothing* (*GM* 36 [Dec. 1766]:591), *Cymon* (*GM* 37 [Jan. 1767]:28–32), *A Peep behind the Curtain* (*GM* 37 [Nov. 1767]:561–62), and *The Irish Widow* (*GM* 42 [Nov. 1772]:528–32). Hawkesworth's coverage of these plays, while generally favorable, was not sycophantic; he judged them by the same standards he applied to drama generally. Of *The Irish Widow* he wrote, for example: "It is manifestly written to exhibit a character which has never before been brought upon the stage; it is sprightly and comic, but its merit lies rather in character than incidents, and the effect of the dialogue rises chiefly from the provincial dialect" (p. 528).

20 *Garrick Letters*, 1:306–7.

21 Ibid., pp. 316–17, 319.

22 *GM* 22 (April 1752):163. The opening paragraphs of this review exhibit his characteristic vigor and force, but the use of the phrase "in my humble opinion" is unlike Hawkesworth. In criticism he was never humble.

23 *Oroonoko* (London, 1775), n. pag. The Larpent MS. of this play (Huntington Library, LA 162) has no prologue. It was introduced during the play's second performance, on December 3, 1759. See Stone, *The London Stage, Part 4: 1747–1776*, 2:759.

24 *Oroonoko* (London, 1778), p. 3.

25 Production details are in Stone, *The London Stage, Part 4: 1747–1776*, 2:759–60 ff. *Biographia Dramatica*, 3:103.

26 *Critical Review* 8 (Dec. 1759):480, 485–86. The review was attributed to Johnson by Stephen Jones in *Biographia Dramatica*, 3:104. See Donald Greene, "The Development of the Johnson Canon," in *Restoration and Eighteenth-Century Literature: Essays in Honor of Alan Dugald McKillop*, ed. Carroll Camden (Chicago: Univ. of Chicago Press, 1963), p. 421.

27 *Edgar and Emmeline: A Fairy Tale*, Huntington Library, Larpent Collection, LA 185, p. 2. Subsequent references to this manuscript appear in the text. There are slight differences between the printed version of the play (London, 1761) and the Larpent MS.

28 Production details are found in Stone, *The London Stage, Part 4: 1747–1776*, 2:840–41 ff. For the last performance see Hogan, *The London Stage, Part 5: 1776–1800*, 3:1748. Arthur Murphy's comment is in *The Life of David Garrick* (London, 1801), 1:366.

29 Hawkesworth also wrote a tragedy, set in Spain, that was never produced, though both Johnson and Mrs. Thrale read and approved of it. See J. D.

Fleeman, *A Preliminary Handlist of Documents & Manuscripts of Samuel Johnson* (Oxford: Oxford Bibliographical Society, 1967), p. 39. *Johnson Letters*, 2:150. *Thraliana*, 1:328.

Chapter V: Hawkesworth and the *Gentleman's Magazine*, 1741–1773

1 *Spectator* no. 10, ed. Donald F. Bond (Oxford: Clarendon Press, 1965), 1:44.

2 *GM* 11 (1741):n. pag., from Preface. Subsequent citations appear in the text.

3 The standard study of the *Gentleman's Magazine* to Cave's death in 1754 is C. Lennart Carlson, *The First Magazine: A History of the "Gentleman's Magazine,"* Brown Univ. Studies, vol. 4 (Providence: Brown Univ. Press, 1938). See also James M. Kuist, "The *Gentleman's Magazine*, 1754–1800: A Study of Its Development as a Vehicle for the Discussion of Literature" (Ph.D. diss., Duke Univ., 1965); idem, *The Works of John Nichols* (New York: AMS Press, 1968); idem, "The *Gentleman's Magazine* in the Folger Library: The History and Significance of the Nichols Family Collection," *Studies in Bibliography* 29 (1976):307–22 (hereafter cited as Kuist, "Nichols Collection"). Kuist is preparing a book-length study of the magazine, which will be a valuable supplement to Carlson. Often overlooked is [John Gough Nichols], "The Autobiography of Sylvanus Urban," *GM* n.s. 46, pt. 2 (1856):2–9, 131–40, 267–77, 531–41, 667–77; n.s. 47, pt. 1 (1857):3–10, 149–57, 282–90, 379–87. Hawkesworth figures prominently in *GM*, n.s. 47: 282–90 and 379–87. Robert Cradock Nichols identifies his brother John Gough Nichols as the author of the "Autobiography" in *Memoir of the Late John Gough Nichols, F.S.A.* (Westminster, 1874), p. 17. James Kuist kindly provided me with this identification.

Johnson's connections with Cave are noted in *YSJ*, pp. 148, 176. Clifford indicates (*YSJ*, p. 253) that Johnson left Cave's employ in the winter of 1743–44. I survey this subject in "Samuel Johnson, John Hawkesworth, and the Rise of the *Gentleman's Magazine*, 1738–1773," *Studies on Voltaire and the Eighteenth Century* (Oxford: the Voltaire Foundation at the Taylor Institution, 1976), 151:31–46. Johnson's "blockhead" comment is in *Life*, 3:19.

4 A close friend, the Reverend John Duncombe, signing himself as "Crito" (identified as Duncombe in Nichols, "Autobiography," *GM*, n.s. 47:286) in a letter to *GM* in Feb. 1779 (49:72), attributes to Hawkesworth poems in the magazine betwen 1746 and 1749 signed "H. Greville" and "J.G." Duncombe is the authority for the list of poems provided by Alexander Chalmers in *The British Essayists*, 23:xiii. Carlson, *The First Magazine*, correctly notes other contributions by "H. Greville" during 1741–42, and his list (pp. 253–54) is the most inclusive, though not complete. For example, Hawkesworth probably wrote, though not as "H. Greville," "The Male-Content reform'd," *GM* 11 (Oct. 1741):548, thus making complete a series of fables from June to December. Calvin Daniel Yost, Jr., refers to the poetry of "H. Greville" without realizing his identity in *The Poetry of the "Gentleman's Magazine": A Study in Eighteenth-Century Literary Taste* (Philadelphia: n.p., 1936), p. 16. R. Freeman, in *Kentish Poets* (Canterbury, 1821) 2:179, asserts—incorrectly, I think—that Hawkesworth did not write any poems as "J.G." There are obvious similarities between the poetry of "H. Greville" and that of "J.G."

5 Nichols in "Autobiography," *GM*, n.s. 47:286 writes: "In 1746 Hawksworth placed at our disposal another store of his poetical compositions, which, together, with a few more by him, which arose incidently during the same period, were inserted from time to time during that and the three following years." Although "H. Greville" disappears from the indexes in the magazine during 1743, 1744, and 1745, two fables—"Affectation expos'd" (*GM* 14 [Dec. 1744]: 671) and "The Vine and Bramble" (*GM* 15 [Nov. 1745]:607)—might be attributed to Hawkesworth. The first an animal fable, and the second a moral tale with political overtones, they resemble Hawkesworth's previous and later poetry in style and substance. A complete list of Hawkesworth's poetry is hardly less difficult to assemble than an account of his prose contributions to the periodical, and no year offers more problems than 1747. Nine poems are assigned to "Mr. Greville" in the index, but six poems in the May issue, all signed with three asterisks, have caused much confusion and debate as to whether Hawkesworth or Johnson wrote them. See *Life*, 1:178–79; Nichols, "Autobiography," *GM*, n.s. 47:286–87; J. Reading, "Poems by Johnson," *Times Literary Supplement*, Sept. 11, 1937; Arthur Sherbo, "Samuel Johnson and Certain Poems in the May 1747 *Gentleman's Magazine*," *Review of English Studies*, n.s. 27 (1966):382–90. These poems are claimed for Johnson by E. L. McAdam, Jr., and George Milne in *Poems*, vol. 6 of the Yale Edition of *The Works of Samuel Johnson* (New Haven and London: Yale Univ. Press, 1964), and, more recently, by J. D. Fleeman in *Samuel Johnson: The Complete English Poems* (Harmondsworth: Penguin Books, 1971). Not be be ignored in the debate over authorship of these poems is the important point that by the late 1740s Hawkesworth exercised considerable control over the *Gentleman's* poetry section.

6 William Cooke, *The Life of Samuel Johnson, LL.D.* (London, 1785), pp. 96–97.

7 BL, Add. MS. 39,901, fols. 36v–39, which also contains two unpublished poems: the first, entitled "Epitaph," is an attack on Edmund Burke (fols. 39–39v); the second, "A Description of London" (fol. 39v), is obviously written in imitation of Swift's "A Description of a City Shower." There were probably transcribed by Mary Hawkesworth.

8 Freeman, *Kentish Poets*, 2:207–8. Johnson, *Letters*, 2:169. Carlson, *The First Magazine*, p. 228. Contrary to Carlson, Hawkesworth submitted poetry to the *Gentleman's* after 1749. Nichols in "Autobiography" *GM*, n.s. 47:286–87, writes that "Hawkesworth's poetical contributions were continued in 1750, and afterwards, either with his own initials, J.H., or altogether anonymously." He assigns to him "The Caterpillar and Butterfly," published in *GM* 20 (Jan. 1750):36–37, the verses following the 1750 preface, "A Sequel to the Origin of Criticism," and those in explanation of the 1754 frontispiece. Poems signed "J.H." occur frequently in 1750 and 1751, and as late as September 1767 one sees the initials appended to an "Ode to Health" (*GM* 37:517), a poem reminiscent of Hawkesworth's earlier efforts.

9 Hawkesworth's extensive service to the *Gentleman's Magazine* remained concealed even to those who knew about the poetry that he contributed. Chalmers writes: "Whether he wrote any prose compositions is doubtful. Mr. DUNCOMBE, on whose authority the above list [of poetry] is given, says nothing of prose" (*British*

Essayists, 23:xiii). Freeman, who generally writes with authority on Hawkesworth's life, comments: "What share he took in the prose department of the magazine at this time [the 1740s], or whether he took any, is not known; later in his life he was considered the principal conductor of it, and it is probably during these years, some of the prose essays were written by him" (*Kentish Poets*, 2:179). Carlson in *The First Magazine*, p. 24, is equally vague: "Just what his connections were with the magazine during Cave's lifetime cannot be determined, but the fact that he was appointed reviewer of new publications in the periodical eleven years after Cave's death suggests that he had been keeping up his connections with it, and with the proprietors, over a period of years."

10 *Johnson on Shakespeare*, ed. Arthur Sherbo, vol. 7 of the Yale Edition of *The Works of Samuel Johnson* (New Haven and London: Yale Univ. Press, 1968), p. 162. See Donald Eddy, "John Hawkesworth: Book Reviewer in the *Gentleman's Magazine*," *Philological Quarterly* 43 (1964):223–38. Eddy is the first to argue persuasively for Hawkesworth's authorship of the X reviews in the *Gentleman's*, though they were attributed to him by Charles Gray, *Theatrical Criticism in London to 1795* (New York: Columbia Univ. Press, 1931), pp. 171–72. Hawkesworth's reviews for the *Monthly Review* are identified in Benjamin Christie Nangle, *The Monthly Review, First Series, 1749–1789: Indexes, Contributors, and Articles* (Oxford: Clarendon Press, 1934), p. 20.

11 I am much indebted to Arthur Sherbo's unpublished study, "Counting Words: The Prose Styles of Samuel Johnson and John Hawkesworth," which not only independently confirmed Eddy's study but significantly expanded upon it, showing that Hawkesworth probably reviewed long before the X reviews. This essay modifies Sherbo's "Samuel Johnson and the *Gentleman's Magazine*, 1750–1755," in *Johnsonian Studies*, ed. James L. Clifford and Donald J. Greene (Cairo: Oxford Univ. Press, 1962), pp. 133–59. I also make extensive use of Donald Earl Keesey, "Dramatic Criticism in the *Gentleman's Magazine*, 1747–1784" (Ph.D. diss., Michigan State Univ., 1964).

12 The habit of using *that* is seen in reviews of *The Summer's Tale* (*GM* 35 [Dec. 1765]:557–60), *The Double Mistake* (*GM* 36 [Jan. 1766]:19–22), and *The English Merchant* (*GM* 37 [March 1767]:126–30). Other examples can be found in *GM* 32 (April 1762):157; *GM* 34 (Aug. 1764):386. There are five uses of *suppose* on p. 78 of Hawkesworth's *Spendthrift* no. 13. The *OED* gives examples of *attone* only as late as the seventeenth century, which suggests that the same spelling in the *Gentleman's* is an idiosyncratic variation. Hawkesworth frequently prefers this unconventional spelling. See his edition of Swift's *Works* (1755 quarto), 1:8 and 14 and the letter to David Henry quoted later in this chapter. The examples of phrases are not manufactured but appear in *GM* 24 (Dec. 1754):542, and *GM* 26 (April 1756):157.

13 Bodleian Library, Add. MS. c. 89, fol. 157. Hawkins, *Life of Johnson*, p. 132.

14 Osborn Sketch, fols. 1, 2. *Universal Magazine* "Memoirs," p. 233. Hawkesworth's role in the parliamentary "debates" is difficult to clarify. James L. Clifford in *YJS*, p. 252, and Benjamin Beard Hoover in *Samuel Johnson's Parliamentary Reporting* (Berkeley and Los Angeles: Univ. of California Press, 1953), p. 212, conclude that Johnson's last debate appeared in the magazine in March

1744. Hawkins, *Life of Johnson*, p. 132, asserts that Hawkesworth succeeded Johnson as the compiler of this popular feature. Donald Greene in "Some Notes on Johnson and the *Gentleman's Magazine*," *PMLA* 79 (1959):77–78, and F. V. Bernard in "Johnson and the Authorship of Four Debates," *PMLA* 82 (1976): 408–19, argue for Johnson's participation in the debates *through* 1744. This would reduce Hawkesworth's involvement in the feature, if, indeed, he had one in the first place. Greene (p. 77) cites the account of Johnson's career in the *European Magazine* during 1784–85, which states that Johnson compiled the debates as long as they were published, a view supported by Nichols, who writes that he did not "recollect that Hawksworth had at any time anything whatever to do with them" ("Autobiography," *GM*, n.s. 47:285). After long review I could come to no conclusion on the basis of internal evidence, though external evidence would seem to support Hawkesworth's claim to some of the "debates." Hawkins, after all, writes as one who knew Johnson and Hawkesworth intimately during these early years; Hawkesworth clearly moved in the orbit of St. John's Gate at the time, proving himself, at least some years later, an able imitator of Johnson's style; and there is evidence that he wrote political material for Sir James Caldwell, including the Irish *Debates*. Although such political writing came late in his career, the connection is still important. See below, Chapter VI.

15 Osborn Collection, Yale University. The letter is a fair copy. David Henry, the magazine's principal editor, is the probable recipient, the man to negotiate with Hawkesworth for an official position in the magazine.

16 *Life*, 4:409.

17 Osborn Sketch, fol. 3. There is evidence in *James Beattie's London Diary, 1773*, ed. Ralph S. Walker, Aberdeen Univ. Studies, no. 122 (Aberdeen: The Univ. Press, 1946), p. 44, that Hawkesworth received better financial terms from Henry. Beattie records, in fact, that Hawkesworth got sole management of the magazine at a salary of £100 per annum after Johnson left. Hawkesworth, of course, never achieved exclusive control of the periodical.

18 Nichols, "Autobiography," *GM*, n.s. 47:284, 286–87, 380.

19 Ibid., p. 287. Initials that are obviously based on names or pseudonyms offer clues to authorship of items in the magazine. Kuist, "Nichols Collection," p. 317, shows how Richard Gough and Samuel Pegge signed themselves, respectively, as "D.H." and "L.E." The signature "H.H." accompanies an article on two poems by Racine (*GM* 17 [Oct. 1747]:472–73) and one on Voltaire's *Mérope* as revised by Aaron Hill (*GM* 19 [April 1749]:171–72). A review of Edward Moore's *Foundling* in March 1748 (18:114–16) is signed "H.G.," probably for "H. Greville," the pseudonym under which Hawkesworth wrote poetry for the periodical. An article on Voltaire (*GM* 38 [Dec. 1768]:556–58), a translation of one of his letters on the Quakers, is signed "J.H.," but Hawkesworth vigorously denied authorship of a piece on Voltaire's *Philosophical Dictionary* (*GM* 35 [Oct. 1765]: 469–72), asserting at the same time that the magazine had never been under his sole control. "I must beg leave to assure you," he writes, "that it is *not*, nor *ever was*, there being in almost every number some things that I never see, and some thing that I do not approve" (Chalmers, *British Essayists*, 23:xviii–xix). For all his protest, Hawkesworth's comments can only be construed to show that his role in the *Gentleman's* was central.

20 *Life*, 1:498. William Kenrick, *Johnson's Shakespeare* (London, 1766), p. 15. Kenrick later asks, "But are not Dr. H——h and Mr. H——y the editors and managers of the Gentlemen's Magazine?" (p. 33).

21 Hawkesworth is the likely author of a long note appended to "The Story of Irene," an excerpt from Vertot's *History of the Knights of Malta* featured in the *Gentleman's* Supplement for 1762, which observes that Johnson's *Irene* had been acted "but nine nights and never been since revived; tho' the parts were allotted to the best performers, though the dramatic unities were strictly observed, and though the sublimest and most important truths were conveyed throughout in the most beautiful and harmonious language" (32:619).

22 *Life*, 1:372–77. The issue of the pension is illuminated in James L. Clifford's *Dictionary Johnson* (New York: McGraw-Hill, 1979), Chapter 16.

23 BL, Add. MS. 35,399, fols. 344 and 346.

24 See James T. Boulton, ed., *Johnson: The Critical Heritage* (New York: Barnes & Noble, 1971), for a convenient summary of Johnson's critical reception. Boulton shows the heavy criticism that Johnson endured during his lifetime, though he does not cite the consistent support provided by the *Gentleman's Magazine*. "The critical response of Johnson's contemporaries was, then," he writes, "voluminous, searching, and frequently personal in the view of the increasing dominance of the man who provoked it. Inevitably, too, because he was essentially a miscellaneous writer Johnson had to endure criticism of very diverse quality. His critics were innumerable" (p. 7).

25 Nichols, "Autobiography," *GM*, n.s. 47:283–84.

26 *Garrick Letters*, 1:235, 249–50, 255, 268, 312, 314.

27 JRULMSS. B 3/10/209 and B 3/16/133.

28 *The Papers of Benjamin Franklin*, ed. Leonard W. Labaree, 21 vols. (New Haven and London: Yale Univ. Press, 1959-), 10:233. Hereafter cited as *Franklin Papers*.

29 Ibid., 12:16.

30 For a valuable account of eighteenth-century book review practices see Edward A. Bloom, " 'Labors of the Learned': Neoclassic Book Reviewing Aims and Techniques," *Studies in Philology* 54 (1957):537–63.

31 Hawkesworth's authorship of this review is confirmed in the *Genuine Works of William Hogarth*, ed. John Nichols and George Steevens (London, 1808), pp. 231–33. Arthur Sherbo kindly provided this information.

32 The following creative pieces and translations from the French might be considered for admission to the Hawkesworth canon: "The Tragical Story of Ludovisio Carantani, a Milanese, and his two Daughters" (*GM* 21 [Feb. 1751]: 72–75); "Rosetta and Chamont. A true Story" (*GM* 25 [Sept.–Oct. 1755]: 401–6, 441–45); "The Trial of Pleasure before the Judge Philosophy" (*GM* 32 [Nov. 1762]:518–20); "The Dream of Irus" (*GM* 35 [July 1765]:323–28); and "The Oracle. A Story from the Greek" (*GM* 36 [Jan. 1766]:9–14). "Rosetta and Chamont" was widely reprinted. See Robert D. Mayo, *The English Novel in the Magazines, 1740–1815* (Evanston, Ill.: Northwestern Univ. Press, 1962), p. 582. Hawkesworth could well have been the author of the following translations from the French: "Wit and Beauty. From the French of Madam de Fagnon" (*GM* 20 [Sept. 1750]:410–13); "Asem and Salned. An Eastern Tale" (*GM* 21 [Dec. and Supplement 1751]:552–55, 604–606), which Mayo, *The English Novel*, p. 172 says

was translated from the *Mercure de France*; "A Mother inexorably unkind" (*GM* 25 [Jan. 1755]:18–20); "The Case of Tantalus fairly stated; or, The danger of Connections with the Great" (*GM* 25 [Feb. 1755]:57–59), which purports to be a French translation submitted by "T.B." and translated by "H.J."; "Anette and Lubin; said to be a true Story. From the French" (*GM* 31 [Sept. 1761]:398–402); "An authentic Narrative of the Death of Anthony Calas, and of the Trial and Execution of his Father, John Calas, for the supposed murder of his Son. From the French" (*GM* 32 [Nov. 1762]:509–13); "Jeanot and Colin: A Story now first translated from the French of M. Voltaire" (*GM* 35 [March 1765]:118–23); "The Trial of Friendship. A Story now first translated from the third Volume of Contes Moraux, just published by Marmontel" (*GM* 35 [June–July 1765]:273–79, 309–15); "An Account of the Life and Writings of George Buchanan; Extracted from the French of M. Le Clerc" (*GM* 36 [May 1766]:212–17); and "Oriental Fables; from the French" (*GM* 36 [Dec. 1766]:558–60). Hawkesworth's authorship of the last item is confirmed by Joseph Cockfield, who comments in a letter to the Reverend Weeden Butler on March 25, 1767: "There were two or three little tales inserted in the latter end of last year in the *Gentleman's Magazine*, for which I believe we were indebted to the Doctor" (Nichols, *Illustrations* 5:775). One measure of Hawkesworth's importance to the magazine is seen in the fact that dramatic criticism virtually ceased at his death in 1773.

33 *Life*, 1:111–12.

Chapter VI: The 1760s

1 *Life*, 2:40–41.

2 *Universal Magazine* "Memoirs," p. 237.

3 Mary Hawkesworth's letter is published in R. Freeman, *Kentish Poets* (Canterbury, 1821), 2:191–92. Hawkesworth confirms that Almoran and Hamet "were originally Characters in a Drama" in a letter to Sir James Caldwell of October 3, 1767 (JRULMS. B 3/16/134). The fracas over *The Chinese Festival* is described by W. J. Lawrence, "The Drama and the Theatre," in *Johnson's England*, 2:178. According to *Biographia Dramatica*, 2:20 and 211, Hawkesworth's tale inspired Gorges Edmund Howard's *Almeyda; or, the Rival Kings* (1769) and Samuel Jackson Pratt's *The Fair Circassian* (1780).

4 *The History of Rasselas, Prince of Abyssinia*, in *Samuel Johnson: Selected Poetry and Prose*, ed. Frank Brady and W. K. Wimsatt (Berkeley and Los Angeles: Univ. of California Press, 1977), p. 73. Hawkesworth, *Almoran and Hamet* (London, 1761), 1:1–2. Subsequent references appear in the text.

5 BL, Add. MS. 5,720, fol. 88 (in Hawkesworth's hand). A few weeks earlier, on February 12, 1761, Sir Harry Erskine had written to Bute that Hawkesworth's pen might be employed in political writing (Central Library, Cardiff, Bute Correspondence). I am grateful to James McKelvy of the University of Connecticut for calling this fact to my attention.

6 *Universal Magazine* "Memoirs," p. 238.

7 Owen Ruffhead, *Monthly Review* 24 (1761):415–16. Leigh Hunt, *Classic Tales* (London, 1817), 4:230. Martha Pike Conant, *The Oriental Tale in England in the*

Eighteenth Century (New York: Columbia Univ. Press, 1908), pp. 70, 95. Johnson's comment is in *GM* 52 (Jan. 1782):19. Paul P. Kies argues that *Almoran and Hamet* may have provided a portion of the love story in Lessing's *Nathan der Weise* (1779) in "Lessing and Hawkesworth," *Research Studies, State College of Washington* 8 (1940):143–44.

8 *Life*, 1:342. Hawkesworth's assessment is in *GM* 29 (1759):186.

9 A concise summary of Franklin's life, which I use here, is Louis K. Wechsler, *Benjamin Franklin: American and World Educator* (Boston: Twayne Publishers, 1976).

10 For Franklin's connections with the *Gentleman's Magazine* see C. Lennart Carlson, *The First Magazine* (Providence: Brown Univ. Press, 1938), pp. 184–86.

11 An excellent account of Polly Stevenson, Franklin, and the Bromley circle is by Whitfield J. Bell, Jr., " 'All Clear Sunshine': New Letters of Franklin and Mary Stevenson Hewson," *Proceedings of the American Philosophical Society* 100 (1956): 521–36. Catherine (1721–75) and Dorothea (1733–1809) Blunt were the granddaughters of Sir John Blunt (1665–1733), the financier ruined in the collapse of the South Sea Company.

12 *Franklin Papers*, 9:327–28.

13 American Philosophical Society, Bradford Collection, MS. in Polly's hand.

14 *Franklin Papers*, 10:232.

15 Both Polly Stevenson and Franklin deferred to Hawkesworth's literary judgment. She consulted Franklin about her revision of a poem by her uncle Thomas Tickell, noting in a letter to Hawkesworth on December 16, 1761, that Franklin "submitted all Alternatives to your better Judgment" (American Philosophical Society, Bradford Collection, MS. in Polly's hand). The poem appeared in *GM* 31 (Dec. 1761):594, entitled, "To a Lady before Marriage. By the late ingenious Mr Tickel; never before published." Wechsler, *Benjamin Franklin*, pp. 117–20, comments on Franklin's "examination." Hawkesworth's review, signed "X," is in *GM* 37 (July 1767):368. (The "X" signature is noted on p. 409 of *GM*, since it was left off the July review.)

16 Hawkesworth's associations with men of science are seen in *Franklin Papers*, 14:152–53, in a letter from Richard Price to Franklin on May 15, 1767, asking him to dine with him, Hawkesworth, Canton, and either Joseph or James Densham. Hawkesworth's election to the Society for the Encouragement of Arts, Manufactures, and Commerce is recorded in the society's manuscript Subscription Book. The best recent study of this important institution is Derek Hudson and Kenneth W. Luckhurst, *The Royal Society of Arts, 1754–1954* (London: John Murray, 1954). Specialized studies include D. G. C. Allan, *William Shipley: Founder of the Royal Society of Arts* (London: Hutchinson, 1968), and my articles "Dr. Johnson and the Society," pts. i and ii, and "John Hawkesworth and 'The Treatise on the Arts of Peace,' " *Journal of the Royal Society of Arts*, 115 (1967), 395–400, 486–91, 645–49.

17 The stove reference is in *Franklin Papers*, 16:226. The cane trick is described in M. Lémontey, *Mémoires de L'Abbé Morellet* (Paris, 1823), 1:203–4. Franklin's letter on "Fix'd air" (carbon dioxide, which could sweeten water on long voyages and was thought to have some medicinal properties) is in *Franklin Papers*, 19:133–34.

See also ibid., p. 125. Hawkesworth's letter of May 15(?) the following week (p. 142) reveals that he had asked Franklin about the process on behalf of an ailing friend. He also invited Franklin to join him, Joseph Banks, and Carl Solander. The last two, both scientists, accompanied Cook on his first Pacific voyage.

18　The definitive biography is Arthur Sherbo, *Christopher Smart: Scholar of the University* (East Lansing: Michigan State Univ. Press, 1967); see especially Appendix A, "Smart's Confinements for Madness" (pp. 266–69). Johnson's comment is in *Life*, 1:397.

19　Sherbo, *Christopher Smart*, p. 130.

20　Nichols, *Illustrations*, 5:809–11. The Reverend Christopher Hunter, Smart's nephew, preserved the original letter.

21　*Life*, 1:182.

22　For a thorough account of this controversy see James Gray " 'More Blood than Brains': Robert Dodsley and the *Cleone* Affair," *Dalhousie Review* 54 (1974):207–27. Johnson's comment is in *Life*, 4:20–21.

23　Hawkesworth's holograph letter of September 14, 1756, is BL, Add. MS. 29,300, fol. 43v. His holograph letter of Dec. 10, 1759, is Huntington Library MS. 12238.

24　The contract with Galley is Bodleian Library, MS. Eng. Misc., c. 143. The British Library copy of the *Spendthrift*, which includes two letters in Hawkesworth's hand, dated May 10 and 14, 1766, establish that he wrote no. 8 (on taste) and no. 13 (on painting). Huntington Library MSS. 12236 and 12239, Hawkesworth to James Dodsley, Dec. 19, 1766, and March 9, 1767 (both in his hand), indicate that he contributed five reviews to Dodsley's *Annual Register* for 1766, including coverage of his own edition of Swift's letters! This aspect of Hawkesworth's reviewing is noted briefly by G. J. Finch, "John Hawkesworth, 'The Gentleman's Magazine,' and 'The Annual Register,' " *Notes & Queries*, n.s. 22 (1975):17–18, and is thoroughly reviewed by James E. Tierney in "Edmund Burke, John Hawkesworth, the *Annual Register*, and the *Gentleman's Magazine*," *Huntington Library Quarterly* 42 (1978):57–72. Five surviving letters that Hawkesworth wrote during the 1760s to Dean Zachary Pearce, bishop of Rochester, indicate again that men of position sought his views and support. Three letters (dated Dec. 9, 1764; Jan. 12, 1765; and Jan. 20, 1765) show Hawkesworth's involvement in a current religious dispute that resulted in a piece signed "J.H." in *GM* 35 (Jan. 1765):26–28, entitled "A Defence of the Bishops for not Attempting to bring about an Alteration in the Articles, and Liturgy of the Church of England; to favour the admission of Dissenters into her Communion." The other two letters deal with Hawkesworth's *Telemachus* (March 9, 1768) and his views on verses by Lord Blessington and Dryden (undated). These are found in Westminster Abbey, Muniment Room and Library, WAM 64373–77. I am grateful to Mrs. Sarah Markham, of Wooton-Under-Edge, Gloucestershire, for calling this material to my attention.

25　The most important collection of material concerning Hawkesworth and Caldwell is found in the John Rylands University Library of Manchester. I draw here on F. Taylor's "Johnsoniana from the Bagshawe Muniments in the John Rylands Library: Sir James Caldwell, Dr. Hawkesworth, Dr. Johnson, and Boswell's Use of the 'Caldwell Minute,' " *Bulletin of the John Rylands Library* 35 (1952):211–47.

26 I quote from JRULMSS. B 3/10/7 (diplomatic post); B 3/16/127 (Lady Bute); B 3/16/129 (Pitt); B 3/19/72 (Townshend); B 3/22/5 (peerage claim); B 3/16/130 (Bagshawe services).

27 JRULMSS. B 3/21/2a and B 3/21/32 (*Account of the Speeches* . . .).

28. JRULMSS. B 3/16/128 (Hawkesworth to Caldwell, Jan. 11, 1763); B 3/21/9a (Dublin fish trade); B 3/26/54 (hymn); B 3/26/56–65 (prayers); B 3/10/272 (Burney reference).

29 JRULMS. B 3/10/79 (on "George"). Carlson, *The First Magazine*, p. 104, and *Life*, 1:501 (Cave's trial). JRULMSS. B 3/10/286 (Caldwell in 1769 to Dr. King at Oxford on projected edition); B 3/10/348 (will); B 3/16/336 and B 3/16/396 (*Voyages* in Ireland).

30 JRULMSS. B 3/16/88 (Faulkner's letter); B 3/16/130 (Hawkesworth's undated response to Caldwell's invitation). The latter accompanies Hawkesworth's draft of Mrs. Bagshawe's memorial to the king (see text at n. 26, above). While Hawkesworth's and Johnson's intimacy ceased after the days of the Ivy Lane Club, their paths crossed on occasion. The rupture suggested in "Recollections of Dr. Johnson by Miss Reynolds" ("Hawkesworth is grown a coxcomb, and I have done with him," she reports Johnson saying) in G. B. Hill, ed., *Johnsonian Miscellanies* (New York: Barnes and Noble, 1966), 2:298, did not last. Hawkesworth, for example, joined Johnson, Goldsmith, Garrick, Colman, and Thornton at a student production of the *Eunuch of Terence* at Westminster School in the early 1760s according to Charles Welsh, *A Bookseller of the Last Century: Being Some Account of the Life of John Newbery* . . . (New York, 1885), p. 124. As late as February 12, 1767, Johnson, writing to Sir James Caldwell, refers to "Our friend Doctor Hawkesworth" (*Johnson Letters*, 1:431). According to Lady Phillipina Knight's annotated *Life of Johnson*, Hawkesworth was among those who slipped out of the room to write down Johnson's conversations. Such action is undated but suggests frequent meetings between the two men. See Charles G. Osgood, "Lady Phillipina Knight and Her Boswell," *Princeton Univ. Library Chronicle* (1943):37–49. As late as April 29, 1769, Hawkesworth joined Johnson and other luminaries at a dinner celebrating the knighting of Sir Joshua Reynolds. See Donald Cross Bryant, *Edmund Burke and His Literary Friends*, Washington Univ. Studies in Language and Literature, no. 9 (St. Louis: Washington Univ. Press, 1939), p. 61. Hawkesworth's letter of December 11, 1767, which mentions Caldwell's sons, is JRULMS. B 3/10/234.

31 JRULMSS. B 3/31/8 (Mrs. Bernard); B 3/10/235 (Lady Kerry).

32 JRULMSS. B 3/10/272 (Lady Mary Howard); B 3/10/276 (Lady Arabella Denny). Sir James Prior, *Life of Edmond Malone* (London, 1860), p. 442. JRULMSS. B 3/10/280 (Lady Arabella Denny); B 3/10/311 (Dowager Lady Shelburne).

33 A useful commentary on Fénelon's classic, on which I draw, is Glenn Negley and J. Max Patrick, eds., *The Quest for Utopia* (New York: Anchor Books, 1962). Negley and Patrick reprint a portion of Hawkesworth's translation issued by G. Gregory.

34 Nichols, *Illustrations*, 5:773–74. This letter reflects Hawkesworth's connections with Dr. Dodd, the famous forger, and John Hoole, another Johnson intimate.

Hawkesworth is said to have introduced Hoole to Johnson and to have written an epilogue to his tragedy, *Cyrus*. See Allen T. Hazen, *Samuel Johnson's Prefaces and Dedications* (New Haven: Yale Univ. Press, 1937), pp. 60–61. In early December 1768, Hawkesworth wrote to Hoole, asking that his name not be attached to the epilogue, though he had already been connected with the piece in the papers. Herman Liebert kindly called my attention to Hawkesworth's letter in the Beinecke Library Yale University Library containing this information.

35 JRULMSS. B 3/10/209 (Jan. 11, 1767); B 3/10/234 (Dec. 11, 1767); B 3/10/236 (March 4, 1768).

36 In a letter to the *Public Advertiser* which appeared on May 24, 1768 (written from Bromley on May 16), notice is given that *Telemachus* will be delivered to subscribers on Monday, May 30, 1768. It is obvious from the number of subscriptions that Sir James had lobbied well in Hawkesworth's behalf. Subscribers' names are from *The Adventures of Telemachus* (London, 1768). Subsequent references to this work and the French version with which I compare it (Leiden, 1761) appear in the text.

37 Yale *Idler & Adventurer*, p. 217.

38 *Monthly Review* 39 (1768): 237. *The Adventures of Telemachus, the Son of Ulysses*, ed. G. Gregory (London, 1795), 1:v–vi.

Chapter VII: Hawkesworth's *Voyages*

1 The best introduction to the subject of Pacific exploration, which I draw on here, is J. C. Beaglehole, *The Exploration of the Pacific*, 3rd ed. (1934; rpt. Stanford, Calif.: Stanford Univ. Press, 1968). Hereafter cited as Beaglehole, *Pacific Exploration*. One of the best specialized studies is Bernard Smith, *European Vision and the South Pacific, 1768–1850* (Oxford: Clarendon Press, 1960). Of more general interest, but carefully researched, are Alan Moorehead, *The Fatal Impact: An Account of the Invasion of the South Pacific, 1767–1840* (London: Hamish Hamilton, 1966), and Alan Villiers, *Captain Cook, the Seamen's Seaman* (1967; rpt. Harmondsworth: Penguin Books, 1970).

2 Beaglehole, *Pacific Exploration*, p. 9. See *GM* 33 (Jan. 1763): opposite p. 32, where the hypothetical southern continent is included in a "Chart of the Antarctic Polar Circle, with the Countries adjoining, According to the New Hypothesis of M. Buache."

3 Beaglehole, *Pacific Exploration*, p. 213.

4 James A. Williamson, "Exploration and Discovery," in *Johnson's England*, 1:122.

5 Beaglehole, *Pacific Exploration*, pp. 233–34.

6 Ibid., p. 237.

7 Beaglehole writes: "He had given New Zealand a sure and defined outline; in less than six months he had charted 2400 miles of coast in a manner as accurate as it was unprecedented" (*Pacific Exploration*, p. 246).

8 Ibid., pp. 257–59.

9 John Hawkesworth, *An Account of the Voyages . . . by Commodore Byron, Captain Wallis, Captain Carteret, And Captain Cook*, 3 vols. (London, 1773). I use the first edition of this work. Hereafter cited in the text as Hawkesworth's *Voyages*. For

details about the editions of the *Voyages* see William Thomas Lowndes, *Bibliographer's Manual of English Literature*, rev. by Henry G. Bohn (London, 1857–71), 2:1014.

10 Charlotte Barrett, ed., *Diary & Letters of Madame D'Arblay, 1778–1840* (London: Macmillan, 1904), 1:9–10.

11 Burney, *Early Diary*, 1:43, 126, 190–91. W. H. Pearson of the University of Auckland kindly called my attention to several valuable letters in the National Library of Australia, Canberra (hereafter NLA), which further establish Hawkesworth's connections with the Burneys. Among these is an undated letter in Hawkesworth's hand (NLA MS. 332/3) that suggests Fanny had asked him to read one of her early literary efforts.

12 Burney, *Early Diary*, 1:133–34. Lord Sandwich was one of Burney's musical patrons. For Burney's German tour, Burney writes, he "was pleased to honour me with recommendatory letters, in his own hand, to every English nobleman and gentleman who resided in a public character in the several cities through which I passed" (Ibid., 1:132, n. 2).

13 I quote from NLA, MS. 332/1 in Hawkesworth's hand. He refers to "your obliging Favour of the 14th," which apparently dates Burney's recommendation to Sandwich. The latter wrote shortly afterwards from the Admiralty: "Lord S: takes this opportunity to return D^r B: his particular thanks, for having made him acquainted with Dr Hawkesworth" (NLA, MS. 332/5, dated 1771). This material clarifies the confusion surrounding the respective roles Burney and Garrick played in gaining Hawkesworth the right to edit the *Voyages*. It amends the views of those who, from Edmond Malone to G.F.R. Barker in the DNB, give Garrick chief credit. Malone, for example, writes that Hawkesworth "was introduced by Garrick to Lord Sandwich, who thinking to put a few hundred pounds into his pocket, appointed him to revise and publish Cook's *Voyages*" (Sir James Prior, *Life of Edmond Malone* [London, 1860], p. 441).

14 Wray's letter is in Nichols, *Illustrations*, 1:140. Again, Garrick's role, not Burney's, is stressed. Hawkesworth's holograph letter to Burney is NLA, MS. 332/2.

15 This letter, in Hawkesworth's hand, is found in the Sandwich Papers at Mapperton House, Dorset, box 18, Corres. 4th Earl, Cook's & Bickerton's Voyages: letters of Barrington & Foster, envelope 1: "Publication of the narrative of the first voyage 1771–1773." Hereafter cited as Sandwich Papers. Victor Montagu, former earl of Sandwich, kindly permitted me to examine the Sandwich Papers.

16 For this summary I use R. W. Harris, *A Short History of Eighteenth-Century England: 1689–1793* (New York: Mentor Books, 1963), pp. 158 ff.

17 Evidence of Hawkesworth's involvement in the company is in the archives of the India Office Records, Commonwealth Office. His stock purchases and transfers were kindly searched for me by C. J. McNally in the Transfer Books and Transfers by Attorney. Entries are as follows: From Smith, Transfers by Attorney, May 1770–Nov. 1772, L–Z, p. 86; to Devaynes, ibid., Aug. 1771–Aug. 1773, A–K, p. 4; from Green, ibid., Transfers, Sept. 1772–Sept. 1773, A–K, p. 52; from Norden, ibid., Oct. 1772–May 1774, L–Z, p. 123. Mrs. Hawkesworth subsequently disposed of the £2,000 of India stock: on January 15,

1774, she sold £1,000 to John Cowley of Walbrook March and £1,000 to William Grainger of Bucklersbury, painter in Transfers, Sept. 30, 1773–Jan. 11, 1776, A–K, pp. 96–97; also in India Office Records, Ledger 5.7. 1769–5.1. 1774, and Ledger 5.1. 1774–5.4. 1783).

18 Hawkesworth's election is noted in India Office Records, Court Book no. 82, April 7, 1773–April 13, 1774. *Garrick Letters*, 2:862.

19 Hawkesworth's installation and attendance at company meetings are noted in Court Book no. 82 (see note 18). His letter to "My dear Madam" (a copy) is in the Osborn Collection at Yale. Such evidence clearly contradicts those who minimized Hawkesworth's participation in the company, from Alexander Chalmers in *The General Biographical Dictionary* (London, 1814), 17:241, who writes that Hawkesworth "probably attended meetings, but took no active share" to G.F.R. Barker in the *DNB*, who states that Hawkesworth "took no active part in their proceedings."

20 *Garrick Letters*, 2:842, 862–63. Boaden, *Garrick Correspondence*, 2:604, 606, 622.

21 Payments for Robertson's *Charles V* and Hume's *History* are noted in *The Journals of Captain Cook on his Voyages of Discovery*, vol. 1, *The Voyage of the "Endeavour," 1768–1771*, ed. J. C. Beaglehole, Hakluyt Society Extra Series, no. 34 (1955; rpt. Cambridge: Cambridge Univ. Press, 1968), p. ccxliii. Hereafter cited as Beaglehole, *Cook's "Endeavour" Journal*. Payments for Johnson's works are found in *Life*, 1:183, 341.

22 Details about Strahan are found in J. A. Cochrane, *Dr. Johnson's Printer: The Life of William Strahan* (Cambridge: Harvard Univ. Press, 1964), pp. 159–61. Strahan's letter to Hume is in *Letters of David Hume to William Strahan*, ed. G. B. Hill (Oxford, 1888), pp. 283–84. Costs of printing the *Voyages* are found in BL, Add. MS. 48,803, Strahan Ledger, fol. 56v (1773), fol. 57 (1775). J. D. Fleeman kindly called to my attention Strahan's bank account in Gosling's branch of Barclay's bank in Fleet Street. This records a number of payments to Hawkesworth from the mid-1750s until his death, and two substantial ones (£1,625 and £2,000) to his widow, obviously for the *Voyages*.

23 BL, Add. MS. 28,104, fols. 45–46, Hawkesworth to Garrick, May 5, 1773 (holograph), printed in Boaden, *Garrick Correspondence*, 1:535. I quote from the original.

24 *Garrick Letters*, 2:867. Hyde Collection, Hawkesworth to Garrick, May 7, 1773 (holograph), printed in Boaden, *Garrick Correspondence*, 1:536. I quote from the original. Garrick's editors are wrong here and above (n. 23) about the dates of Hawkesworth's letters. Mary Hawkesworth's June 12 letter is Folger Library, MS. w.b. 487, item 8. Her June 20 letter is in the Hyde Collection. Both are in her hand.

25 The dispute with Parkinson is covered succinctly by J. C. Beaglehole in *Cook's "Endeavour" Journal*, pp. ccliii–cclv, and in *The "Endeavour" Journal of Joseph Banks, 1768–1771*, ed. J. C. Beaglehole, 2nd ed. (Sydney: Angus & Robertson, 1963), 1: 56–61. Hereafter cited as Beaglehole, *Banks's "Endeavour" Journal*. I examined the suit in Chancery, which appears mainly to have been a delaying tactic to prevent the publication of Parkinson's journal. The secretary of the Public Record Office

kindly provided me with the following information: "The Chancery Bill Book for 1773 (IND. 14474) shows that the action between John Hawkesworth and Stanfield Parkinson, Charles Clarke, and John Jacquery started in Hilary Term 1773 and that the plantiff's Six Clerk was Mitford. Mitford's Six Clerk Cause Book (IND. 4119) shows that Whittington was the defendants' Six Clerk and that the plaintiff's Bill was filed on 26 January 1773, Parkinson's Answer on 5 May 1773 and a Rejoinder on 10 June 1773. The Bill and Answer are to be found among Chancery Proceedings under our reference C. 12/1624/8. The Index to Decrees and Orders of 1773 (IND. 1820) lists Orders in the case and in the Decree and Order Book (C. 33/439) at folios 159, 240, 249 and 251 (Hilary Term), folios 256 and 304 (Easter Term) and folios 345, 543, 544 (Trinity Term)." The last entry in this case appears to be on Friday, June 15, 1773. This was six days after Hawkesworth's edition appeared, and the aim of the injunction—to prevent prior publication by Parkinson—succeeded.

26 Hawkesworth's letter to "My dear Madam," a copy, is in the Osborn Collection at Yale.

27 Ibid. See Beaglehole, *Cook's "Endeavour" Journal*, p. cclv, for the role of Dr. John Fothergill in this dispute. Also a Quaker, he was a member of Stanfield Parkinson's meeting.

28 Joseph Cradock, *Literary and Miscellaneous Memoirs* (London, 1828), 1:132–33, 4:184.

29 *James Beattie's London Diary, 1773*, ed. Ralph S. Walker (Aberdeen: The Univ. Press, 1946), p. 36.

30 Mapperton House, Dorset, Sandwich Papers.

31 Cradock, *Memoirs*, 4:185–87.

32 Osborn Sketch, fol. 4.

33 *Horace Walpole's Correspondence with William Mason*, ed. W. S. Lewis, Grover Cronin, Jr., and Charles H. Bennett (New Haven: Yale Univ. Press, 1955), vol. 28 of the Yale Edition of *Horace Walpole's Correspondence*, ed. W. S. Lewis (1937–1974), pp. 86, 94, 96. *Horace Walpole's Correspondence with Madame Du Deffand and Mademoiselle Sanadon*, ed. W. S. Lewis and Warren Hunting Smith (New Haven: Yale Univ. Press, 1939), vol. 5 of Yale *Walpole Correspondence*, p. 383. The £1,000 Walpole mentions was apparently part of an earlier financial settlement. In the *Public Advertiser* for July 17, 1773, "a Seaman" wrote: "It was originally proposed to pay the Doctor a Sum of Money for his Trouble, in which Event any clever Bookseller was equal to the Task of vending the Book to the Public. It was, however, afterwards thought more proper to give him the Property of the Book that he might make the most of it." Hawkesworth obviously benefited from exclusive rights to this valuable property.

34 *Mrs. Montagu, "Queen of the Blues": Her Letters and Friendships from 1762–1800*, ed. Reginald Blunt (London: Constable, n. d.), 1:279.

35 *Letters from Mrs. Elizabeth Carter to Mrs. Montagu*, ed. Montagu Pennington (London, 1817), 2:202, 207, 209.

36 *The Journal of the Rev. John Wesley, A.M.*, ed. Nehemia Gurnock (London: Charles H. Kelly, 1915), 6:7. Beaglehole, *Cook's "Endeavour" Voyage*, p. ccxlix. *The*

Correspondence of William Cowper, ed. Thomas Wright (London: Hodder and Stoughton, 1904), 2:109. Although Cowper's letter is dated October 6, 1783, he apparently refers to Hawkesworth's *Voyages*.

37 *Life*, 2:247–48, 1:471. There are many references to South Sea exploration in Boswell's *Life*.

38 Dalrymple's *Letter* and his *Observations*, both written in 1773, are found in the British Library in *A Collection of Charts and Memoirs*, published by Alexander Dalrymple (London, 1772). I quote from pp. 2 and 7 of the *Observations*. I am unable to explain the discrepancy of the dates other than to guess that the pamphlets were bound in the volume of the earlier date.

39 I quote from BL, Add. MS. 33,977, fols. 26–27. This is printed in *Carteret's Voyage Round the World, 1766–1769*, ed. Helen Wallis, Hakluyt Society Second Series, nos. 124–25 (Cambridge: Cambridge Univ. Press, 1965), 2:503–4. Dr. Wallis identifies the recipient of the letter as Joseph Banks, though the salutation refers to "Gentlemen," perhaps Strahan and Cadell.

40 Wallis, *Carteret's Voyage*, 1:3. Carteret's lists of objections to Hawkesworth's text are at ibid., 2:504–9.

41 *The Journals of Captain James Cook*, vol. 2, *The Voyage of the "Resolution" and "Adventure," 1772–1775*, ed. J. C. Beaglehole, Hakluyt Society Extra Series, no. 35 (1961; rpt. Cambridge: Cambridge Univ. Press, 1969), p. 661. Cook at this time did not realize that Hawkesworth used Banks's somewhat derogatory comments about this island. Charles Ryskamp and Frederick A. Pottle, eds., *Boswell: The Ominous Years, 1774–1776* (New York: McGraw-Hill, 1963), pp. 308–9.

42 "A Christian" is identified as Joseph Cockfield by Nichols, *Illustrations*, 5:753.

43 The assessment of Hawkesworth's *Voyages* in the major periodicals of the time—the *Critical Review*, the *Monthly Review*, and the *Annual Register*—was generally more moderate, though—with the exception of the *Gentleman's Magazine*, with which Hawkesworth was connected—all expressed reservations about aspects of the work. The *Monthly Review*, for example, regretted that Hawkesworth was "not always equally clear and unembarrassed in his philosophical reflections" (49:141). The *Annual Register* for 1773 alluded as well to the philosophical excesses of the volumes, the reviewer commenting: "We could wish too, that speculative opinions of dark and difficult subjects had been omitted; whatever their merit may be, we may truly say, *non erat his locus*. Such is the dissertation upon and denial of, a particular providence" (16:267).

44 Pennington, *Mrs. Elizabeth Carter to Mrs. Montagu*, 2:218–19. Sir William Forbes, *An Account of the Life and Writings of James Beattie* (Edinburgh, 1806), 1:396.

45 *Life*, 5:281–82, 280.

46 *Life*, 2:104. Beaglehole, *Cook's "Endeavour" Journal*, p. 381.

47 I quote from *An Epistle from Mr. Banks. . . .* This is a supposed "second edition," "printed at Batavia, for Jacobus Opano" and sold in London by John Swan and Thomas Axtele, n. d., p. 11. It is found in the Bodleian Library, Bodwin Pamphlets 1492, Miscellaneous Poems 1755–1774, Tract 16. For the general satiric and literary reaction to Hawkesworth, see Smith, *European Vision*, pp.

28–35. Also useful is Clara Rebecca Lesher, *The South Sea Islanders in English Literature, 1519–1798* (Chicago: Univ. of Chicago Libraries, 1940), a partial publication of her 1937 Univ. of Chicago Ph.D. dissertation.

48 A word about the collations to follow is in order. I compare Hawkesworth's text with printed editions of the journals of Cook, Banks, and Carteret edited by J. C. Beaglehole and Helen Wallis (see notes 21, 25, and 39, above) and with *Byron's Journal of His Circumnavigation, 1764–1766*, ed. R. E. Gallagher, Hakluyt Society Second Series, no. 122 (Cambridge: Cambridge Univ. Press, 1964). There is no printed edition of Wallis's journal, and I compare Hawkesworth with the original in the Public Record Office (Adm 55/35). Since Hawkesworth is known to have worked directly from Byron's journal (National Maritime Museum MS. 57 /053), I have also consulted this manuscript as well as a fair copy of Cook's journal in the Public Record Office (Ship's Logs Supplementary, Series II, Adm 55/40). This, J. C. Beaglehole writes, "is apparently the copy handed over to the Admiralty at the end of the voyage and is possibly that from which Hawkesworth worked" (Beaglehole, *Cook's "Endeavour" Journal.* pp. ccxxiii–ccxxiv). References to these works for purposes of comparison with Hawkesworth appear in the text. In addition to the valuable editions cited above, one should consult W. H. Pearson, "Hawkesworth's Alterations," *Journal of Pacific History* 7 (1972): 45–72.

49 Beaglehole, *Banks's "Endeavour" Journal*, 1:276.

50 *Horace Walpole's Correspondence with the Countess of Upper Ossory, 1761–1777*, ed. W. S. Lewis and A. Dayle Wallace (New Haven: Yale Univ. Press, 1965), vol. 32 of Yale *Walpole Correspondence*, pp. 127–28.

51 Beaglehole, *Cook's "Endeavour" Journal*, p. ccxlvi. Cradock, *Memoirs*, 1:135. The issue is obviously complex, and one must consider such evidence as the comment of a correspondent in *Baldwin's London Weekly Journal* for May 22, 1773, who wrote that the captains were ill-treated in the whole matter and forced into silence: "Their Journals and Papers are seized by their Superiors; nor are they suffered to preserve the smallest Memorandum of Scrap or Paper relating to these Expeditions; nay, farther, they are enjoined, with the Spirit of a Tribunal resembling the Spanish Inquisition, an eternal Silence upon the Subject." Truth here may be embellished with a good deal of hyperbole.

52 *Adventurer*, 1:19. Yale *Idler & Adventurer*, 2:298–99. A valuable essay, which indirectly justifies Hawkesworth's approach to Cook, is Arthur Sherbo's "Johnson's Intent in the *Journey to the Western Islands of Scotland*," *Essays in Criticism* 16 (1966): 382–97. Concerning theories of travel literature of the time Sherbo writes: "Most important in [Johnson's] and in those of his contemporaries was what reflections the traveller made upon what he saw" (p. 385). Sherbo also details the praise the *Journey* received from various reviewers for Johnson's "reflections."

53 Gallagher, *Byron's Journal*, p. lxxvi.

54 Pearson, "Hawkesworth's Alterations," p. 64.

55 Wallis, *Carteret's Voyage*, should be consulted on this difficult issue. See esp. 2:504–9.

56 Quoted in Beaglehole, *Cook's "Endeavour" Journal*, p. 85.

57 For a careful assessment of the white man's behavior in this part of the world, see W. H. Pearson, "European Intimidation and the Myth of Tahiti," *Journal of Pacific History* 4 (1969): 199–217.

58 Beaglehole, *Cook's "Endeavour" Journal*, p. ccliii. The best recent appreciation of the *Voyages* is by E. H. McCormick, *Omai, Pacific Envoy* (Auckland: Auckland Univ. Press, 1977). Working independently, Mr. McCormick and I came to similar conclusions about the importance of Hawkesworth's text.

59 Helen Wallis, "John Hawkesworth and the English Circumnavigators," *Commonwealth Journal* 6 (1963): 171.

Chapter VIII: The Final Days

1 *A New and General Biographical Dictionary* (London, 1784) 6:477. Sir James Prior, *Life of Edmond Malone* (London, 1860), p. 441. Boaden, *Garrick Correspondence*, 1:535. Charles Robert Leslie and Thomas Taylor, *Life and Times of Sir Joshua Reynolds* (London, 1865) 1:429. Leslie Stephen, *Samuel Johnson* (London, 1882), p. 71.

2 Prior, *Life of Edmond Malone*, p. 441. *GM* 33 (Feb. 1763) 51. The book reviewed here was John Awsiter's *Account of the Effects of Opium as a Poison.* . . . In a review of a medical text in *GM* 38 (Aug. 1768): 384, Hawkesworth wrote that opium "taken in such a quantity as to kill, produces distraction, convulsions, and agony not to be exceeded by the effect of poisons less deceitful in their first effects." The 1768 review is signed "X" (the signature Hawkesworth used) and refers the reader to the 1763 review of Awsiter's book.

3 *Garrick Letters*, 2:862. Mary Hawkesworth's holograph letter is in the Hyde Collection. Burney, *Early Diary*, 1:263–64.

4 Hawkesworth, *Swift.*, 1:71.

5 Hyde Collection. A note at the top of the MS., probably in Mary Hawkesworth's hand, indicates the time of dictation.

6 Duncan Isles, "The Lennox Collection," *Harvard Library Bulletin* 19 (1971): 169–70. See also ibid., pp. 43–44, for a letter from Hawkesworth to Charlotte Lennox that dates their friendship from as early as April 30, 1756. India Office Records, Court Book no. 82, April 7, 1773–April 13, 1774.

7 In its death notices for November 1773, the *Gentleman's Magazine* commented: "At Dr. Grant's, in Lime street, of a slow fever, John Hawkesworth, LL.D. of Bromley, in Kent; a gentleman well known and highly esteemed in the literary world, and author of several elegant English compositions" (43:582). Madame D'Arblay, *Memoirs of Doctor Burney* (London, 1832), 1:278–79.

8 Hawkesworth's burial is recorded in the register of the Bromley parish church of St. Peter and St. Paul.

9 Shaw, *Memoirs*–Piozzi *Anecdotes*, pp. 122–23. *Thraliana*, 1:328. JRULMS. B 3/10/459.

10 Burney, *Early Diary*, 1:262. In her letter of June 14, 1776 (JRULMS. B 3/10/457), Mary Hawkesworth wrote to Caldwell: "I hop'd before this time to have transmitted to you an Account of the Publication of my long expected Work, but have had it delay'd, as I fear'd I should by our friend Doctor Johnson to whose

Judgment I wish'd to commit the Papers for such a Selection as will I hope do Honour to the Author." The July 20 letter is JRULMS. B 3/10/459. *Johnson Letters*, 2:150, 152, 168.

11 *Johnson Letters*, 2:168–69.
12 In a letter to Sir James Caldwell, written on August 27, 1777 (JRULMS. B 3/16/144), Mary Hawkesworth discussed possible means of publication of the edition, including publication by subscription.
13 *Adventurer*, 4:244.
14 *Life*, 3:19.
15 *Life*, 1:222, 252.

Index

This index is full though not exhaustive. I have not indexed all geographical locations; neither have I indexed matter in the notes except to draw attention to works by Hawkesworth and aspects of his life not treated fully in the text.

Adam, Robert, 76
Addison, Joseph: *Tatler*, 18, 29, 33, 85; *Spectator*, 18, 29, 42, 44, 85, 86; *The Campaign*, 142; mentioned, xiv, 32, 35, 45, 47, 130
Admiralty: authorizes publication of H's *Voyages*, 142; *Voyages* read at, 173; mentioned, xiv, 139, 151, 154, 157, 158, 181, 196
Akenside, Mark, 22, 87
Alexander the Great, 41
Allen, Mrs. Stephen. *See* Burney, Mrs.
American Philosophical Society, 119
Amhurst, Geoffrey, 14
Anne, Queen of England, 55, 142, 145
Annual Register: sketch of H's character, 10–11; on H's mind and speech, 21; H's reviews for, 127, 218*n24*
Anson, George, 1st Baron Anson, 138, 144
Archbishop of Canterbury. *See* Herring, Dr. Thomas
Aristotle, 95, 143
Armstrong, Dr. John, 143
Arne, Thomas, 84
Augusta (Sandwich yacht), 151, 153, 154
Australia, 138, 140. *See also* New Holland

Bagshaw, Rev. Thomas, 22, 28, 191
Bagshawe, Catherine, *née* Caldwell, 129
Bagshawe, Samuel, 129
Balboa, Vasco Nuñez de: first sights Pacific, 137
Baldwin, H., 191
Banks, Joseph: journals altered by H, 169–70, 181–84; mentioned, 121, 139, 140, 142, 145, 147, 149, 150, 152, 154, 155, 158, 167, 172, 173, 174, 176

Barbados, xiv, 24
Baretti, Joseph: *A Journey from London to Genoa . . .* , 108
Barker, Dr. Edmund, 23, 46
Barnard, Sir Frederick Augusta, 112
Barré, Colonel Isaac, 122
Barrington, William Wildman Barrington, 2nd Viscount, 134
Barry, James, 143
Bartolozzi, Francesco, 190
Barwell, Mrs., 123
Bates, Mr., 151
Bathurst, C., 48
Bathurst, Dr. Richard, 23, 29, 30, 31
Beaglehole, J. C., 137, 138, 139, 140, 156, 170, 173, 186
Beattie, Dr. James: *London Diary 1773*, 151; mentioned, 166
Beattie, Mrs., 166
Becket, Thomas, 148, 149
Beckford, William: *Vathek*, 117
Bedford, John Russell, 4th Duke of, 129
Bell Hotel (Bromley), 13, 14, 15
Berenger, Richard, 77
Berkeley, Charles, 2nd Earl of, 54, 55
Berkeley, Dr. George, 157
Bernard, Mrs. M., 131
Bethell, Hugh, 131
Bickerton, Sir Richard, 150
Biographia Dramatica: praises H's *Oroonoko*, 81
Birch, Dr. Thomas, xiv, 22, 63, 105
Blacking, Mr. (Bromley surgeon), 21
Blenheim, battle of, 142
Blomer family (Bromley), 14
Blunt, Catherine, 119
Blunt, Dorothea (Dolly), 119

229

DESIGNED BY MIKE JAYNES
COMPOSED BY PIED TYPER, LINCOLN, NEBRASKA
MANUFACTURED BY CUSHING-MALLOY, ANN ARBOR, MICHIGAN
TEXT AND DISPLAY LINES ARE SET IN JANSON

Library of Congress Cataloging in Publication Data
Abbott, John Lawrence.
John Hawkesworth : eighteenth-century man of letters.
Includes bibliographical references and index.
1. Hawkesworth, John, 1715?–1773. 2. Authors,
English—18th century—Biography. 3. Great Britain—
Intellectual life—18th century. I. Title.
PR3506.H866Z5 1982   828'.609   81–69811
ISBN 0–299–08610–0   AACR2